Words of Life 2012

Words of Life 2012

Daily Reflections for Your Spirit

Edited by Suzanne Nussey

NOVALIS

© 2012 Novalis Publishing Inc.

Cover design and layout: Audrey Wells
Cover illustration: Sue Todd (www.suetodd.com)

Published by Novalis

Publishing Office
10 Lower Spadina Avenue, Suite 400
Toronto, Ontario, Canada
M5V 2Z2

Head Office
4475 Frontenac Street
Montréal, Québec, Canada
H2H 2S2

www.novalis.ca

Cataloguing data available from Library and Archives Canada

Printed in Canada.

We acknowledge the financial support of the Government of Canada through the
Canada Book Fund for business development activities.

Since 1997, *Words of Life* has offered readers a Scripture passage along with a daily reflection and prayer to support their spiritual practice. This edition presents a "best of" collection from recent years: specially selected reflections from *Words of Life*, with Sunday reflections drawn from *Living with Christ*, follow Year B of the Church's lectionary for 2012.

As a reader and writer, I know the power of words to comfort or confound, to create or destroy. Words are like the air we breathe and the food we eat; we can't function without them. *Words of Life* authors have chosen their words carefully. While providing helpful insights into the daily readings, they also offer us honest words that reflect our own responses to challenging Scripture passages, sometimes taking us in an unanticipated direction. I like their unpredictability and their fresh vision of the old familiar verses and stories.

During his temptation in the desert, Jesus quotes the words of an Old Testament writer: "A person does not live by bread alone, but by every word that comes from the mouth of God." In the eucharist we receive Jesus, the Word made flesh, as bread for our journey on earth. In Scripture, we receive God's word to nourish and sustain our spiritual lives. As you take time to read the daily reflections in *Words of Life*, may you find words that encourage, challenge and renew your life in Christ as you live and speak God's unchanging words of love to a hungry world.

Suzanne Nussey

Editor

Num 6: 22-27; Ps 67; Gal 4: 4-7; Lk 2: 16-21

I t was a life-changing moment when Mary said "Yes!" to God's plan of salvation. Two thousand years later, Mary's yes continues to echo and bear fruit in the hearts and lives of people everywhere. Like Mary, we are invited to say yes to God as we work to build God's kingdom.

Today we honour Mary, the mother of God, for her courage and selflessness, her faith and devotion. We also treasure her as our mother. Mary knows what it is to feel vulnerable; she had worries and fears. Still, her trust in God carried her as she carried her baby in her womb; that trust was rewarded when shepherds, guided by angels, came to pay homage to the infant Jesus.

My only child, a son, was born on a starry night in December. A close friend came to see us in the hospital the next afternoon: our first visitor. Gazing at this tiny newborn resting in her arms, she said softly, "Now I know how the shepherds felt." As a mother, I have pondered these words in my heart ever since. They lead me to a hay-strewn stable where Mary, filled with joy, is embracing the Son of God.

Like the shepherds who found their way to Bethlehem, we are on a journey of discovery. Mary, our mother, travels with us: listening, guiding, loving and leading us to Christ.

**God of love, may I trust in you as Mary did,
all the days of my life.**

S ing a new song to the Lord;
he has done wonderful things!
By his own power and holy strength
he has won the victory.
The Lord announced his victory;
he made his saving power known to the nations.
He kept his promise to the people of Israel
with loyalty and constant love for them.
All people everywhere have seen
the victory of our God.
Sing for joy to the Lord, all the earth;
praise him with songs and shouts of joy!   *Psalm 98: 1-4*

> "...with loyalty and constant love for them."

Unending love

One balmy October evening, as I walked among the fallen leaves, a splash of colour caught my eye. Reaching down, I picked up a maple leaf, each yellow- and red-flecked tip perfectly intact. I marvelled briefly at this wonder, then let it drift back to the ground.

I continued on, absorbing the splendour of the multi-coloured leaves dancing in the wind, and the sound of dried-up leaves crunching underfoot.

Suddenly, my eyes were opened to something greater than nature's beauty. In a moment of insight I realized that I'd held in my hand a symbol of God's faithfulness. God, whose loyalty and love craft the seasons' remarkable cycles, also promises to stay by me with unending love.

Your unfaltering loyalty and love
draw me to sing your praises, my God.

See how much the Father has loved us! His love is so great that we are called God's children – and so, in fact, we are. This is why the world does not know us: it has not known God. My dear friends, we are now God's children, but it is not yet clear what we shall become. But we know that when Christ appears, we shall be like him, because we shall see him as he really is…. Whoever sins is guilty of breaking God's law, because sin is a breaking of the law. You know that Christ appeared in order to take away sins, and that there is no sin in him. So everyone who lives in union with Christ does not continue to sin. · *I John 2: 29; 3: 1-6*

"…we are called God's children."

God's child

After my parents died, one of the ways my sorrow and grief revealed itself was through the painful awareness that I was no longer anyone's child. There was no one left who had held me as a baby crying for food, who encouraged me as a child nervously going off to school, who put up with me as an adolescent struggling with the Great Questions of Life, who hoped with me as a young man trying to find his place.

It sounds strange for a middle-aged husband and father to feel like a bereft orphan – but there you have it.

So I find John's words comforting and touching. It's reassuring to know that the lonely child, deep inside, is Someone's child.

Your Son, Jesus, invited us to call you Abba, Father. Thank you for your life-giving love.

John was standing with two of his disciples, when he saw Jesus walking by. "There is the Lamb of God!" he said. The two disciples heard him say this and went with Jesus. Jesus asked, "What are you looking for?" They answered, "Where do you live, Rabbi?"(This word means "Teacher.") "Come and see," he answered.... So they went with him and saw where he lived, and spent the rest of that day with him. One of them was Andrew, Simon Peter's brother. At once he found his brother Simon and told him, "We have found the Messiah." (This word means "Christ.") Then he took Simon to Jesus. Jesus looked at him and said, "Your name is Simon son of John, but you will be called Cephas." (This is the same as Peter and means "a rock.")   *John 1: 35-42*

"What are you looking for?"

The true rock

When I first met my husband-to-be, I did not know what I was looking for. Yet, like the disciples, I responded to the invitation to "Come and see." Over the weeks and months that followed, we discovered a deep love – a love that brought healing to past hurts, a love that opened us to the future.

Eight years into our marriage, my husband was diagnosed with cancer. When he died, I felt as if I'd lost everything. Our shared love, the rock upon which I'd built my life, had been shattered.

With time, I've come to recognize the true rock – the source of any love – is, in fact, God's love. Turning to God in my despair, I find the courage to love again.

Lord, when my life seems to have lost all meaning, gather me up in your deep and unshakable love.

The next day Jesus decided to go to Galilee. He found Philip and said to him, "Follow me." Now Philip was from Bethsaida, the city of Andrew and Peter. Philip found Nathanael and told him, "We have found the one whom Moses wrote about in the book of the Law and whom the prophets also wrote about. He is Jesus son of Joseph, from Nazareth."

"Can anything good come from Nazareth?" Nathanael asked.

"Come and see," answered Philip.

When Jesus saw Nathanael coming to him, he said about him, "Here is a real Israelite; there is nothing false in him!" Nathanael asked him, "How do you know me?" Jesus answered, "I saw you when you were under the fig tree before Philip called you."

"Teacher," answered Nathanael, "you are the Son of God! You are the King of Israel!"   *John 1: 43-51*

"Can anything good come from Nazareth?"

False judgments

As the new school term begins, I try not to second-guess our decision to send our children to the local neighbourhood school. It's a small school, without lots of bells and whistles. There are plenty of "better" schools available – with higher testing scores and state-of-the-art resources.

I sometimes wonder if anything good might come from a place that is often overlooked. Nathanael's words in today's reading challenge me.

For centuries, it seems, we have been judging others based on where they come from. And, for centuries, we have been wrong.

Lord, teach me to leave my own prejudices at home.

Praise your God, O Zion!
He keeps your borders safe
and satisfies you with the finest wheat.
He gives a command to the earth,
and what he says is quickly done.
He spreads snow like a blanket
and scatters frost like dust.
He sends hail like gravel;
no one can endure the cold he sends!
Then he gives a command, and the ice melts;
he sends the wind, and the water flows.
He gives his message to his people,
his instructions and laws to Israel.

Psalm 147: 12-20

"…and the ice melts…"

New growth

The days of teetering between winter and spring are challenging ones
– especially for a gardener. When it's been a long winter, I'm just
itching to get my fingers into some warm earth. It's hard to believe
that the possibility of green, new life exists underneath the blanket
of snow.

But inevitably, it happens. The first shoots of a crocus nudge me
out of my winter ill-humour. My faith is restored. I believe again. My
energy is renewed, and anything is possible!

Each year it is the same. I know spring will return, but my faith
is fragile. The bright crocuses are like miracles. They remind me to be
patient, to be attentive, and to be open to the surprise of God's presence and power.

**Creator God, open my heart to possibilities of new
growth. Indeed, with you all things are possible!**

Thehere was a wedding in the town of Cana in Galilee. Jesus' mother was there, and Jesus and his disciples had also been invited to the wedding. When the wine had given out, Jesus' mother said to him, "They are out of wine."

"You must not tell me what to do," Jesus replied. "My time has not yet come."

Jesus' mother then told the servants, "Do whatever he tells you...."

Jesus said to the servants, "Fill these jars with water.... Now draw some water out and take it to the man in charge of the feast." They took him the water, which now had turned into wine, and he tasted it.... He called the bridegroom and said, "Everyone else serves the best wine first, and after the guests have drunk a lot, he serves the ordinary wine. But you have kept the best wine until now!"

John 2: 1-12

> "Do whatever he tells you..."

A mother's wisdom

A fascinating detail in today's reading, the story of Jesus' first miracle, is the way Mary seems to "push" him toward it. Jesus even rebukes her, saying, "You must not tell me what to do." But Mary seems to know his time has come.

From the beginning, Mary knew who Jesus was. She always knew his calling.

All young adults have to break the ties with their mother. But, at the same time, all know that their mother is the one who knows them best.

Devotion to Mary is a celebration of the wise mother – the one who knows us better than we know ourselves. The one who often encourages us and leads us to become our best selves.

Thank you, God, for wise mothers.

Isa 60: 1-6; Ps 72; Eph 3: 2-3, 5-6; Mt 2: 1-12

A news commentator on North American TV made the flippant remark that the notion of a one-family world is naive and stupid. He said, "Anyone who believes that needs to get real and grow up or shut up. We need to defend ourselves against the other, especially the stranger." Unfortunately, these sentiments are shared by many.

The feast of the Epiphany gives us cause to rejoice that another kind of world is possible. Today's readings invite us to celebrate the  immigrant and the stranger in our midst. Matthew's gospel presents foreigners bringing gifts to the Christ child in Bethlehem. We know nothing of their origins other than that they came from far-off Eastern lands carrying the best they had. How different the world would be if everyone received the foreigner as "gift" rather than "threat"! Different values and customs can enrich, rather than deprive, a culture.

Another important aspect prevails in today's story: the lie. Herod lies to the foreigners, saying he desires to do homage to the newborn child. Herod distorts the truth, which gives birth to violence. Often, the truth about immigrants and foreigners is distorted, giving rise to prejudice.

Let us remember that we are all strangers to each other, extending the hand of friendship and truth. This one family around the table truly becomes a manifestation of God.

God, our creator, help us to reach out in friendship to strangers rather than push them away.

Listen now, my people, and come to me;
come to me, and you will have life....
My thoughts," says the Lord, "are not like yours,
and my ways are different from yours.
As high as the heavens are above the earth,
so high are my ways and thoughts above yours.
My word is like the snow and the rain
that come down from the sky to water the earth.
They make the crops grow
and provide seed for planting and food to eat.
So also will be the word that I speak –
it will not fail to do what I plan for it;
it will do everything I send it to do."

Isaiah 55: 1-11

"My word is like the snow and the rain..."

Words of life

One of the earliest and most telling photographs of me shows a toddler standing on a chair at a kitchen table, looking closely at a newspaper spread before him.

Since then, I have rarely been without a book nearby. I read the newspaper daily to see what's going on. And, for almost 30 years, I have made my living by moving words around on paper, trying to find exactly the right word to express what needs to be expressed.

You would be right if you concluded that I have a hunger for words and their meanings. But most words are fluff – without real sustenance, and my restless appetite is rarely satisfied.

The Lord promises better, and I wonder, "Are these the words that will nourish?"

Lord, I am hungry. Nourish me with your words.

"**N**o one is holy like the Lord; there is none like him, no protector like our God…. For the Lord is a God who knows, and he judges all that people do…. The people who once were well fed now hire themselves out to get food, but the hungry are hungry no more…. The Lord kills and restores to life; he sends people to the world of the dead and brings them back again. He makes some people poor and others rich; he humbles some and makes others great. He lifts the poor from the dust and raises the needy from their misery. He makes them companions of princes and puts them in places of honour. The foundations of the earth belong to the Lord; on them he has built the world." *1 Samuel 2:1-8*

> "…and raises the needy from their misery."

A song of praise

How I resonate with today's hymn of praise! Like Hannah, my heart sang for joy as I gazed at my newborn son, Daniel. It's easy enough to rejoice, sing, even jump for joy at a birth – especially a long-awaited, much-longed-for one like Samuel's. But, putting today's reading in its context, doesn't it strike you as odd that Hannah sings at the very moment she is offering up her precious son to God?

Even though she would one day lose Jesus to death on a cross, Mary sang her *Magnificat* using words similar to Hannah's, rejoicing that God's love would be revealed through him.

Cuddling my baby close, I acknowledge that he is not really mine, but God's. And every day, I try to remember to "offer up" Daniel to God's loving service.

**Lord, I offer you this child whom you have given to me.
May he grow to reveal your love to others.**

J esus and his disciples, including James and John, left the synagogue and went straight to the home of Simon and Andrew. Simon's mother-in-law was sick in bed with a fever, and as soon as Jesus arrived, he was told about her. He went to her, took her by the hand, and helped her up. The fever left her, and she began to wait on them.

After the sun had set and evening had come, people brought to Jesus all the sick and those who had demons. All the people of the town gathered in front of the house. Jesus healed many who were sick with all kinds of diseases and drove out many demons. He would not let the demons say anything, because they knew who he was.

Mark 1: 29-39

> "Jesus healed many who were sick."

Recovery

Last summer I took my mother with me to a wonderful old resort in the country. Unfortunately, she had a serious allergic reaction to something in the lodge. After a few days she started coughing and wheezing. Her breathing became laboured and her chest was sore; we had to leave right away. Back home, away from the old building, Mom started feeling better immediately; her recovery was like a miracle. My relief was enormous.

How did Peter feel when Jesus healed his mother-in-law? The gospels are too matter-of-fact, making it sound so easy: "Jesus healed many who were sick." Behind that simple statement were individual stories: mothers and fathers, children and in-laws feeling relief, gratitude and awe in the face of sudden recovery from serious illness.

Lord of healing and hope, your presence in this world brings wholeness and serenity to the sick.

A man suffering from a dreaded skin disease came to Jesus, knelt down, and begged him for help. "If you want to," he said, "you can make me clean." Jesus was filled with pity, and reached out and touched him. "I do want to," he answered. "Be clean!" At once the disease left the man, and he was clean. Then Jesus spoke sternly to him and sent him away at once, after saying to him, "Listen, don't tell anyone about this. But go straight to the priest and let him examine you...." But the man went away and began to spread the news everywhere.   *Mark 1: 40-45*

> "If you want to, you can make me clean."

Ready to help

A close friend of mine has a problem with gambling. She has borrowed money from everyone; she's even admitted to stealing from the company where she works. She's tried counselling a few times, but hasn't been able to stay with it. Sometimes she feels worthless and defeated.

But there is nothing within the human spirit that God cannot help fix. Regardless of who we are, where we've been, or what we've done, God stands with open arms, ready to assist.

In today's passage, Jesus not only assures the man that he is willing to help, but immediately frees him from his ailment. Whatever prevents me from leading a fulfilled life can be overcome when I ask for – and allow myself to receive – God's help.

**God, help me to turn to you
when I want to "clean up" the messes in my life.**

Jesus was preaching the message to them when four men arrived, carrying a paralyzed man. Because of the crowd, however, they could not get the man to him. So they made a hole in the roof right above the place where Jesus was. When they had made an opening, they let the man down, lying on his mat. Seeing how much faith they had, Jesus said, "My son, your sins are forgiven."

Some teachers of the Law thought to themselves, "This is blasphemy! God is the only one who can forgive sins!" Jesus knew what they were thinking, so he said, "Is it easier to say to this paralyzed man, 'Your sins are forgiven,' or to say, 'Get up, pick up your mat, and walk'?" … So he said, "I tell you, get up, pick up your mat, and go home!" The man got up, picked up his mat, and hurried away.

Mark 2: 1-12

> "So they made a hole in the roof…"

Risking it all

Thomas Merton once wrote in his journal, "Suddenly there is a point where religion becomes laughable. Then you decide you are nevertheless religious."

It is almost comical to think of a couple of men cutting a hole in the roof because they were unable to push through the crowd around Jesus. I imagine the look on the face of the house's owner when he sees his roof broken, and the other, more decorous bystanders who have to step aside to avoid being hit on the head by falling roof tiles! It could just as well be a scene from a Laurel and Hardy movie.

These roof-breakers will do anything to get to Jesus – even risk ridicule. But the point is that Jesus is happy to see them, even more so because of their laughable means of entry.

Lord, give me the grace to become even laughable, so long as it brings me closer to you.

A crowd came to Jesus, and he started teaching them. As he walked along, he saw a tax collector, Levi son of Alphaeus, sitting in his office. Jesus said to him, "Follow me." Levi got up and followed him.

Later on Jesus was having a meal in Levi's house. A large number of tax collectors and other outcasts was following Jesus, and many of them joined him and his disciples at the table. Some teachers of the Law, who were Pharisees, saw that Jesus was eating with these outcasts and tax collectors, so they asked his disciples, "Why does he eat with such people?"

Jesus heard them and answered, "People who are well do not need a doctor, but only those who are sick. I have not come to call respectable people, but outcasts."   *Mark 2: 13-17*

> "I have not come to call respectable people, but outcasts."

Beyond appearances

In a world that is so complex and unclear, how we long for structures to tell us who we are and what we should do!

The law told the Pharisees who they were and what they were to do. And here is Jesus challenging, questioning, breaking the mould… again. Making it difficult and confusing. Making it real. Today, I am faced with the "outsiders," the ones who don't fit in. How easy it is to close myself off, to protect my little world. Maybe the great challenge in a pluralistic society is to live by my chosen values, but not divide the world into "us" and "them." To accept the unfamiliar and even unsettling ways of others. To see beyond the external. To see the person.

God, help me live Jesus' challenge to reach out to those in need, rather than to stand in judgment.

1 Sam 3: 3-10, 19; Ps 40; 1 Cor 6: 13-15, 17-20; Jn 1: 35-42

D o you remember, as a child, not being able to walk at your own pace and having to run along beside a parent who was in a hurry? Now I do it to my own daughter. Hurry up, I say, we'll be late. And when I am working to a deadline, I don't welcome her interruptions. Even worse, I don't even hear them.

Jesus has a mission and an approaching deadline. Yet when he becomes aware of two young men following him, instead of ignoring them or hurrying ahead, he turns and asks them what they are looking for. They answer that they want to know where he lives. "Come and see," he replies.

To join this rabbi they do not have to listen to a lecture denouncing other sects or learn a bunch of special rules or rituals. This rabbi turns to *them*, aware that they are following him, and asks them what their hearts truly desire. Then he invites them to get to know him, to spend time with him.

Jesus also invites us to come and see. As he asks us to come closer, do we know our own heart's desires? In following him, may we join our neighbours with an open heart, journeying together to where Jesus lives.

Jesus, help me hear your invitation to come closer to you.

Some people came to Jesus and asked him, "Why is it that the disciples of John the Baptist and the disciples of the Pharisees fast, but yours do not?"

Jesus answered, "Do you expect the guests at a wedding party to go without food? Of course not…. But the day will come when the bridegroom will be taken away from them, and then they will fast.

"No one uses a piece of new cloth to patch up an old coat, because the new patch will shrink and tear off some of the old cloth, making an even bigger hole. Nor does anyone pour new wine into used wineskins, because the wine will burst the skins, and both the wine and the skins will be ruined. Instead, new wine must be poured into fresh wineskins."

Mark 2: 18-22

> "New wine must be poured into fresh wineskins."

Changes

I like the idea of change; it's just that I don't like *changes*. At the office, we recently came up with a well-thought-out plan for changing the positions of our workstations. It made sense, but in my heart of hearts, I would have much preferred that things stay the way they were. Or better yet, that everyone else change, and I stay the same.

New is good, but old is so comfortable. Now that computers are a familiar, even automatic way of putting my thoughts on paper, I forget the resistance I initially felt to giving up my typewriter. I still hoard yellow pads of paper, but rarely use them. But I keep them… just in case.

Change is necessary; change is good. However, change is not always comfortable.

Lord, when the very thought of doing things differently leaves me fearful, help me stay open to your word.

The Lord said to Samuel, "How long will you go on grieving over Saul? I have rejected him as king of Israel. But now get some olive oil and go to Bethlehem, to a man named Jesse, because I have chosen one of his sons to be king...." Samuel did what the Lord told him to do....

Jesse brought seven of his sons to Samuel. And Samuel said to him, "Do you have any more sons?" Jesse answered, "There is still the youngest, but he is out taking care of the sheep."

"Tell him to come here," Samuel said. "We won't offer the sacrifice until he comes." So Jesse sent for him. He was a handsome, healthy young man, and his eyes sparkled. The Lord said to Samuel, "This is the one – anoint him!" Samuel took the olive oil and anointed David in front of his brothers.   *1 Samuel 16: 1-13*

> **"...and anointed David in front of his brothers."**

Marked for life

There's something a little embarrassing about being singled out. Especially when you're a teenager, desperately trying to belong to the group.

Through most of my younger years, I was a teacher's pet. If I got singled out, it was usually for some kind of commendation. Occasionally, I got disciplined. The cause of this special attention didn't really matter. Good or bad, the effect was the same – to isolate me from my peers.

By all accounts, young David was quite self-confident. But I wonder, sometimes, how he felt about being singled out in front of his brothers. Did he, like Joseph, want to lord it over them? Did he sense that they resented his favoured status? Did he retreat to his fields in relief?

I don't want to live in the limelight, Lord.
Please let me serve you in the comfortable shadows.

There was a man who had a paralyzed hand…. Some people were there who wanted to accuse Jesus of doing wrong; so they watched him closely to see whether he would cure the man on the Sabbath. Jesus said to the man, "Come up here to the front." Then he asked the people, "What does our Law allow us to do on the Sabbath? To help or to harm? To save someone's life or to destroy it?"

But they did not say a thing. Jesus was angry as he looked around at them, but at the same time he felt sorry for them, because they were so stubborn and wrong. Then he said to the man, "Stretch out your hand." He stretched it out, and it became well again. So the Pharisees… made plans to kill Jesus.   *Mark 3: 1-6*

"…at the same time he felt sorry for them."

Out of compassion

Did Jesus struggle with this situation? It would have been so easy to respond in anger… so hard to live by his rule of love.

I, too, have been forced to confront difficult situations in my work or personal life – structures that are unjust, relationships that are unhealthy. My anger is good, since it prompts me to action. However, I'm reminded that Jesus responded not from his anger but out of compassion.

How difficult it is to pause and listen to that quiet voice within. After all, isn't my anger justified? I need to be reminded that I am not alone: God is acting in me and through me to address the situation.

God, help me to find the courage to fight injustice and the wisdom to act out of love, not anger.

A large crowd followed Jesus…. All these people came to Jesus because they had heard of the things he was doing.

Jesus told his disciples to get a boat ready for him, so that the people would not crush him. He had healed many people, and all the sick kept pushing their way to him in order to touch him. And whenever the people who had evil spirits in them saw him, they would fall down before him and scream, "You are the Son of God!" Jesus sternly ordered the evil spirits not to tell anyone who he was.

Mark 3: 7-12

> "All the sick kept pushing their way to him."

A brief respite

Working in what's called a "helping profession," I often have the experience of people pressing around me, demanding that I meet their needs. Sometimes I feel overwhelmed, almost suffocated, by their demands for attention.

When the crowd was pressing around Jesus, to touch him and be healed, he had an innovative solution. He got into a boat where he could still teach them, but have some distance.

What are the creative solutions in my life, the "boats" that allow me some distance and prevent me from being consumed by others' needs? Perhaps it's a few minutes of prayer, a humorous comment that helps me see the situation from a fresh perspective, a chat with someone who loves and affirms me.

**Jesus, when I'm feeling overwhelmed, help me
to find creative solutions to the problems I face.**

Jesus went up a hill and called to himself those he wanted. They came to him, and he chose twelve, whom he named apostles. "I have chosen you to be with me," he told them. "I will also send you out to preach, and you will have authority to drive out demons."

These are the twelve he chose: Simon (Jesus gave him the name Peter); James and his brother John, the sons of Zebedee (Jesus gave them the name Boanerges, which means "Men of Thunder"); Andrew, Philip, Bartholomew, Matthew, Thomas, James son of Alphaeus, Thaddaeus, Simon the Patriot, and Judas Iscariot, who betrayed Jesus.

Mark 3: 13-19

"Jesus gave him the name Peter..."

Called by name

When my daughter was only a few hours old, a nurse came into my room, took the baby in her arms, and stood by the window gazing at her. I lay in the bed looking at the winter light falling on the two of them. The nurse said, "This child is very peaceful, and very strong." I have marvelled ever since at that nurse's perception of my daughter's character.

When Jesus called the apostles to him, he gave some of them new names that characterized their gifts. He named them with deep love and faith in them.

I had already named my daughter as soon as she was born, but in some sense the nurse was giving her that new name. What is God's loving name for me?

Lord, help me to hear the loving name you call me by, and to be true to it throughout my life.

Then Jesus went home. Again such a large crowd gathered that Jesus and his disciples had no time to eat. When his family heard about it, they set out to take charge of him, because people were saying, "He's gone mad!"

Mark 3: 20-21

> "...people were saying, 'He's gone mad!'"

Mad or holy?

All parents hope their children grow up kind and compassionate – within reason. Jesus, however, seemed unreasonably compassionate. In fact, the crowds considered him mad because his compassion exceeded their imaginations.

Saint Francis was locked up by his father at first. Mother Teresa's superiors tried to talk her out of living among the poor. Dorothy Day had friends who thought she was foolish for devoting her life to the "worthless" poor. And some people considered both Oscar Romero and Martin Luther King "mad" for the risks they took.

Compassion, I guess, is a good thing – until it hinders personal success or challenges social norms. Then it starts to look like madness – or holiness, depending on whether your perspective is the world's or God's.

**God, inspire me today, even if only in small ways,
to be madly compassionate.**

Jonah 3: 1-5, 10; Ps 25; 1 Cor 7: 29-31; Mk 1: 14-20

There's an ancient story of three demons who argued about the best way to destroy Christianity. One said, "Let's tell Christians there is no heaven. Take away the reward and their mission will collapse." Another said, "Let's tell Christians there is no hell. Take away fear of punishment and their mission will collapse." The third demon spoke: "There's a better way. Tell them there's no hurry and the whole Christian enterprise will collapse."

Today we see Jesus' public ministry begin in an atmosphere of urgency: "The time is fulfilled, and the kingdom of God has come near." Making his way along the Sea of Galilee, Jesus exhorts Simon and Andrew, "Come, follow me." Immediately they abandon their nets and follow. When he calls James and John, they too join Jesus immediately, leaving behind their father and their work. For them, there is no question about Jesus' call and their response.

In today's hectic world, we may often find our resolve to follow the gospel being diverted. We find good excuses for delay; we miss opportunities for forgiving, healing and comforting, for providing for those in need. Life rushes around us, people move on or die, and the opportunity for reconciliation and loving service may be lost forever.

Like Jesus and those first followers, we must seize the day now and respond to the call, lest the whole Christian enterprise collapse because there is no hurry.

**Lord Jesus, stir me out of my complacency so that
I follow you today and every day.**

S ome teachers of the Law were saying, "He has Beelzebul in him! It is the chief of the demons who gives him the power to drive them out."

So Jesus called them to him and spoke to them in parables: "How can Satan drive out Satan? If a country divides itself into groups which fight each other, that country will fall apart. If a family divides itself into groups which fight each other, that family will fall apart. So if Satan's kingdom divides into groups, it cannot last, but will fall apart and come to an end."

"No one can break into a strong man's house and take away his belongings unless he first ties up the strong man; then he can plunder his house."
Mark 3: 22-30

> "If a family divides itself…"

Family bonds

In one bedroom, a nine-year-old girl watches reruns on her TV. Upstairs, her teenage sister listens to "her" music. Their mother is heading off to the fitness club; their father eats his supper while watching a news report about runaways. A normal family, pulled in many directions.

How easy it is to lose touch with those who share our lives. In pursuing our own dreams, we risk waking up one day in a house of strangers.

How can I participate in the public sphere without losing sight of the centrality of "family"? Outside influences demand so much and pull me in many directions. How can I keep my family as my focus and continue to remain open to the demands of others in their need?

**Dear God, give me the strength and wisdom
to keep my house together.**

Then Jesus' mother and brothers arrived. They stood outside the house and sent in a message, asking for him. A crowd was sitting around Jesus, and they said to him, "Look, your mother and your brothers and sisters are outside, and they want you."

Jesus answered, "Who is my mother? Who are my brothers?" He looked at the people sitting around him and said, "Look! Here are my mother and my brothers! Whoever does what God wants is my brother, my sister, my mother."

Mark 3: 31-35

"They stood outside the house…"

Moving away

A mother is looking for her son. Her strange and wonderful son, who was moving away from her, toward his destiny. Why was she looking for him? Why did she wait outside the house? Did she feel he was hanging around with the wrong crowd?

Now it's my turn to stand and watch as my children move off into the world. They've had friends who've had troubles – with school, with parents, with drugs. Sometimes it scares me. How can I say everyone is a child of God and is worthy of friendship, but also protect my own children?

I can't imagine what Mary went through as she saw the dangers mounting. I admit to hoping that, when my children reach out to others, it doesn't cost them as much.

**Dear God, help my children live their destiny.
Give them the strength to do it well.**

A s Saul was coming near the city of Damascus, suddenly a light from the sky flashed around him. He fell to the ground and heard a voice saying to him, "Saul, Saul! Why do you persecute me?"

"Who are you, Lord?" he asked.

"I am Jesus, whom you persecute," the voice said...." Saul got up from the ground and opened his eyes, but could not see a thing....

Ananias entered the house where Saul was, and placed his hands on him. "Brother Saul," he said, "the Lord has sent me – Jesus himself, who appeared to you on the road as you were coming here. He sent me so that you might see again and be filled with the Holy Spirit." At once something like fish scales fell from Saul's eyes, and he was able to see again.   *Acts 9: 1-22*

> "Something like fish scales fell from Saul's eyes…"

Eyes wide open

I live a quiet life. Unlike Saul, I haven't spent time running around arresting Christians or threatening them with murder. But I do understand him, at least a little.

After all, Son of God, rising from the dead, eternal life – it all sounds pretty wacky. Rather than kill the inexplicable, however, my response is to dismiss it – in a polite, non-confrontational way, of course.

Saul, lucky fellow, receives a beam of light, a voice from heaven, and temporary blindness. That certainly gets your attention.

I, in keeping with my quieter doubts and gentler rejection, get only a nagging sense that maybe there's more to this than meets the eye. That, absurdly, maybe it's me who's wacky.

Lord, my eyes are open, but I do not see.
Take away the scales.

After this the Lord chose another seventy-two men and sent them out two by two, to go ahead of him to every town and place where he himself was about to go. He said to them, "Go! I am sending you like lambs among wolves. Don't take a purse or a beggar's bag or shoes; don't stop to greet anyone on the road. Whenever you go into a house, first say, 'Peace be with this house.' If someone who is peace-loving lives there, let your greeting of peace remain on that person; if not, take back your greeting of peace.... Whenever you go into a town and are made welcome, eat what is set before you, heal the sick in that town, and say to the people there, 'The kingdom of God has come near you.'"

Luke 10: 1-9

> "Don't take a purse or a beggar's bag or shoes..."

Tools for the journey

I think Jesus was worried about the disciples as they set off on their own. Worried about their safety, their well-being, the reception they would receive "out there."

Although the disciples didn't carry "a purse or a beggar's bag or shoes," they did carry the "tools" they would need for their journey. They carried, within their hearts, the example of how Jesus had lived among them – aware of the danger that surrounded him, yet always willing to share God's love with others.

Perhaps Jesus' last-minute advice is much like the words of caution I give my children as they leave home. Instead of worrying, I need to remind myself that they, too, carry the "tools" to help them be in this world.

Loving God, when I am fearful, give me the knowledge that you are with me every step of the way.

The kingdom of God is like this. A man scatters seed in his field. He sleeps at night, is up and about during the day, and all the while the seeds are sprouting and growing…. The soil itself makes the plants grow and bear fruit…. When the grain is ripe, the man starts cutting it with his sickle, because the harvest time has come.

"What shall we say the kingdom of God is like?" asked Jesus. "It is like this. A man takes a mustard seed, the smallest seed in the world, and plants it in the ground. After a while it grows up and becomes the biggest of all plants. It puts out such large branches that the birds come and make their nests in its shade."

Mark 4: 26-34

> "The kingdom of God is like…a mustard seed."

Small acts of kindness

When I read the story *Les Misérables*, I was moved by the way the Bishop's single act of kindness transforms the life of the escaped convict, Jean Valjean. When Valjean is caught stealing the Bishop's candlesticks, the Bishop simply says to the police, "He didn't steal them; I gave them to him." That moment turns Valjean's life around. He finds hope and new meaning in life and goes on to do good for others.

That single act of kindness is like the mustard seed.

My forgiveness toward someone who has wronged me, my word of encouragement to someone in despair, my gesture of welcome to a stranger: these can be the mustard seed that will grow and bear fruit in that person's life in ways that I may never know.

**O God, may I be aware of how important
my small gestures of love can be for someone else.**

Jesus said, "Let us go across to the other side of the lake." So the disciples got into the boat in which Jesus was already sitting.... Suddenly a strong wind blew up, and the waves began to spill over into the boat, so that it was about to fill with water. Jesus was in the back of the boat, sleeping with his head on a pillow. The disciples woke him up and said, "Teacher, don't you care that we are about to die?"

Jesus stood up and commanded the wind, "Be quiet!" and he said to the waves, "Be still!" The wind died down, and there was a great calm. Then Jesus said, "Why are you frightened? Do you still have no faith?"

Mark 4: 35-41

> "Why are you frightened?"

Within the storm

Picture the scene: a storm is raging all around; the waves reach higher and higher. As they go down between the swells, the disciples cannot see over them. It is dark, black. The men are small, insignificant before the forces arrayed against them.

How often I feel small, and the storm within me so out of control. It is hard to have faith – that I have been given the strength to cope. Faith that I, like Jesus, can tell the waves, "Be still." I have had to face so many storms: Will I fit in? What will I do with my life? And now there is the mortgage, sick children, work... so many fears.

"Why are you frightened? Do you still have no faith?" Let it go. You'll be fine. I am here.

**Dear God, you give me strength to weather the storms.
Help me trust that you are there with me.**

Deut 18: 15-20; Ps 95; 1 Cor 7: 32-35; Mk 1: 21-28

When I was in university, I had a professor who, to this day, stands out in my mind. His teaching style was dynamic and alive, and there was substance to what he taught. You might say he taught with authority. In today's gospel, the people are captivated by both the style and the substance of Jesus' teaching. "They were astounded at his teaching, for he taught them as one having authority." They just had to listen to him!

Long before the time of Christ, the book of Deuteronomy predicted that God would raise up a prophet who would speak with authority. If God's people were to remain faithful, they would heed the words of this prophet. In a similar vein, the psalmist implores the people to listen to God's voice with open and grateful hearts.

In today's second reading, Paul answers questions posed by the people of Corinth about vocations in life. At the heart of his teaching is our need to keep focused on God no matter what our walk of life. The key is discerning the life that the Lord has called us to, something we can do if we heed his words.

As we go about our week, may God's word find a home in our minds and hearts. May we always listen for God's voice and follow Jesus' teaching given to us with love and authority.

Lord Jesus, may your teaching echo in my heart each and every day.

have so many enemies, Lord,
so many who turn against me!
They talk about me and say,
"God will not help him."
But you, O Lord, are always my shield from danger;
you give me victory
and restore my courage.
I call to the Lord for help,
and from his sacred hill he answers me.
I lie down and sleep,
and all night long the Lord protects me.
I am not afraid of the thousands of enemies
who surround me on every side.

Psalm 3: 1-6

"I have so many enemies, Lord…"

So many enemies…

I have never known war first-hand, so I cannot relate fully to the experience of today's psalmist: "I have so many enemies…." I realize, however, that I *can* relate to the underlying emotions of the psalm.

The enemies in my life are not so much "people" as they are "voices." They seem to lie in wait, attacking me when and where I am most vulnerable. When I am overwhelmed by the demands of home and work, they goad me into giving up. When I feel lonely, they tell me I am unlovable. When I worry about making ends meet, they remind me that poverty lurks just around the corner.

But my experience shows that these voices cannot defeat me: God's love fills me, giving me victory over my fears.

Dearest God, when my fears threaten to overwhelm me, remind me that you are with me through it all.

There was a woman who had suffered terribly from severe bleeding for twelve years, even though she had been treated by many doctors. She had spent all her money, but instead of getting better she got worse all the time. She had heard about Jesus, so she came behind him, saying to herself, "If I just touch his clothes, I will get well."

She touched his cloak, and her bleeding stopped at once; and she had the feeling inside herself that she was healed of her trouble. At once Jesus knew that power had gone out of him, so he turned around in the crowd and asked, "Who touched my clothes...?"

The woman realized what had happened to her, so she came, trembling with fear, knelt at his feet, and told him the whole truth. Jesus said, "My daughter, your faith has made you well. Go in peace, and be healed of your trouble."   *Mark 5: 21-43*

> "She touched his cloak..."

True healing

My friend Janet lives with lupus, a chronic and debilitating disease. Someday, medical science may cure her; in the meantime, her only hope is the hem of Jesus' cloak.

Janet isn't waiting for a medical miracle, though I'm certain she'd welcome one. Instead, she embraces a miracle of a different sort – the grace of living each day to its fullest, being as present as possible to her husband, her children, her friends and herself. She isn't "known" by her disease, but instead by her wry wit, her warm love and her good cheer.

Not every day, of course, but most days, Janet does manage to touch the hem of Jesus' cloak simply by living well in this moment – and then in the next, and in the next.

God, let me make the most of life, one moment at a time.

Jesus went back to his hometown, followed by his disciples. On the Sabbath he began to teach in the synagogue. Many people were there; and when they heard him, they were all amazed. "Where did he get all this?" they asked. "What wisdom is this that has been given him? How does he perform miracles? Isn't he the carpenter, the son of Mary, and the brother of James, Joseph, Judas and Simon? Aren't his sisters living here?" And so they rejected him.

Jesus said to them, "Prophets are respected everywhere except in their own hometown and by their relatives and their family." He was not able to perform any miracles there, except that he placed his hands on a few sick people and healed them. *Mark 6: 1-6*

> "And so they rejected him."

Finding our path

There was a lot of unspoken jealousy and competition in the neighbourhood where I grew up. It wasn't about possessions and social status. It focused more on the children: whose children would turn out well and whose would not. Even now, when I return home, I get an update on how everyone is doing – as though there's some kind of scorecard.

I hear the same jealousy and competitiveness in today's reading. Jesus' neighbours wanted to pull him down because he seemed to have moved beyond them.

Growing up, we were told, "Be the best you can be," and "Follow your dreams." Often, when we tried to heed that advice, we were ostracized by our peers. It's not always easy to let our true light shine.

**Lord, give me the confidence to let my own light shine.
Help me when I am jealous of others.**

T he Holy Spirit was with [Simeon] and had assured him that he would not die before he had seen the Lord's promised Messiah. Led by the Spirit, Simeon went into the Temple. When the parents brought the child Jesus into the Temple to do for him what the Law required, Simeon took the child in his arms and gave thanks to God: "Now, Lord, you have kept your promise, and you may let your servant go in peace. With my own eyes I have seen your salvation, which you have prepared in the presence of all peoples...."

There was a very old prophet, a widow named Anna.... She never left the Temple; day and night she worshipped God, fasting and praying. That very same hour she arrived and gave thanks to God and spoke about the child to all who were waiting for God to set Jerusalem free.   *Luke 2: 22-40*

"...and you may let your servant go in peace."

Go in peace

Old Simeon saw Jesus, and felt his life was now complete. To skeptical minds like mine, the timing seems too pat, too coincidental. But I remember visiting Mrs. Powell in hospital. She was so puffed up with cancer she couldn't speak. I wasn't even sure she knew I was there. I held her hand, muttered a few words and fled, feeling utterly helpless and useless.

But she refused to die. Until her daughter's wedding. Then, and only then, she let go of life and slipped away.

The human spirit is remarkably tenacious. If Mrs. Powell could stay alive by sheer force of will until her daughter was married, I see no reason why Simeon couldn't hang on until he saw the promised Messiah.

Jesus, I'm a little jealous of Simeon, Anna and Mrs. Powell. I wish I knew what would make my life complete.

Herodias held a grudge against John and wanted to kill him, but she could not because of Herod. Herod was afraid of John because he knew that John was a good and holy man....

Finally Herodias got her chance. It was on Herod's birthday, when he gave a feast for all the top government officials, the military chiefs, and the leading citizens of Galilee. The daughter of Herodias came in and danced, and pleased Herod and his guests. So the king said to the girl, "What would you like to have? I will give you anything you want...." So the girl went out and asked her mother, "What shall I ask for?"

"The head of John the Baptist," she answered.... This made the king very sad, but he could not refuse her because of the vows he had made in front of all his guests.   *Mark 6:14-29*

"...he knew that John was a good and holy man..."

Knowing the truth, but...

Blinded by lust – one can imagine him leering as the young girl dances before him – Herod commits the ultimate crime. And yet, Herod knew in his heart that "John was a good and holy man."

Herod not only lacked the will to do what he knew was right (welcome to the club!), but also was blind to what would really make him happy.

Today, in a society that worships consumption and treats women as commodities, I am bombarded with messages that tell me "You'll be happy if you look like this..., or drive this car..., or buy this product...."

Herod did not listen to the voice in his heart. I must try to listen to mine and act accordingly.

Lord, let me hear your voice within me and follow it.

The Lord appeared to Solomon in a dream and asked him, "What would you like me to give you?" Solomon answered, "O Lord God, you have let me succeed my father as king, even though I am very young and don't know how to rule…. So give me the wisdom I need to rule your people with justice and to know the difference between good and evil…."

The Lord was pleased that Solomon had asked for this, and so he said to him, "I will give you more wisdom and understanding than anyone has ever had before or will ever have again. I will also give you what you have not asked for: all your life you will have wealth and honour, more than that of any other king… and I will give you a long life."

1 Kings 3: 4-13

> "So give me the wisdom I need…"

Wisdom and understanding

When I turn to God to ask for help, wisdom is not often at the top of my list. Help to find the car keys seems to be my most urgent request these days!

It's rare for me to stop and think about what I truly need. I tend to ask God for help either in the middle of a crisis or at the end of a long day when clear thinking and a sense of the bigger picture are well beyond my grasp.

Perhaps Solomon's wisdom lay in his ability to reflect on what he truly needed. He knew that it was important to consider the larger community and his place in it. How might my requests change if I do the same?

God, may I recognize my need for wisdom more often.

Job 7: 1-4, 6-7; Ps 147; 1 Cor 9: 16-19, 22-23; Mk 1: 29-39

We sometimes say, 'There's no rest for the wicked." For Job, troubled and even angry with God, there seems to be no rest even for the just. Despite his anger at God, however, Job remains in his heart a person of faith and prayer.

Paul endured suffering as well. For the sake of the gospel, he became the servant of all, forfeiting everything so that no obstacle might stand between the gospel and those to whom he proclaimed it. The blessings the gospel brings were reward enough for him.

By contrast, the crowds in today's gospel hunt Jesus down, unable or unwilling to see who he is beyond the cures. Unlike Simon's mother-in-law, they do not yet understand that service to others is required of those who have been saved by Christ. Jesus does not leave them behind out of coldness on his part; he does so in order to proclaim the real message of salvation, which is not about incidental healings, but about a Messiah who will win salvation for all through his suffering and death.

In the face of human misery, the very best words of comfort do not explain away suffering, but proclaim the good news that Christ bore our sickness and endured our suffering. Rather than watching our suffering from afar, Christ has been and is with us, offering healing to the broken-hearted through a share in his resurrection. For this, we offer grateful praise.

**Lord Jesus, be with me in my suffering
and bring me true healing.**

They crossed the lake and came to land at Gennesaret, where they tied up the boat. As they left the boat, people recognized Jesus at once. So they ran throughout the whole region; and wherever they heard he was, they brought to him the sick lying on their mats. And everywhere Jesus went, to villages, towns, or farms, people would take their sick to the marketplaces and beg him to let the sick at least touch the edge of his cloak. And all who touched it were made well.

Mark 6: 53-56

> "And all who touched it were made well."

True faith

But what about those who didn't get to touch the edge of his cloak? Two days ago, Kayci's mother died after routine surgery. She experienced complications – and Jesus' cloak was nowhere in sight. Why are some healed while others are not? I don't know.

Honestly, I don't think today's reading will comfort those who grieve Mary Beth's death right now. But I do know this much. When tragedy strikes – without warning or explanation – and when healing doesn't happen, faith cannot be the blind conviction that this tragedy was somehow for the best.

Sometimes all you can do is reach out with compassion to the family and friends who are grieving. That reaching out is the real faith – even when it doesn't find a cloak to touch.

Dear Jesus, help me touch one person with compassion today – and let that touch bring some healing into the world.

The Pharisees and the teachers of the Law asked, "Why is it that your disciples do not follow the teaching handed down by our ancestors…?" Jesus answered, "How right Isaiah was! You are hypocrites, just as he wrote: 'These people, says God, honour me with their words, but their heart is really far away from me.'"

Jesus continued, "You have a clever way of rejecting God's law in order to uphold your own teaching. For Moses commanded, 'Respect your father and your mother….' But you teach that if people have something they could use to help their father or mother, but say, 'This is Corban' (which means, it belongs to God), they are excused from helping their father or mother. In this way the teaching you pass on to others cancels out the word of God."

Mark 7: 1-13

> "…but their heart is really far away from me."

God in the questions

Some days I really sympathize with the Pharisees and their penchant for the rules. As an elementary school teacher, I seem to spend a lot of time enforcing school rules that have a million and one exceptions. My students are always eager to point out the contradictions they see – and it drives me crazy!

Often the more I try to pin things down with rules, the more ridiculous they become. My students' constant questioning reminds me that God isn't found in the rules. God is found in my willingness to be surprised.

Sure, a set of foolproof rules would be handy. But if I had a big rulebook, I'd miss out on the chance to discover God as I wrestle with the questions.

God, remind me to look for you beyond the rules.

The queen of Sheba travelled to Jerusalem.... When she and Solomon met, she asked him all the questions that she could think of. He answered them all; there was nothing too difficult for him to explain....

The queen of Sheba said, "What I heard in my own country about you and your wisdom is true! But I couldn't believe it until I had come and seen it all for myself. But I didn't hear even half of it; your wisdom and wealth are much greater than what I was told.... Praise the Lord your God! He has shown how pleased he is with you by making you king of Israel. Because his love for Israel is eternal, he has made you their king so that you can maintain law and justice."

1 Kings 10: 1-10

> "...she asked him all the questions that she could think of."

Asking questions

As a journalist, I've learned to hold back my own reaction to a person's comments and instead to ask another question based on what they have just said. Once in a while, the person ends up telling me things that are very important to them but that they have never been able to fully articulate before, because no one has ever taken the time to listen. Those are moments of privilege for both of us.

The Queen of Sheba had learned one of the great arts of conversation: she knew how to listen. She didn't keep interrupting Solomon with her own opinion; she just kept asking, probing, hungry to understand.

How often do I genuinely learn from others' insights, or delight in their accomplishments, without constantly imposing my own?

**Lord, give me the generosity of spirit to listen,
and then listen some more.**

Jesus went away to the territory near the city of Tyre…. A woman, whose daughter had an evil spirit in her, heard about Jesus and came to him at once and fell at his feet. The woman was a Gentile, born in the region of Phoenicia in Syria. She begged Jesus to drive the demon out of her daughter. But Jesus answered, "Let us first feed the children. It isn't right to take the children's food and throw it to the dogs." "Sir," she answered, "even the dogs under the table eat the children's leftovers!" Jesus said to her, "Because of that answer, go back home, where you will find that the demon has gone out of your daughter!" She went home and found her child lying on the bed; the demon had indeed gone out of her.

Mark 7: 24-30

> "Sir, even the dogs under the table eat the children's leftovers."

Courage to persevere

The human heart has many longings, and few of those longings are satisfied without some effort. An old adage says: "There's a cost to everything!" Often, when I've had to struggle to reach a goal, I find that I treasure what I've gained even more.

Because she loved her daughter, the Phoenician woman struggled to overcome barriers. First she found the courage to make her way through the crowd. Then, in spite of rejection, she humbled herself before Jesus and persevered with her request for healing for her daughter.

When a colleague criticizes me, or a friend rejects me, or my family fails to understand me, I am called to overcome these obstacles as I try to grow in faith and love.

**Lord, give me courage to set my goal –
and the stubbornness to achieve it.**

S ome people brought Jesus a man who was deaf and could hardly speak, and they begged Jesus to place his hands on him. So Jesus took him off alone, away from the crowd, put his fingers in the man's ears, spat, and touched the man's tongue. Then Jesus looked up to heaven, gave a deep groan, and said to the man, "Ephphatha," which means, "Open up!"

At once the man was able to hear, his speech impediment was removed, and he began to talk without any trouble. Then Jesus ordered the people not to speak of it to anyone; but the more he ordered them not to, the more they told it. And all who heard were completely amazed. "How well he does everything!" they exclaimed. "He even causes the deaf to hear and the dumb to speak!"

Mark 7: 31-37

> "...gave a deep groan..."

The miracle

I teach at a school for adults. Many of my students have problems that make it difficult for them to learn. Sometimes, no matter how hard they try, and no matter how hard I try, it doesn't seem to work.

On one occasion a young woman said to me, "I guess I'm just too stupid." And she began to cry. What I would have given to be able to give a deep groan and perform a miracle, as Jesus did. But I couldn't, and her situation remained the same.

Eventually she had to lower her sights and switch programs. She seemed to accept her limitations. It always amazes me how people forge bravely on in a world that has not been generous to them. Maybe that's the miracle.

Dear God, help me to recognize and tear down obstacles that stand in the way of others.

Jesus said, "I feel sorry for these people, because they have been with me for three days and now have nothing to eat. If I send them home without feeding them, they will faint as they go...."

His disciples asked him, "Where in this desert can anyone find enough food to feed all these people?"

"How much bread do you have?" Jesus asked. "Seven loaves," they answered. Jesus took the seven loaves, gave thanks to God, broke them, and gave them to his disciples to distribute to the crowd; and the disciples did so. They also had a few small fish. Jesus gave thanks for these and told the disciples to distribute them too. Everybody ate and had enough. Then the disciples took up seven baskets full of pieces left over.   *Mark 8: 1-10*

> "Where in this desert can anyone find enough food...?"

Expect the unexpected

One reason I like the disciples is that they are rarely wise; instead, they are often ordinary and dull, just like me. You would think that after spending months and years with Jesus, they would have learned to look for the unexpected, to delight in witnessing God's grace in action. But here they are again, seeing only what is right in front of their noses.

I don't judge them harshly because I see myself in their plodding focus on the obvious. I, too, see the "facts" right in front of me. How can anyone solve widespread poverty? Environmental degradation? Economic injustice? It's all too much. It can't be done.

I can see Jesus smiling at them while ignoring their negative words, just as he smiles at me while ignoring mine: "Well, what have you got? Let's begin there."

Lord, help me to see life through your eyes, and to respond.

Lev 13: 1-2, 45-46; Ps 32; 1 Cor 10: 31 — 11.1; Mk 1: 40-45

What a dramatic story in today's gospel, one that goes to the heart of Jesus' spontaneous and compassionate response to suffering. An old Bible I have reads, "With warm indignation, Jesus stretched out his hand." I love that phrase "warm indignation." It expresses the anger and the love that Jesus feels about the obvious injustice experienced by this person who has leprosy and is rejected by his community. It is Jesus' righteous passion that prompts his gesture of *com*-passion.

We can easily summon a multitude of reasons why we cannot or should not help people who are suffering: "I've done enough!" "They've hurt me, so why should I help them?" "It's their own fault and they need to take responsibility for their lives." While these reasons may be valid, we can't use them to justify our anger or unwillingness to offer assistance. We may be right, but being right and angry is not the same thing as righteous anger!

When we stretch out our hand with "warm indignation" to help someone, we accept that the world is broken and unfair. Then we move from looking for someone or something to blame to wanting to be a loving person. A good question we can ask ourselves is this: "Do I want to be right in this situation or do I want to be loving?" They are often not the same thing!

**God of love, teach me to show my love to others,
even when it's the last thing I want to do.**

S ome Pharisees came to Jesus and started to argue with him. They wanted to trap him, so they asked him to perform a miracle to show that God approved of him. But Jesus gave a deep groan and said, "Why do the people of this day ask for a miracle? No, I tell you! No such proof will be given to these people!"

He left them, got back into the boat, and started across to the other side of the lake.

Mark 8: 11-13

> "Why do the people of this day ask for a miracle?"

Show me!

The Pharisees are usually synonymous with trickery and ill will. So I'm a bit surprised to find myself siding with them today.

Maybe they were trying to trap Jesus. But then again, maybe they were simply trying to find out the truth. After all, *if* Jesus had performed a miracle for them, wouldn't that have answered their question, once and for all?

If I stood on a hill tomorrow and said, "Cure cancer" or "End world poverty" and it happened instantly, wouldn't that resolve my own doubts and prove that Jesus was God's chosen one?

But then I hear Jesus' heartfelt groan and watch his back as he sails to the other side of the lake. And I realize that I still don't get it.

**Lord, give me understanding,
and help me see who you are.**

Happy are those who remain faithful under trials, because when they succeed in passing such a test, they will receive as their reward the life which God has promised to those who love him. If we are tempted by such trials, we must not say, "This temptation comes from God." For God cannot be tempted by evil, and he himself tempts no one. But we are tempted when we are drawn away and trapped by our own evil desires....

Do not be deceived, my dear friends! Every good gift and every perfect present comes from heaven; it comes down from God, the Creator of the heavenly lights, who does not change or cause darkness by turning. By his own will he brought us into being through the word of truth, so that we should have first place among all his creatures.   *James 1:12-18*

> "...who remain faithful under trials..."

Choosing to believe

Reeling from the news that my husband only had six to twelve months to live, I realized that I was faced with a choice. I could either deny and try to escape from that harsh reality, becoming bitter about what was "being done to me," or I could live fully whatever difficulties lay ahead, believing that life is good. While I couldn't change the final outcome, I could decide *how* I would face its challenges.

Nine years later, I realize that I face that same choice every day. I want to live believing that life is a gift from a loving God. But it's not always easy. There are times when I feel I can barely get through the day.

Deciding to believe in God's loving-kindness is a conscious choice I must make each and every day.

Lord, help me to meet my trials head on,
believing that you are with me in the midst of it all.

They came to Bethsaida, where some people brought a blind man to Jesus and begged him to touch him. Jesus took the blind man by the hand and led him out of the village. After spitting on the man's eyes, Jesus placed his hands on him and asked him, "Can you see anything?"

The man looked up and said, "Yes, I can see people, but they look like trees walking around."

Jesus again placed his hands on the man's eyes. This time the man looked intently, his eyesight returned, and he saw everything clearly. Jesus then sent him home with the order, "Don't go back into the village."

Mark 8: 22-26

> "Don't go back into the village."

Process what you preach

After finishing high school, I decided to live with a L'Arche community. It was my first time away from home, as well as my first experience of Christian community.

Being young and full of enthusiasm, I wanted to share this new experience with my family and friends. While my parents were pleased with my new-found outlook on life, a few of my close friends were not so impressed.

Like the blind man in today's reading, I was touched by Jesus and I could see life more clearly. But, as Jesus cautioned the blind man, I needed to "go home" – to let this experience settle and take hold deep within me. Instead, against Jesus' advice, I ran back to the "village," to tell everyone of my experience.

Lord, remind me to allow the experience of your love to take hold deep within me.

Jesus and his disciples went away to the villages near Caesarea Philippi. On the way he asked them, "Tell me, who do people say I am?"

"Some say that you are John the Baptist," they answered; "others say that you are Elijah, while others say that you are one of the prophets."

"What about you?" he asked them. "Who do you say I am?"

Peter answered, "You are the Messiah."

Then Jesus ordered them, "Do not tell anyone about me."

Then Jesus began to teach his disciples: "The Son of Man must suffer much and be rejected by the elders, the chief priests, and the teachers of the Law. He will be put to death, but three days later he will rise to life."

Mark 8: 27-33

> "Who do you say I am?"

Asking the question

A few years ago I moved far away from family and friends to an isolated community in northern Ontario. It was a challenging year for me: making new friends, starting a new job, adapting to a new language and culture.

In the silence and stillness of those long winter nights, I had lots of time for reflection and prayer. Looking back over those months, I see that God's love was working in me – prodding me, guiding me, asking me the question that Jesus asked the disciples.

That time spent in reflection helped me to grow in my spiritual life. And when asked to give Jesus my answer to his question, I was able to respond with deep conviction: "Jesus, you are my Saviour, my Beloved."

Jesus, continue to instill in me the desire for silence and reflection so I can know you better.

Jesus told the crowd: "If any of you want to come with me, you must forget yourself, carry your cross, and follow me. For if you want to save your own life, you will lose it; but if you lose your life for me and for the gospel, you will save it. Do you gain anything if you win the whole world but lose your life? Of course not! There is nothing you can give to regain your life. If you are ashamed of me and of my teaching in this godless and wicked day, then the Son of Man will be ashamed of you when he comes in the glory of his Father with the holy angels.

"I tell you, there are some here who will not die until they have seen the kingdom of God come with power."

Mark 8: 34 – 9: 1

> "If any of you want to come with me, you must carry your cross..."

Cross or resurrection?

My crosses tend to be people. People with one-track minds. People who prejudge issues. People who whine constantly. They sit beside me on planes. They single me out in a crowd. They put me on committees.

To balance that, my resurrections also tend to be people. Resurrections happen when an acquaintance unexpectedly turns into a friend. When a face lights up with a smile. When, on the telephone, I hear delight in someone's voice.

Crosses drain life; resurrections restore it. Sometimes there's not much difference between my crosses and my resurrections. Some of these people can't return much for what I try to give them. But spending time with them makes me feel good.

And I hope I'm not one of the crosses they have to bear.

**God, let me take up my crosses gladly,
confident that they can turn into resurrections.**

Just think how large a forest can be set on fire by a tiny flame! And the tongue is like a fire. It is a world of wrong, occupying its place in our bodies and spreading evil through our whole being. It sets on fire the entire course of our existence with the fire that comes to it from hell itself. We humans are able to tame and have tamed all other creatures – wild animals and birds, reptiles and fish. But no one has ever been able to tame the tongue. It is evil and uncontrollable, full of deadly poison. We use it to give thanks to our Lord and Father and also to curse other people, who are created in the likeness of God. Words of thanksgiving and cursing pour out from the same mouth. My friends, this should not happen!

James 3: 1-10

> "And the tongue is like a fire."

The power of words

Once, when my daughter was three, she was angry at me and said something hurtful. Like the good parent I was trying to be, I gently reminded her that words are powerful and that hers had hurt my feelings. She looked me straight in the eye and said, "Good. I wanted them to."

Somehow I managed to keep from laughing, and made a mental note not to be so smarmy next time. But I also noted that my young daughter clearly understood the effect words can have on others.

I, too, know the power of words. Yet sometimes I forget or, even worse, like my daughter, I deliberately speak words meant to hurt. Harsh words come so easily and can be so hard to undo.

Lord, words can be used like a sharp knife.
Give me wise judgment in my use of them.

Isa 43: 18-22, 24-25; Ps 41; 2 Cor 1: 18-22; Mk 2: 1-12

Early in his ministry, Jesus travelled the countryside, proclaiming the proximity of the kingdom of God and demonstrating his gentle love for those in need of his healing power. Now a crowd has followed him home, thirsting to hear the good news. Today, Mark recounts for us a heartfelt example of how first-century "thinking outside the box" brought wholeness to one particular person.

Among those who had come to Jesus' home were a paralyzed man and his four friends. Realizing that there was no way to reach

Jesus in the conventional way, they had the audacity to climb to the rooftop of his house, hoist their friend up, then lower him into the room where Jesus sat. By their act of faith, these friends became the vehicle by which the paralyzed man was able to experience Jesus' gentle healing touch.

Today, that same faith can inspire us to daring action on behalf of those in need and especially on behalf of those who seek justice. Our willingness to think outside the box can open us to the amazing power of Jesus' promise that "the one who believes in me will also do the works that I do and, in fact, will do greater works than these" (John 14:12). Do we have the audacity to believe that we, too, can create a world where all can be healed and made whole?

**Jesus, help me find creative ways to reach you
when the usual ways seem blocked.**

A man in the crowd [said], "Teacher, I brought my son to you, because he has an evil spirit in him and cannot talk…. Have pity on us and help us, if you possibly can!" "Yes," said Jesus, "if you yourself can! Everything is possible for the person who has faith." The father at once cried out, "I do have faith, but not enough. Help me have more!"

Jesus… gave a command to the evil spirit. "Deaf and dumb spirit," he said, "I order you to come out of the boy and never go into him again!" The spirit screamed, threw the boy into a bad fit, and came out….

The disciples asked Jesus privately, "Why couldn't we drive the spirit out?" "Only prayer can drive this kind out," answered Jesus; "nothing else can." *Mark 9: 14-29*

> "Everything is possible for the person who has faith."

Faith and healing

This story sounds so out of sync in our age of scientific explanations. How am I to understand this story?

I think of a friend who, on two occasions, attempted suicide. Real attempts, not "just" cries for help. Now, some years later, still in a twelve-step program, still recovering, he credits his success as a husband and father to a greater power and his faith in that power. When he talks, he sounds different: there's a ring of reality to what he says. He is changed.

If you'd asked him some years ago how he could shake the abysmal darkness he experienced, how he could exorcise his demons, he would have said (and indeed did say): "I can't believe I ever will."

"Everything is possible for the person who has faith."

God, I struggle with my own demons, and I can't seem to change. Help me when I despair and lose faith.

Jesus and his disciples left that place and went on through Galilee…. They came to Capernaum, and after going indoors Jesus asked his disciples, "What were you arguing about on the road?" But they would not answer him, because on the road they had been arguing among themselves about who was the greatest. Jesus sat down, called the twelve disciples, and said to them, "Whoever wants to be first must place himself last of all and be the servant of all." Then he took a child and had him stand in front of them. He put his arms around him and said to them, "Whoever welcomes in my name one of these children, welcomes me; and whoever welcomes me, welcomes not only me but also the one who sent me."

Mark 9: 30-37

"…one of these children…"

A child's love

Not long ago, as I walked down a hospital corridor, I found myself approaching an elderly woman. Sitting in her wheelchair, she looked quite unhappy. I wondered what words of comfort I could offer her.

A young boy, who could not have been more than four, was coming from the other end of the hallway. He happily bounced toward the wheelchair, holding his mother's hand. When he came alongside of it, he gave the woman in the wheelchair a huge smile, a cheery wave and a bright two-note "Hi."

I marvelled at his spontaneous and loving ministry that came straight from the heart. I felt I was standing in the presence of pure and genuine life. Yes, in welcoming the children, I welcome Jesus.

Lord, may I welcome all children with open arms, recognizing your life-giving spirit in their eyes.

Here we are, then, speaking for Christ, as though God himself were making his appeal through us. We plead on Christ's behalf: let God change you from enemies into his friends! Christ was without sin, but for our sake God made him share our sin in order that in union with him we might share the righteousness of God.

In our work together with God, then, we beg you who have received God's grace not to let it be wasted. Hear what God says: "When the time came for me to show you favour, I heard you; when the day arrived for me to save you, I helped you."

2 Corinthians 5: 20 – 6: 2

> "Here we are, then, speaking for Christ…"

In Christ's name

Several years before he died, my father gave me power of attorney. Not until later did I realize what an enormous act of trust that was. The power of attorney gave me the same authority he had – over his property, his bank accounts, his business affairs. I could act in his name.

The third great commandment says, "You shall not take the name of the Lord in vain." My father trusted me not to take his name in vain.

Jesus, too, gave his disciples a kind of power of attorney. "Even the demons obeyed us," they exulted, "when we gave them a command in your name." That took enormous trust on Jesus' part. Now we, like Paul, are trusted to speak in his name.

God, may I always speak in your name
faithfully and lovingly.

"Today I am giving you a choice between good and evil, between life and death. If you obey the commands of the Lord your God, which I give you today, if you love him, obey him, and keep all his laws, then you will prosper and become a nation of many people.... But if you disobey and refuse to listen, and are led away to worship other gods, you will be destroyed – I warn you here and now.... I am now giving you the choice between life and death, between God's blessing and God's curse, and I call heaven and earth to witness the choice you make. Choose life. Love the Lord your God, obey him and be faithful to him, and then you and your descendants will live long in the land that he promised to give your ancestors, Abraham, Isaac, and Jacob."

Deuteronomy 30: 15-20

> "Choose life."

Good and evil

Who wouldn't choose life over death, good over evil? When I consider the choices in such stark terms, my decision seems easy. But today I can choose to visit my aunt who is housebound, or I can telephone her, or I can do nothing. None of these choices is evil, but they are not equally loving or good.

Life is full of choices. I once read that life is a continuum and we constantly move either in the direction of good or in the direction of evil. Not every decision is definitive, but we need to be moving in the right direction.

This image is helpful when I want to choose good over evil with one grand, magnificent flourish, rather than inching along, one small step at a time.

Dear Lord, forgive my impatience. Help me remain faithful to you in the little things.

The people ask, "Why should we fast if the Lord never notices?" The Lord says to them, "The truth is that at the same time you fast, you pursue your own interests and oppress your workers. Your fasting makes you violent, and you quarrel and fight. Do you think this kind of fasting will make me listen to your prayers? When you fast, you make yourselves suffer…. Is that what you call fasting? Do you think I will be pleased with that?

"The kind of fasting I want is this: Remove the chains of oppression and the yoke of injustice, and let the oppressed go free. Share your food with the hungry and open your homes to the homeless poor. Give clothes to those who have nothing to wear, and do not refuse to help your own relatives."

Isaiah 58: 1-9

> "…do not refuse to help your own relatives."

Closer to home

I notice that today's reading ends with "do not refuse to help your own relatives." When I hear about feeding the hungry and giving shelter to the homeless, I feel overwhelmed. The problems "out there" seem so big, and my efforts seem so insignificant.

I agree that I must not forget the needs of the hungry and the homeless. But neither can I overlook the needs of those closer to home. I must be honest with myself and acknowledge when I've been defensive or self-righteous with members of my family. When I've quarrelled needlessly. When I've not tried to find a peaceful settlement of our differences.

Today, I will try to lift the burden of misunderstanding that I've placed on someone's shoulders and bring peace to that relationship.

Lord, today I will look at my relationships within my family. I will reach out to one person in a gesture of peace.

After this, Jesus went out and saw a tax collector named Levi, sitting in his office. Jesus said to him, "Follow me." Levi got up, left everything, and followed him.

Then Levi had a big feast in his house for Jesus, and among the guests were a large number of tax collectors and other people. Some Pharisees and some teachers of the Law who belonged to their group complained to Jesus' disciples. "Why do you eat and drink with tax collectors and other outcasts?" they asked.

Jesus answered them, "People who are well do not need a doctor, but only those who are sick. I have not come to call respectable people to repent, but outcasts."

Luke 5: 27-32

"Levi got up and left everything…"

Following through

What an extraordinary story! Jesus comes up to the tax official sitting in his office and says, "Follow me." And the tax collector gets up, leaves his lucrative position of power and sets off with Jesus.

Sometimes the big, difficult decisions come easily to me: I respond in a moment of grace. Impulsively I reach out to someone who has been my enemy, or speak against an abuse of power in my workplace. I make the decision to walk away from an unhealthy friendship.

It's following through that's difficult: holding firm when I've made the first step. Levi probably had second thoughts when he realized how poor and vulnerable Jesus was. What made Levi an apostle was that he persevered with his daring deed.

**Teach me, Lord, to follow my good
and generous impulses when you call me to act.**

Gen 9: 8-15; Ps 25; I Pet 3: 18-22; Mk 1: 12-15

The season of Lent is our time to prepare to celebrate the death and resurrection of Jesus. It might seem easier to get to Easter without passing through this time of reflection and restraint, but that is not the path to conversion envisioned by today's readings.

Jesus prepared for his ministry by living in the wilderness for 40 days, a time of privation he was sorely tempted to cut short. In the Bible, the wilderness is not only a place of testing; it is also a place of encounter with God. If you have ever lived through a period of forced unemployment, a failed relationship or the loss of a loved one, you may be able to imagine how devastating a "wilderness experience" can be. In such difficult moments, it is hard to reimagine the radical fullness of life to which God continually invites us.

Yet after the tremendous destruction of the flood, God offered Noah a covenant that was extended to "every living creature ... for all future generations." Peter's letter reminds us that Christ suffered for us all: the righteous and the unrighteous. No matter how difficult our wilderness experience, we remember that it was the Spirit that "drove" Jesus there in preparation for his ministry. Let us embrace Lent, this time of God that has come near, so we can join Jesus in the journey of good news that leads to Easter!

**Lord, be with me in the desert of Lent
as I prepare my heart for the joy of Easter.**

"The King will say, 'Come, you that are blessed by my Father! Come and possess the kingdom…. I was hungry and you fed me, thirsty and you gave me a drink; I was a stranger and you received me in your homes, naked and you clothed me; I was sick and you took care of me, in prison and you visited me.' The righteous will then answer him, 'When, Lord, did we ever see you hungry and feed you, or thirsty and give you a drink? When did we ever see you a stranger and welcome you in our homes, or naked and clothe you? When did we ever see you sick or in prison, and visit you?' The King will reply, 'I tell you, whenever you did this for one of the least important of these followers of mine, you did it for me.'"

Matthew 25: 31-46

> "When did we ever see you a stranger…?"

Habits of the heart

Sometimes people don't see the good they do. Maybe the habit of love becomes so ingrained, they don't even know they're being good anymore.

Growing up, I never noticed it in my mother. Like the people in today's reading, I imagine her saying, "Lord, when did we ever see you hungry…?" Yet, when someone died, she'd be making egg salad sandwiches. If a neighbour's spouse walked out on them, they'd be sitting at our kitchen table. If the husband of the woman down the street drank up the grocery money, my mother would say: "Here's a little something until payday."

If someone complimented her, she'd reply, "I'm only doing what I'm supposed to do." Her favourite prayer was "O Lord, I am not worthy…." Guess what, Mom? I disagree; I think you were very worthy.

**Lord, help me give of myself in little ways,
so that helping others becomes a habit.**

"**M**y word is like the snow and the rain
that come down from the sky to water the earth.
They make the crops grow
and provide seed for planting and food to eat.
So also will be the word that I speak –
it will not fail to do what I plan for it;
it will do everything I send it to do."

Isaiah 55: 10-11

> "My word is like the snow and the rain…"

Rain and snow

I sense it's a good thing that Isaiah was never in Saskatchewan when the rain threatens to cause permanent damage to your skull as it lashes down with frightening violence. And that he never had to walk across the High Level Bridge in Edmonton during a skin-scraping February blizzard. Accordingly, God's promise to Isaiah has a certain Mediterranean warmth to it.

But of course, through Isaiah, God is also speaking to me – here and now. And it's up to me to find meaning through my own experience and situation.

As much as I want the benign kindness of God in the form of gentle spring showers, I know that God's voice also calls to me in the extremes of storms and blizzards.

**Dear God, please give me the courage
to become more than your fairweather friend.**

O nce again the Lord spoke to Jonah. He said, "Go to Nineveh, that great city, and proclaim to the people the message I have given you." So Jonah obeyed the Lord and went to Nineveh, a city so large that it took three days to walk through it. Jonah started through the city, and after walking a whole day, he proclaimed, "In forty days Nineveh will be destroyed!"

The people of Nineveh believed God's message. So they decided that everyone should fast, and all the people, from the greatest to the least, put on sackcloth to show that they had repented....

God saw what they did; he saw that they had given up their wicked behaviour. So he changed his mind and did not punish them as he had said he would.

Jonah 3: 1-10

"So he changed his mind..."

Mercy and love

A tow truck scours the streets of our neighbourhood, looking for illegally parked vehicles. It gleams black and silver. Emblazoned above the cab in bright letters are the words "Expect No Mercy." Every time I see it, I imagine Jonah sitting behind the wheel. I think of him prowling the streets of Nineveh, warning of the severe judgment awaiting those whose meters have almost run out.

God's response in today's reading boggles my mind. Mercy is not something I'm very good at. I prefer to think about the just punishments waiting for those who have hurt me, rather than to look for ways I could be merciful.

Today I will look at my habit of judging harshly, and I will take one small step toward changing it.

Forgiving God, teach me to reach out to others with a merciful touch.

I thank you, Lord, with all my heart;
I sing praise to you before the gods.
I face your holy Temple,
bow down, and praise your name
because of your constant love and faithfulness....
You answered me when I called to you;
with your strength you strengthened me
When I am surrounded by troubles,
you keep me safe....
You will do everything you have promised;
Lord, your love is eternal.
Complete the work that you have begun.
Psalm 138: 1-3, 7-8

> "...you strengthened me."

Strength in weakness

My children and I have been watching a spider that has stretched her web between the garage and our honeysuckle tree. We've become quite attached to her. Each day we go to check on her progress. The last few nights have been windy and I've been afraid we'll find her gossamer strands in tatters.

And yet the web remains. Some strands have been broken, but the spider persists: she repairs and rebuilds. What seems so vulnerable, so fragile, is actually strong, surprisingly resilient.

There are times when my resources are stretched. Rather than panicking, I might think of this little spider that lets the web of her life stretch and bend through the windy days, believing that the calm days for repairing will come.

**Thank you, God, for the small signs of strength
that inspire me.**

From the depths of my despair I call to you, Lord.
Hear my cry, O Lord;
    listen to my call for help!
If you kept a record of our sins,
who could escape being condemned?
But you forgive us,
so that we should stand in awe of you.
I wait eagerly for the Lord's help,
and in his word I trust.
I wait for the Lord
more eagerly than sentries wait for the dawn –
than sentries wait for the dawn.

Psalm 130: 1-6

"From the depths of my despair…"

Forgiveness

What was the psalmist's despair? And when was he feeling that despair? The dark, rainy days in early spring are the worst for me – when winter stretches its fingers, holding on. That's when I struggle with the memories of all I've done and can't undo, should have done and didn't. All the hurtful words I've spoken that can never be unsaid.

And what of those whose sins are more serious? Who got drunk, then killed someone while driving home? Seduced someone's spouse, and destroyed a family? Lost wife and kids through an addiction? What are the depths of their despair on dark, rainy nights? Those whom we would judge.

The psalmist says, "But you forgive us…." This is the great mystery: God forgives. We can be forgiven. And so must we forgive ourselves. And others.

**Loving God, forgive my sins.
Give me the courage to forgive myself, and others.**

Y ou have heard that it was said, 'Love your friends, hate your enemies.' But now I tell you: love your enemies and pray for those who persecute you, so that you may become the children of your Father in heaven. For he makes his sun to shine on bad and good people alike, and gives rain to those who do good and to those who do evil. Why should God reward you if you love only the people who love you? Even the tax collectors do that! And if you speak only to your friends, have you done anything out of the ordinary? Even the pagans do that! You must be perfect – just as your Father in heaven is perfect."

Matthew 5: 43-48

"Love your enemies…"

Love your enemies

Is Jesus *really* asking me to love Adolf Hitler? To love the people who flew the planes into the Twin Towers on 9/11? To love those who kill innocent civilians in the many war-torn cities around the world?

All who visit – or even think about – Ground Zero find themselves moved to pray for the thousands of people who were killed in that attack. And some pray for those who flew the planes that day.

Jesus seems to be asking me to do the near impossible. But he knows (from personal experience, in fact) that it is the only way to peace – in ourselves and in our world.

O God, do you understand the demands you make on those who want to follow you? Help me accept that kind of demand.

Gen 22: 1-2, 9-13, 15-18; Ps 116; Rom 8: 31-35, 37; Mk 9: 2-10

Today's readings call for reflection on our trust in God, who gives us life and all we have, who blesses us even when all hope seems lost. The first reading tells us that God asked Abraham to sacrifice his only son, Isaac. Abraham unhesitatingly said "Yes." God spared Isaac's life and blessed Abraham abundantly, "because you have obeyed my voice."

Paul reminds us that God gave up his own Son for us. Jesus died on a cross; as his followers, we are called to carry our daily crosses. A loved one with an incurable disease, a broken relationship... In painful moments, God asks us to trust and God will shower us with blessings.

Mark's gospel story is *awe*-some: Jesus takes three disciples to a mountaintop and is transfigured before their eyes. As they behold Jesus clad in "dazzling white," God's voice is heard saying, "This is my Son, the Beloved; listen to him!" How graced they were to share this intimate moment!

We are called to intimacy with God, to listen to the voice of Jesus speaking in our hearts, to walk in Jesus' footsteps so we may be transfigured. Throughout Lent, may we reply "Yes" when God asks something difficult of us. When God calls us home, may we be welcomed with the words "This is my child, the beloved!"

God of love, I find it hard to trust. Open my heart to you.

I prayed to the Lord my God and confessed the sins of my people. I said, "Lord God, you are great, and we honour you. You are faithful to your covenant and show constant love to those who love you and do what you command.

"We have sinned, we have been evil, we have done wrong…. We have not listened to your servants the prophets, who spoke in your name to our kings, our rulers, our ancestors, and our whole nation. You, Lord, always do what is right, but we have always brought disgrace on ourselves…. You are merciful and forgiving, although we have rebelled against you. We did not listen to you, O Lord our God, when you told us to live according to the laws which you gave us through your servants the prophets."

Daniel 9: 3-10

> "…and confessed the sins of my people."

Society's sin

Daniel confessed "the sins of his people." What sins of my people would I confess today? I know I couldn't get away with the hypocrisy of confessing another person's personal sins. Of course, I am tempted to do that, and that in itself is a sin.

Daniel had something else in mind. He was talking about social sin. I don't know what sin he was confessing, but there are still many to choose from today. Sins like letting millions in Africa die of AIDS and famine – because, in our wealth, we find we are not wealthy enough. Sins like preferring tax cuts to offering health care to the poor and a living wage to immigrants. In fact, our list may be longer than Daniel's.

**Lord, your prophets confessed their collective sins.
Help me to recognize ours.**

"... Listen to what the Lord is saying to you. Pay attention to what our God is teaching you. ... Wash yourselves clean. Stop all this evil that I see you doing. Yes, stop doing evil and learn to do right. See that justice is done – help those who are oppressed, give orphans their rights, and defend widows." ... Because the Lord is righteous, he will save Jerusalem and everyone there who repents. But he will crush everyone who sins and rebels against him; he will kill everyone who forsakes him....

Isaiah 1: 10, 16-20, 27-28, 31

> "Listen to what the Lord is saying to you."

Love and limits

How can I reconcile my image of God – as always patient and kind – with the one presented in today's reading? What would push a loving God to speak and act so strongly?

I think I've often confused loving with not imposing any limits. It's taken me a while to learn when to be patient and when to say, "Enough is enough! I won't take this anymore!" Also, there have been times when I have pushed the patience and limits of those I love. Their willingness to challenge me has been the wake-up call I needed.

Perhaps today's reading is saying that, while there are no limits to God's love, when my words and actions are unloving and unacceptable, God will say, "Enough is enough."

**Loving God, help me to recognize your limits
so that I may act justly.**

Keep me safe from the trap that has been set for me;
shelter me from danger.
I place myself in your care.
You will save me, Lord;
you are a faithful God....
I hear many enemies whispering;
terror is all around me.
They are making plans against me,
plotting to kill me.
But my trust is in you, O Lord;
you are my God.
I am always in your care;
save me from my enemies,
from those who persecute me.   *Psalm 31: 4-5, 13-15*

"They are making plans against me…"

Blinded by suspicion

I'm not proud of this incident. When I was still in high school, an acquaintance telephoned, saying, "Carl and I wanted to invite you over to join us." I didn't go. I thought they were up to something. I accused them of plotting ways to humiliate me. In truth, I had no grounds for my suspicions – except suspicion itself.

If the psalmist was writing about the nation of Israel, then I can understand the writer's suspicions. Israel was a small nation, a pawn of the larger powers that dominated the region.

But if it's about an individual, I can't help wondering if he, too, had bad days when he thought everyone was conspiring against him.

I trust you, God. I really do.
Free me from my secret doubts and fears.

"There was once a rich man who dressed in the most expensive clothes and lived in great luxury every day. There was also a poor man named Lazarus, covered with sores, who used to be brought to the rich man's door, hoping to eat the bits of food that fell from the rich man's table.... The poor man died and was carried by the angels to sit beside Abraham at the feast in heaven. The rich man died and was buried, and in Hades, where he was in great pain.... He called out, 'Father Abraham! Take pity on me, and send Lazarus to dip his finger in some water and cool off my tongue....' But Abraham said, 'Remember, my son, that in your lifetime you were given all the good things, while Lazarus got all the bad things. But now he is enjoying himself here, while you are in pain. Besides all that, there is a deep pit lying between us, so that those who want to cross over from here to you cannot do so.'"

Luke 16: 19-31

> "...there is a deep pit lying between us..."

All by myself

Jean-Paul Sartre once wrote that "Hell is other people." I think the pain of isolation is far worse.

How terrible it is for the rich man to know he cannot undo the past. Worse still, he cannot change the future by warning others of the consequences of his selfishness. A gulf now separates him from those he loves. His isolation is complete.

Our culture encourages me to fend for myself and to live by the creed "No compromise." When I get caught up in my own needs and neglect the needs of others, I live by that creed. When I shut the door on the poor, I live by that creed. After all, who is there to compromise with when I'm concerned only with myself?

**Lord, help me to reach out to others
with compassion today.**

Jacob loved Joseph more than all his other sons, because he had been born to him when he was old. He made a long robe with full sleeves for him. When his brothers saw that their father loved Joseph more than he loved them, they hated their brother....

Joseph's brothers plotted against him and decided to kill him. They said to one another, "Come on now, let's kill him and throw his body into one of the dry wells...."

Reuben heard them and tried to save Joseph. "Let's not kill him," he said. "Just throw him into this well in the wilderness, but don't hurt him...." When Joseph came up to his brothers, they ripped off his long robe with full sleeves. Then they took him and threw him into the well. *Genesis 37: 3-4, 12-13, 17-28*

> "...and threw him into the well."

Sibling rivalry

I've thrown my brother down many a well over the years, though never intentionally. Last summer, as we sat out on the deck, my mother told me something I didn't want to hear. "Your brother has always felt that he has lived under your shadow." My immediate response was to dismiss such a preposterous idea. But she persisted. "He always looked up to you and somehow felt he could never live up to the standards you set."

"But he's running the company's division, doing an executive MBA, has two kids, has built an extension on his house all by himself, and is a marathon cyclist!"

Then I realized how I, too, have kept a list of accomplishments that I can serve up as resentments whenever necessary.

Dear God, let me learn to celebrate – rather than count – the differences between me and others.

P raise the Lord, my soul!
All my being, praise his holy name!
Praise the Lord, my soul,
and do not forget how kind he is.
He forgives all my sins
and heals all my diseases.
He keeps me from the grave
and blesses me with love and mercy....
He does not keep on rebuking;
he is not angry forever.
He does not punish us as we deserve
or repay us according to our sins and wrongs.
As high as the sky is above the earth,
so great is his love for those who honour him.   *Psalm 103: 1-4, 9-12*

"...so great is his love..."

Faithfulness

My beloved Irish setter, Brick, died last year, worn out by a lifetime of epilepsy. In one sense, his death freed me from a prison of pills and exercise regimes, of arranging for dog sitters and, occasionally, repairing the damage caused by his playful spirit.

But I miss him terribly. He was always glad to see me. He always trusted me. He loved me unconditionally.

My daughter gave me a politically incorrect T-shirt. Its caption refers to a "dyslexic agnostic" pondering "if there is a Dog." Is it pure coincidence, I wonder, that "dog" and "God" use the same letters in English? Because the relationship between God and me, as portrayed in today's reading, sometimes seems uncommonly like the relationship I knew with my dog.

**I wish I could be as faithful to you, God,
as my dog was to me. Thank you for your unending love.**

Sunday | MARCH 11

Ex 20: 1-17; Ps 19; 1 Cor 1: 18, 22-25; Jn 2: 13-25

Have you ever found out that a person you assumed you knew wasn't the person you thought they were? If I'm honest, I have to admit that today's gospel leaves me feeling this way. The Jesus we hear about today seems to be a world away from the one who blesses children and has such compassion for sinners. The gentle and loving Jesus is someone with whom we long to have a relationship. But a Jesus who gets mad and even overturns tables in his fury? That's a different matter.

Perhaps the reason we are uneasy with the image of Jesus in today's gospel is that it challenges us and moves us beyond our comfort zone. It leads us to ask ourselves what kinds of things Jesus would change or overturn in *us*. What would he cleanse in the temple of *our* lives if we let him in?

Each Lent, for 40 days we are challenged to allow Jesus to enter our lives to cleanse us of apathy or jealousy or hatred or despair or whatever does not nurture our relationship with God and others. As we continue our Lenten journey, may we open ourselves ever more deeply to the purifying power of the One who loved us enough to take our sins to the cross.

**Jesus, I long to know you.
Help me to welcome you into my life.**

Naaman, the commander of the Syrian army, was a great soldier, but he suffered from a dreaded skin disease. In one of their raids against Israel, the Syrians had carried off a little Israelite girl, who became a servant of Naaman's wife. One day she said to her mistress, "I wish that my master could go to the prophet who lives in Samaria! He would cure him of his disease." ... So Naaman went with his horses and chariot and stopped at the entrance to Elisha's house. Elisha sent a servant out to tell him to go and wash himself seven times in the Jordan River, and he would be completely cured of his disease.... So Naaman went down to the Jordan, dipped himself in it seven times, as Elisha had instructed, and he was completely cured.

2 Kings 5: 1-15

> "...and he was completely cured."

A simple request

How was it that Naaman found healing and an experience of God? First, he was desperate, suffering from a disease with no known cure. Second, he paid attention to a servant girl and took her advice to heart. In venturing forth to visit a prophet in neighbouring Israel, he let go of his national pride. And by listening again to a servant he was able to let go of the heroic and follow the simple way asked for by Elisha. In short, Naaman learned humility.

In my own life, too, it is often only when I am in a desperate situation, when my pride comes crumbling down, that I can hear and trust in those ordinary people in my life who are right beside me.

Lord, may I have the humility to receive the wisdom of the people in my life.

Peter came to Jesus and asked, "Lord, if my brother keeps on sinning against me, how many times do I have to forgive him? Seven times?"

"No, not seven times," answered Jesus, "but seventy times seven, because the kingdom of heaven is like this. Once there was a king who decided to check on his servants' accounts.... The king said to the servant, 'I forgave you the whole amount you owed me, just because you asked me to. You should have had mercy on your fellow servant, just as I had mercy on you.' The king was very angry, and he sent the servant to jail to be punished...."

Jesus concluded, "That is how my Father in heaven will treat every one of you unless you forgive your brother from your heart."

Matthew 18: 21-35

> "You should have had mercy on your fellow servant..."

Pass it on

In so many areas of life, I rarely get to keep what I have received. I am blessed in receiving and I am blessed in passing it on. To keep something for myself is to interrupt the flow.

Think of a pipe that carries water from one spot to another: in receiving the water and passing it along, the pipe is washed. If one end of the pipe is blocked and the water cannot pass through, then the water stagnates and the pipe rusts.

No doubt it costs to give to and forgive others... as the Lord gives to and forgives me. But for me to hold onto what I have received not only deprives others, it also blocks God's saving action in my life.

Open my hands, Lord, to receive
***and* to share what I have been given.**

"Do not think that I have come to do away with the Law of Moses and the teachings of the prophets. I have not come to do away with them, but to make their teachings come true. Remember that as long as heaven and earth last, not the least point nor the smallest detail of the Law will be done away with – not until the end of all things. So then, whoever disobeys even the least important of the commandments and teaches others to do the same, will be least in the kingdom of heaven. On the other hand, whoever obeys the Law and teaches others to do the same, will be great in the kingdom of heaven."

Matthew 5: 17-19

> "...to make their teachings come true."

The purpose of the law

When I got my first job, I wanted to impress my boss. I arrived before starting time; I never took my full lunch hour; and even if I had finished all my assigned tasks, I found something meaningless to keep me occupied until it was quitting time.

As I became more involved in my work – and more confident – I stopped worrying about the clock and began to concentrate more on what we were trying to do as a team. I hadn't done away with my timetable. Instead, I got better at fulfilling its purpose.

My life is richer when I stop worrying about the details of God's law and concentrate on its purpose: to guide me toward a life of truth, justice and love.

**Lord, help me to commit myself
to your holy purpose for my life.**

" **I** did command them to obey me, so that I would be their God and they would be my people. And I told them to live the way I had commanded them, so that things would go well for them. But they did not obey or pay any attention. Instead, they did whatever their stubborn and evil hearts told them to do, and they became worse instead of better. From the day that your ancestors came out of Egypt until this very day I have kept on sending to you my servants, the prophets. Yet no one listened or paid any attention. Instead, you became more stubborn and rebellious than your ancestors.

"So, Jeremiah, you will speak all these words to my people, but they will not listen to you; you will call them, but they will not answer."

Jeremiah 7: 23-28

> "…speak all these words to my people…"

Keep trying

Sometimes I feel that no one is listening to me. Not my kids (muddy boots left in the hall), my husband (gym clothes rotting away beside the washer), my students (homework left at home). Even the cat seems bent on breaking my spirit (furballs heaved onto the living room carpet)! How can I build a bridge of faith over the anger and disappointment I feel?

At first glance, today's reading offers little solace. God's anger is deep; it is painful. And yet, despite angry words, God does not abandon the people of Israel. God sends Jeremiah in… again. At least the lines of communication are open.

The next time I feel like turning away, I might try to use Jeremiah as a model of my own.

God, I know you understand my disappointments. Help my actions reflect a love that is deeper than my anger.

A teacher of the Law came to [Jesus] with a question: "Which commandment is the most important of all?" Jesus replied, "The most important one is this: 'Love the Lord your God with all your heart, with all your soul, with all your mind, and with all your strength.' The second most important commandment is this: 'Love your neighbour as you love yourself.' There is no other commandment more important than these two."

The teacher of the Law said, "It is true, as you say… you must love God with all your heart and with all your mind and with all your strength; and you must love your neighbour as you love yourself. It is more important to obey these two commandments than to offer on the altar animals and other sacrifices to God."

Mark 12: 28-34

> "…you must love your neighbour as you love yourself."

One rule

Not long ago, a friend of mine joined Overeaters Anonymous. Her guiding principle has become HALT: she doesn't eat when she's Hungry, Angry, Lonely or Tired. Living with an eating disorder means she is no longer in touch with her true hunger. Rules are required to guide and regulate her eating habits.

What about my own life? I know that when I fill myself with fast food or junk food I lose the taste for truly good and healthy food. Similarly, when I opt for "instant intimacy" and shallow relationships, I lose the hunger for true and healthy love.

When faced with a decision, instead of looking to many rules, I need to stop and ask: Is my choice based on the greatest rule of all, God's law of love?

**Lord, keep my heart hungry for the love
that makes me whole, free and alive!**

"I will abandon my people until they have suffered enough for their sins and come looking for me. Perhaps in their suffering they will try to find me."

The people say, "Let's return to the Lord! He has hurt us, but he will be sure to heal us; he has wounded us, but he will bandage our wounds, won't he...?"

But the Lord says, "Israel and Judah, what am I going to do with you? Your love for me disappears as quickly as morning mist; it is like dew, that vanishes early in the day. That is why I have sent my prophets to you.... What I want from you is plain and clear: I want your constant love, not your animal sacrifices. I would rather have my people know me than burn offerings to me."

Hosea 5: 15 – 6: 6

"What I want from you is plain and clear..."

Simplicity itself

I am, without a doubt, part of the best-educated generation that has ever lived. I know about history, science, math, great works of art and literature. I even know how computers work! I have read my fill of theological and spiritual works to help me try to understand who God is and what God wants of me.

But I'm not sure that this knowledge has helped me very much. There are even times when I feel paralyzed by the vast stores of information to which I have access. I sometimes think that knowing so much has taken me further from the truth, not closer.

But here it is, simple as can be: God wants to be known and loved. And that's it. The rest is details.

Lord, the road to you is cluttered with thoughts and words. Help me clear a simple path to walk along.

2 Chr 36: 14-17, 19-23; Ps 137; Eph 2: 4-10; Jn 3: 14-21

Many people in the world today have experienced some form of exile or separation from home, family or livelihood. Often this state is accompanied by loneliness, fear, even a sense of abandonment by God. The Israelites experienced exile as a result of their lack of faithfulness to God. Yet today's first reading shows us that God never forgot them. In time they were sent home to rebuild the Temple and to practise their faith again. They recognized anew God at work, healing and restoring life.

Jesus, in today's gospel, reveals that God's love extends to all humanity. In the sign of his cross, we see into the heart of God: mercy and compassion, not condemnation. Anyone who but looks to God with eyes of faith will be saved. This happens by grace, says Paul, not by our own efforts. It comes through the gift of Christ sharing with us the life of God.

Whatever obstacles we might face, the sign of the cross motivates and sustains us to go confidently into the world, bearers of a message that is truly liberating. Together with Christ we allow ourselves to be a sign of God's mercy and compassion. Through our actions we play a vital part in God's plan for the salvation of all humanity and the very earth upon which we dwell.

God of grace, lead me out of exile into the freedom of loving you and everyone I meet.

When God promised Abraham and his descendants that the world would belong to him, he did so, not because Abraham obeyed the Law, but because he believed and was accepted as righteous by God....

And so the promise was based on faith, in order that the promise should be guaranteed as God's free gift to all of Abraham's descendants – not just to those who obey the Law, but also to those who believe as Abraham did.... So the promise is good in the sight of God, in whom Abraham believed – the God who brings the dead to life and whose command brings into being what did not exist. Abraham believed and hoped, even when there was no reason for hoping. ... That is why Abraham, through faith, "was accepted as righteous by God."

Romans 4: 13, 16-18, 22

> "...even when there was no reason for hoping."

Reason to believe

It's easy to believe in God or trust that God loves me when things are going well, but that isn't always the way life is. There have been times when I have experienced intense sorrow, pain or disappointment, times when I thought God had abandoned me or no longer loved me.

Abraham is called our "father in faith." He left his family and homeland to go to an unknown land God had promised him. And although he and his wife were well past childbearing years, they trusted God's promise of countless descendants.

I have a long way to go before I have that kind of faith. Still, I draw hope from people like Abraham and Sarah. They are proof that such faith is humanly possible.

Lord, may I trust you in bad times as well as in good. Give me the gift of faith.

Jesus went to Jerusalem for a religious festival. Near the Sheep Gate in Jerusalem there is a pool with five porches; in Hebrew it is called Bethzatha. A large crowd of sick people were lying on the porches – the blind, the lame and the paralyzed. A man was there who had been sick for thirty-eight years. Jesus saw him lying there, and he knew that the man had been sick for such a long time; so he asked him, "Do you want to get well?"

The sick man answered, "Sir, I don't have anyone here to put me in the pool when the water is stirred up; while I am trying to get in, somebody else gets there first."

Jesus said to him, "Get up, pick up your mat, and walk." Immediately the man got well; he picked up his mat and started walking.

John 5: 1-16

> "Do you want to get well?"

True healing

This seems a strange question for Jesus to ask someone who has been crippled for 38 years. But the moment of true healing is perhaps in how the man answers.

I tend to rush in 20 different directions at once, and my efforts end up scattered and diffuse. But do I want to change? I'm attached to the identity of a busy person. Doing important things. Never idle. Part of me dreads the intense focus that God wants my work to have; I'm afraid of failure.

Perhaps the man in today's reading needs to let go of his vision of himself as a man cursed by fate never to make it into the healing pool. Jesus is asking him to take this first step.

**Holy Spirit, tear down the barriers
I've built against your healing love.**

" The Lord says to his people,
  "I will guard and protect you
  and through you make a covenant
with all peoples...."
Sing, heavens! Shout for joy, earth!
The Lord will comfort his people....
But the people of Jerusalem said,
"The Lord has abandoned us!
He has forgotten us."
So the Lord answers,
"Can a woman forget her own baby
and not love the child she bore?
Even if a mother should forget her child,
I will never forget you."

Isaiah 49: 8-15

"Can a woman forget her own baby?"

Dependent on God

Recently the newspaper carried a terrible story of a young mother
who abandoned her two small children for more than a week. The
children died as a result of her neglect. "How can this be?" I cried.
"How could she forget her own babies?" As a mother, I found this
impossible to fathom. It's unnatural; it's hard to accept. And yet, it
happens.

When Isaiah tells me that God will not forget me, I am comforted. Like a child dependent on its mother for food, for warmth,
for water, for love, I rely on God. While human parents may let their
children down, I know that in God all my needs will be met, all my
desires will be known, all my tears will be wiped away.

**Lord, I depend on your love and care every day.
Thank you for always remembering me.**

The Lord said to Moses, "Hurry and go back down, because your people, whom you led out of Egypt, have sinned and rejected me…. They have made a bull-calf out of melted gold and have worshipped it and offered sacrifices to it. They are saying that this is their god, who led them out of Egypt. I know how stubborn these people are. Now, don't try to stop me. I am angry with them, and I am going to destroy them. Then I will make you and your descendants into a great nation."

But Moses pleaded with the Lord his God and said, "Lord, why should you be so angry with your people whom you rescued from Egypt with great might and power? Stop being angry; change your mind and do not bring this disaster on your people…." So the Lord changed his mind and did not bring on his people the disaster he had threatened.   *Exodus 32: 7-14*

"So the Lord changed his mind…"

Challenging authority

I don't know if I'm more amazed with the courage of Moses (after all, who likes to challenge the boss?), or with the fact that, with a good argument, it's possible to change God's mind. Way to go, Moses!

In today's reading, God listens to Moses' challenge. God is open to suggestion and is willing to change. How different from the image of God that I grew up with! The God of my childhood was all knowing, all powerful, righteous and always right.

I wonder if I try to be that way with my students at school or with my children at home. Do they see me as someone who is not to be challenged, or am I someone who is willing to listen?

God, give me the wisdom to listen with a heart that is willing to change.

Some of the people of Jerusalem said, "Isn't this the man the authorities are trying to kill? Look! He is talking in public, and they say nothing against him! Can it be that they really know that he is the Messiah? But when the Messiah comes, no one will know where he is from. And we all know where this man comes from."

As Jesus taught in the Temple, he said in a loud voice, "Do you really know me and know where I am from? I have not come on my own authority. He who sent me, however, is truthful. You do not know him, but I know him, because I come from him and he sent me."

Then they tried to seize him, but no one laid a hand on him, because his hour had not yet come.

John 7: 1-2, 10, 25-30

"Do you really know me?"

Standing with

Today's reading reminds me of the old spiritual "Nobody knows the trouble I've seen. Nobody knows my sorrow." And I think of people I know, of friends...

Some have lost spouses – suddenly or after long, horrific struggles. Some have walked into bedrooms to find their babies dead in cribs. Some have had marriages go sour and spent years living like strangers in their own homes. Some have worries over children whom they fear they're losing to drugs and alcohol. Some, as adolescents, were abused by adults they trusted.

I try not to say, "Yes, I know how you feel," because I don't. How can I truly know how someone else feels? But I can stand with them, and try. Perhaps, just for a moment, I can help them feel less alone.

Dear Lord, may I reach out to others and stand with them, and in so doing, come to know you.

S ome of the people in the crowd heard him and said, "This man is really the Prophet!" Others said, "He is the Messiah!" But others said, "The Messiah will not come from Galilee! The scripture says that the Messiah will be a descendant of King David and will be born in Bethlehem, the town where David lived." Some wanted to seize him, but no one laid a hand on him.

When the guards went back, the chief priests and Pharisees asked them, "Why did you not bring him?"

The guards answered, "Nobody has ever talked the way this man does!"

"Did he fool you, too?" the Pharisees asked them... "Study the Scriptures and you will learn that no prophet ever comes from Galilee."
John 7: 40-53

> "Nobody has ever talked the way this man does!"

An unlikely prophet?

"Dear William, I want to thank you for the kind words that you spoke at Eric's funeral. I know that his parents were comforted by your thoughts, as were the other children and adults there.

"Words have great power, and I want to thank you for reminding me of this. When you said that Eric deserved to be remembered, it reminded me that every day I need to remember the people who are special to me.... You have a natural gift for touching other people's souls. Thank you, William, for touching mine. You are a very special person. Susan."

Prophets come in all shapes and sizes. How wonderful that Susan recognized and affirmed this eleven-year-old boy's gift to her and to the community.

Lord, give me ears to hear and eyes to recognize the prophets I will meet today – especially those close to home.

Jer 31: 31-34; Ps 51; Heb 5: 7-9; Jn 12: 20-33

There are times (perhaps you share this) when I read the gospels and think: What would it feel like to be part of that crowd listening to Jesus? Imagine being there when Jesus tells a story or gestures in your direction! Would I understand the profound nature of what Jesus is saying? Or would I miss the point entirely? Fortunately, I have the benefit of the entire gospels and the luxury of time to reflect.

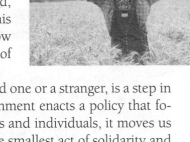

The grain of wheat dying and bearing much fruit is one of my favourite examples. The whole purpose of Jesus' death (and resurrection) was to make a positive change in the way people relate to God, to one another and to creation. Has this event made a difference in our lives? How much fruit has resulted from the death of this single grain?

Each act of kindness, toward a loved one or a stranger, is a step in the right direction. Every time a government enacts a policy that focuses on the well-being of communities and individuals, it moves us forward on the right path. And even the smallest act of solidarity and support that we show for people around the world who are working for justice and liberation is another move forward.

As our Lenten journey nears its conclusion, may we profit from the gospels and our reflection, to "get the message" and work for a bountiful harvest.

Lord, help me to stand in solidarity with my brothers and sisters around the world who are crying out for justice.

The Lord sent another message to Ahaz: "Ask the Lord your God to give you a sign. It can be from deep in the world of the dead or high up in heaven." Ahaz answered, "I will not ask for a sign. I refuse to put the Lord to the test."

To that Isaiah replied, "Listen, now, descendants of King David. It's bad enough for you to wear out the patience of people – do you have to wear out God's patience too? Well, then, the Lord himself will give you a sign: a young woman who is pregnant will have a son and will name him 'Immanuel.'" (This name in Hebrew means "God is with us.")

Make your plans! But they will never succeed. Talk all you want to! But it is all useless, because God is with us.

Isaiah 7: 10-14, 8: 10

> "...the Lord himself will give you a sign..."

A fierce love

One night, my seven-year-old son and I had a terrible scene: a great stubborn match over bathtime. As I finally picked him up and carried him to the tub, he screamed and beat my shoulders with his fists.

In my own anger I responded, "Ben, if you really want to hurt me, just hit me in the face." To my shame he just kept on wailing and said, "No!"

"Why?" I challenged.

"Because I love you!" he screamed in reply.

I did not know such a fierce love existed that could restrain itself, proclaim itself, in the midst of a temper tantrum. At this low point in my fathering, God's presence showed up as a sign unasked for, but given anyway.

Holy Spirit, keep me open to those signs you send me, especially when I am not looking for them.

The Israelites left Mount Hor... but on the way the people lost their patience and spoke against God and Moses. They complained, "Why did you bring us out of Egypt to die in this desert, where there is no food or water?" Then the Lord sent poisonous snakes, and many Israelites were bitten and died. The people said to Moses, "We sinned when we spoke against the Lord and against you. Now pray to the Lord to take these snakes away." So Moses prayed.... Then the Lord told Moses to make a metal snake and put it on a pole, so that anyone who was bitten could look at it and be healed. So Moses made a bronze snake and put it on a pole. Anyone who had been bitten would look at the bronze snake and be healed.

Numbers 21:4-9

> "...could look at it and be healed."

A painful lesson

Last fall my daughter was excited as she started her first day of kindergarten. But as time went on, she became discouraged.

It turned out that at recess she'd stand alone – watching the others play, too shy to join in. I ended up literally having to drag her out the door in the mornings. She would cry bitterly, and I felt like crying, too. Why had I brought her into this wilderness? Surely she's too young to have to experience such loneliness and alienation.

Moses' bronze serpent was a symbol both of the dangers that surrounded the Israelites and of God's faithfulness. I need that bronze serpent – to acknowledge my daughter's pain and to remind me that God is with her and will lead her through it.

God, help me believe that you are with us on our journey, and that the evil in the world will not have the final word.

Jesus said, "If you obey my teaching, you are really my disciples; you will know the truth, and the truth will set you free."

"We are the descendants of Abraham," they answered, "and we have never been anybody's slaves...."

"If you really were Abraham's children," Jesus replied, "you would do the same things that he did. All I have ever done is to tell you the truth I heard from God, yet you are trying to kill me...."

"God himself is the only Father we have," they answered, "and we are his true children." Jesus said, "If God really were your Father, you would love me, because I came from God and now I am here. I did not come on my own authority, but he sent me."

John 8: 31-42

> "If you obey my teaching..."

True disciples

When our kids were young, we read to them constantly. We must have read *The Chronicles of Narnia* by C. S. Lewis at least three times to successive ages of kids.

In the seventh book of the series, *The Last Battle*, a soldier turns up whose religious practice is to worship a diabolical god. Though he worships this false god, all his life he is judged as worthy by the true God: "No service which is vile can be done to me and none which is not vile can be done to him."

Dorothy Day put it another way when she said that atheists she knew, who sacrificed their lives to struggle for peace and serve the poor, were, in truth, lovers of Christ.

Lord, may I refrain from judging others.
You alone know what lies hidden in our hearts.

God said, "I make this covenant with you: I promise that you will be the ancestor of many nations. Your name will no longer be Abram, but Abraham, because I am making you the ancestor of many nations. I will give you many descendants, and some of them will be kings. You will have so many descendants that they will become nations.

"I will keep my promise to you and to your descendants…. I will be your God and the God of your descendants. I will give to you and to your descendants this land in which you are now a foreigner. The whole land of Canaan will belong to your descendants forever…."

God said to Abraham, "You also must agree to keep the covenant with me, both you and your descendants in future generations."

Genesis 17: 3-9

> "…and the God of your descendants."

God lives here

One of my earliest childhood memories is of a visit to my great-grandmother's house. I was fascinated by the icons hanging on the walls in her tiny kitchen. There were images of Mary, Jesus, and a few saints – but none of God!

When I asked my grandmother about this, she showed me a flickering flame dancing in a ruby red glass. God lived on a small shelf in my great-grandmother's kitchen.

Now, with my own daughters, I often light candles on our table. One of their favourite lights is a small red glass. A rosy glow warms their faces as they gaze on it. I recall the flickering ruby shadows that once lit my grandmother's profile. And I know God lives here, too.

God, you grace my home in light and shadow. Thank you.

My God is my protection,
and with him I am safe.
He protects me like a shield;
he defends me and keeps me safe....
Praise the Lord!
The danger of death was all around me;
the waves of destruction rolled over me.
The danger of death was around me,
and the grave set its trap for me.
In my trouble I called to the Lord;
I called to my God for help.
In his temple he heard my voice;
he listened to my cry for help.

Psalm 18: 1-6

> "In my trouble I called to the Lord."

Going home to God

For months, as cancer slowly took my mother away, death lapped at me like steady, rolling waves that grew higher every day. It was often a struggle to keep my head above water.

But my mother remained unperturbed. As she weakened physically, her inner strength increased and she grew more and more serene. She accepted with gratitude whatever life offered to her.

I marvelled at this and wondered where she found her strength.

Now I realize that, in her own quiet way, she had called on God. God had been her strong fortress, providing her safety and protection – not from death, which comes to us all, but from the terror of death. She was already safe at home, even before she left us.

**Lord, be my protector
– not just on my last day, but every day.**

Many who had come to visit Mary saw what Jesus did, and they believed in him. But some of them returned to the Pharisees and told them what Jesus had done. So the Pharisees and the chief priests met with the Council and said, "What shall we do? Look at all the miracles this man is performing! If we let him go on in this way, everyone will believe in him, and the Roman authorities will take action and destroy our Temple and our nation!"

One of them, named Caiaphas, who was High Priest that year, said, "What fools you are! Don't you realize that it is better for you to have one man die for the people, instead of having the whole nation destroyed?"

John 11:45-57

> "What shall we do?"

Faced with a choice

Recently a friend confided in me that she'd fallen in love. Unfortunately, the man she loved was married. She found herself in a "no-win" situation: if she cut off the relationship, she risked losing a dear friend, a soul mate; if she chose to have an affair, she would hurt others and betray her very core. She agonized over the decision. The answer is obvious, you say. But is it?

Most difficult decisions we face are over two "good" things. That's what makes them so hard.

"What shall we do?" the Pharisees and chief priests ask. Should they believe in Jesus and his message of healing and forgiveness, or should they defend and protect their nation? An obvious choice. Or was it?

**Lord, in times of turmoil and questioning,
keep my heart and mind open to your word.**

Is 50: 4-7; Ps 22; Phil 2: 6-11; Mk 14: 1 – 15: 47

Recently, as someone dear to me struggled through a difficult period of depression and self-doubt, I realized more than ever how deeply the wound of loneliness can penetrate a person's life. It is a wound we all experience at some time and it can be more painful than any bodily suffering.

No one knew this better than Jesus. Even more agonizing than thorns, scourge and nails is his experience of rejection and abandonment. The crowds who had acclaimed him a short time earlier now clamour for his death. Betrayed by Judas, denied by Peter, in the end Jesus is deserted by every one of his followers. Even the faithful women can only watch helplessly from a distance.

Beneath the darkened midday sky, the terrible cry is wrenched from Jesus: "My God, my God, why have you forsaken me?" In this moment, the Saviour of the world tastes the depth of human loneliness – the sense of being abandoned even by God.

The passion narrative humbles us as we see the extent to which Jesus has entered into our human condition. He is, indeed, like us in all things but sin.

And, of course, the story does not end there, in the shadow of the cross. The journey of this week, like the journey of our lives, leads through death to new life in the blazing light of resurrection.

**Lord Jesus, walk with me through my suffering
and lead me to the joy of new life.**

The Lord says,
"Here is my servant, whom I strengthen –
the one I have chosen, with whom I am pleased.
I have filled him with my Spirit,
and he will bring justice to every nation...."
God created the heavens and stretched them out;
he fashioned the earth and all that lives there;
he gave life and breath to all its people.
And now the Lord God says to his servant,
Through you...
I will bring light to the nations.
You will open the eyes of the blind
and set free those who sit in dark prisons."

Isaiah 42: 1-7

"You will open the eyes of the blind..."

The gift of sight

"Dr. Jane," as I called her during the brief time we worked together, had difficulties with today's reading. For her, blindness was not symbolic but linked to her unique genetic circumstances and juvenile diabetes. She did not expect to have her vision miraculously restored. Her blindness was not a metaphor, but a tedious fact of daily life, a litany of "smashing crack-ups" that could send objects flying and cause bruises on her arms and legs.

She reminded me that "sight" is indeed an interior concept, a gift. She worked tirelessly, finding her way as a blind physician in a seeing world.

I, too, must find a way, through my inner turbulence of darkness and doubt.

Dear God, I'm not looking for miracles – just a sense that no matter where I drift, you will keep me safe.

J esus said, "Now the Son of Man's glory is revealed; now God's glory is revealed through him…. My children, I shall not be with you very much longer. You will look for me; but I tell you now what I told the Jewish authorities, 'You cannot go where I am going.' And now I give you a new commandment: love one another. As I have loved you, so you must love one another. If you have love for one another, then everyone will know that you are my disciples."

"Where are you going, Lord?" Simon Peter asked him.

"You cannot follow me now where I am going," answered Jesus; "but later you will follow me."

"Lord, why can't I follow you now?" asked Peter. "I am ready to die for you!"

John 13: 21-33, 36-38

"…but later you will follow me."

Love one another

The day-to-day demands of parenting three young children alone had taken their toll. One night, after a particularly challenging day, I whispered my dead husband's name: "How I wish I could see you again. Can't I join you now?" And, in the stillness of the night, I heard him say, "No, not yet. The children still need you."

Just as Peter wanted to follow Jesus, I wanted to follow my husband – to the grave and beyond. And, like Peter, I received a gentle reminder: "As I have loved you, so you must love one another."

I know that I have been loved – and loved deeply – in my life. And I know I must find the strength to continue to give my children the love and support they need.

**Dear Jesus, how hard it is to follow you
in the everyday demands of life. Give me strength.
Give me hope. Give me love.**

The Sovereign Lord has taught me what to say,
so that I can strengthen the weary.
Every morning he makes me eager
to hear what he is going to teach me.
The Lord has given me understanding,
and I have not rebelled or turned away from him.
I bared my back to those who beat me.
I did not stop them when they insulted me....
But their insults cannot hurt me
because the Sovereign Lord gives me help.
I brace myself to endure them.
I know that I will not be disgraced,
for God is near,
and he will prove me innocent.

Isaiah 50:4-9

"The Lord has given me understanding..."

In face of violence

Lately, when I drop my son off at school, I've noticed kids bullying other kids. I watch closely. When necessary, I intervene, because my heart goes out to the ones who are too little, too fragile or too innocent to put a bully in their place.

Bullying doesn't stop when children leave school. I see it happening between my neighbours, within families, in my community, and between countries fighting for land and power.

I find it hard to turn my back on insults and acts of violence directed at me or at those I love. But I know that if I follow Jesus' example of peace, justice and forgiveness, no real harm can come to me.

**Jesus, give me the strength and courage
to follow your example.**

Jesus rose from the table, took off his outer garment, and tied a towel around his waist. Then he poured some water into a washbasin and began to wash the disciples' feet and dry them with the towel around his waist. He came to Simon Peter, who said, "Never at any time will you wash my feet!"

"If I do not wash your feet," Jesus answered, "you will no longer be my disciple."

Simon Peter answered, "Lord, do not wash only my feet, then! Wash my hands and head, too...."

After Jesus had washed their feet... he said, "I, your Lord and Teacher, have just washed your feet. You, then, should wash one another's feet. I have set an example for you, so that you will do just what I have done for you." · *John 13: 1-15*

> "I have set an example for you…"

An example

With the miracles, the sermons and the teaching, it's only after this humble event that Jesus says, "I have set an example for you."

We had a pastor who was a great speaker; I remember loud exhortations, stiff-lipped faces. Me? I was scared. The sermons, I guess, had their desired effect.

A very different man followed. At gatherings, he was always in the background – Christmas baskets arranged by him, but always delivered by someone else. Events took place as the church became the centre of the community; someone else always spoke.

Not a great speaker. Not an eminent theologian... seemingly. He told me once, with characteristic humility, "I just try to find out what people need, and give it to them."

Lord, let me follow your example.
Help me to serve others.

Simon Peter and another disciple followed Jesus. That other disciple went with Jesus into the courtyard of the High Priest's house, while Peter stayed outside by the gate. Then the other disciple went back out, spoke to the girl at the gate, and brought Peter inside. The girl at the gate said to Peter, "Aren't you also one of the disciples of that man?"

"No, I am not," answered Peter....

The High Priest questioned Jesus about his disciples and about his teaching. Jesus answered, "I have always spoken publicly to everyone; all my teaching was done in the synagogues and in the Temple, where all the people come together. I have never said anything in secret. Why, then, do you question me? Question the people who heard me...." Then Annas sent him, still tied up, to Caiaphas the High Priest. *John 18: 1 – 19: 42*

"Aren't you also one of the disciples of that man?"

Facing the pain

My Congolese friends tell me stories about the war that tore their country apart. They say the lucky ones were those who made it to refugee camps. Those who didn't, mostly women and children, experienced a kind of hell on earth. I don't want to hear these stories – I try not to believe them, or try to detach myself, or find relief in blaming someone.

In today's reading, Pilate is intrigued by Jesus, but he doesn't even give Jesus the dignity of a full hearing, his "day in court." Guilty of avoidance, he hands him over to Caiaphas. Peter pretends he never knew the man who changed his life.

Today, of all days, I'll try not to flinch from looking deep into my Lord's eyes as he dies.

Lord, give me the courage to head straight into suffering until I find you.

G ive thanks to the Lord, because he is good,
and his love is eternal.
Let the people of Israel say,
"His love is eternal.…
His power has brought us victory –
his mighty power in battle!"
I will not die; instead, I will live
and proclaim what the Lord has done.
The stone which the builders rejected as worthless
turned out to be the most important of all.
This was done by the Lord;
what a wonderful sight it is!   *Psalm 118: 1-2, 16-17, 22-23*

"Give thanks to the Lord, because he is good."

Unsettling words

For some reason he can't explain, his eight-year-old son convinced him to go to this year's Good Friday service. "Everyone from St. Benedict's school is going to be there. Come on, Dad. Let's go!"

He was overwhelmed by what happened to him there. He knew "the story" but he didn't expect the effect it would have on him. He and his wife had seen the movie *The Passion of the Christ*, but this was totally different. There was something about the faces of the people around him – listening to the readings and processing to venerate the cross. His son grabbed him by the hand and practically dragged him forward.

Today, he's still taking it all in, trying to understand the place it might have in his life.

**O God, in these busy times,
help me to leave room for your voice.**

Sunday | **APRIL 8**

Acts 10: 34, 37-43; Ps 118; Col 3: 1-4 or 1 Cor 5: 6-8; Jn 20: 1-18

Sometimes, particularly when I read today's scriptures, I imagine what it would be like to have met the newly risen Jesus: to have been one of the group who ate and drank with him after he rose from the dead; to have been Mary of Magdala, the apostle to the apostles, who encountered her beloved Lord in the garden; to have been the disciples who first recognized him in the breaking of the bread after the journey from Jerusalem to Emmaus. How lucky they all were!

Then I give my head a shake. How can I feel any less privileged than those men and women? Any less intimate with the risen Christ? When I gather with my brothers and sisters for eucharist each Sunday, he speaks to me through the voice of the lector and the priest, who let us hear his voice here and now. Through the priest's ministry, I join the risen Christ in his sacrifice, the one who breaks the bread for us gathered here this Easter Day, and wishes us the same peace that he offered to his disciples 2,000 years ago. When I share in holy communion, I not only am taken more deeply into my risen Lord, but become more fully one with the rest of his risen body.

Christ is truly risen and present among us whenever we gather for eucharist – if only our faith is alert enough to perceive his presence.

**Lord, open my ears to hear you
and my eyes see you each and every day.**

P rotect me, O God; I trust in you for safety.
I say to the Lord, "You are my Lord;
    all the good things I have come from you...."
I praise the Lord, because he guides me,
and in the night my conscience warns me.
I am always aware of the Lord's presence;
he is near, and nothing can shake me.
And so I am thankful and glad,
and I feel completely secure,
because you protect me from the power of death...
You will show me the path that leads to life;
your presence fills me with joy....   *Psalm 16: 1-2, 5, 7-11*

"...and in the night my conscience warns me."

Sleepless nights

Strange that in this joyous song, the psalmist mentions his conscience hunting him down in his sleep. I, too, am one for whom the night is often difficult. Whatever the cause – be it something I'm anxious about doing, or something I regret having done – in the night it comes, waking me. No escape.

How many nights did Jesus spend alone, misunderstood, seeing the inexorable approach of his agony? His conscience saying, "No, you must not stop. You must drink from this cup."

Yet his anxious nights ended, along with his agony. In the morning, the tomb was empty. Resurrection! Resurrection that's not possible without the agony.

For me, too, the night often brings not only sleepless rumination, but the answer or the courage I seek. Resurrection. The dawn does come.

**Lord, when you send me sleepless nights,
let me strain to hear the sound of your voice.**

Early on Sunday morning, Mary Magdalene went to the tomb and saw that the stone had been taken away from the entrance.

Mary stood crying outside the tomb. While she was still crying, she bent over and looked in the tomb and saw two angels there dressed in white, sitting where the body of Jesus had been. "Woman, why are you crying?" they asked. She answered, "They have taken my Lord away, and I do not know where they have put him!" Then she turned around and saw Jesus standing there; but she did not know that it was Jesus. "Woman, why are you crying?" Jesus asked her. "Who is it that you are looking for...?"

Jesus said to her, "Mary!" She turned toward him and said in Hebrew, "Rabboni!" (This means "Teacher.")

John 20: 11-18

"Who is it that you are looking for?"

Present to others

My life is so cluttered – with things to do or to buy, with news to catch up on – that it is hard to stay focused like Mary Magdalene in her grief over Jesus' death, and in her joy when she recognized him after his resurrection. She had stood by the cross and watched Jesus' agonizing death. She was the first to proclaim that he had risen: he is alive!

How can I recognize Jesus in the pain and sorrow of others? Maybe I won't see it at first – after all, Mary Magdalene thought Jesus was the gardener! But if I try to simplify my life, so that people always come first, then perhaps I will be able to see Jesus in everyone I meet.

Lord, may I learn to be present – in small ways – to those who suffer within my community.

There was a man who had been lame all his life. Every day he was carried to the gate to beg for money from the people who were going into the Temple. When he saw Peter and John going in, he begged them to give him something. Peter said, "Look at us!" So he looked at them, expecting to get something from them. But Peter said to him, "I have no money at all, but I give you what I have: in the name of Jesus Christ of Nazareth I order you to get up and walk!" Then he took him by his right hand and helped him up. At once the man's feet and ankles became strong; he jumped up, stood on his feet, and started walking around.... When the people recognized him as the beggar who had sat at the Beautiful Gate, they were all surprised and amazed at what had happened to him.

Acts 3: 1-10

> "...expecting to get something from them."

Comfort or challenge

Frank McNair established the first mental health clinic in British Columbia's interior. When he died, the church was jammed with people who came to pay their respects. But not because he had a soft touch. The doctor giving the eulogy commented, "If people needed to be challenged, we referred them to Frank. If they needed comforting, we referred them to his colleague."

The beggar at the gate expected comforting. Peter challenged him. He took the beggar's hand and hoisted him to his feet. And the man danced around, rejoicing.

How did Peter do it? All we know is it could not have been a psychosomatic illness, because the people *knew* this man. He really had been crippled, and now was healed.

I find it so hard to know whether to comfort someone or challenge them. Guide me, Lord.

S uddenly the Lord himself stood among the disciples and said to them, "Peace be with you...." He said this and showed them his hands and his feet. They still could not believe, they were so full of joy and wonder....

Then he said to them, "These are the very things I told you about while I was still with you: everything written about me in the Law of Moses, the writings of the prophets, and the Psalms had to come true."

Then he opened their minds to understand the Scriptures, and said to them, "This is what is written: the Messiah must suffer and must rise from death three days later, and in his name the message about repentance and the forgiveness of sins must be preached to all nations."

Luke 24: 35-48

"...they were so full of joy and wonder..."

Embracing all of life

"Say 'yes' to the best, and 'no' to the rest!" advised the retreat's motivational speaker. "Position yourself so that wonderful opportunities help to propel you forward." So why did I leave the presentation feeling unhappy and unmotivated?

I find myself wondering how Jesus managed to fill his disciples with "joy and wonder," while the speaker on that weekend retreat left me feeling empty and dissatisfied.

Jesus showed his disciples – through his words and his actions – that suffering and death are part of life, and that God promises to be with us through those hard times.

Do I believe that true happiness comes from living through *all* experiences – and not only the "wonderful" ones? That by embracing illness, loss, suffering and death, I will find peace?

Lord, when I want to turn away from the demands of life, help me turn back with open arms, as you did.

S imon Peter said, "I am going fishing…." So they went out in a boat, but all that night they did not catch a thing. As the sun was rising, Jesus stood at the water's edge, but the disciples did not know that it was Jesus. Then he asked them, "Young men, haven't you caught anything?"

"Not a thing," they answered. He said to them, "Throw your net out on the right side of the boat, and you will catch some." So they threw the net out and could not pull it back in, because they had caught so many fish.

The disciple whom Jesus loved said to Peter, "It is the Lord!"

John 21: 1-14

> "… the disciples did not know that it was Jesus."

Another way

I have such a soft spot for Jesus' disciples – they're so weak and human, just like me. Here they display two of my favourite personal failings: blindness and stubbornness.

How often in my life have I followed their fishing technique: try something that doesn't work. Try it again. Repeat. Keep at it; maybe it will work this time. Don't give up now, you've only been at it all night. What's that? Try it another way? Well, what do you know? It works!

How often in my life have I, too, failed to see the Lord right before me – delivering mail, at the checkout counter, signing out my books at the library, asking for help with homework.

But the disciples learned. Maybe I will, too.

**Lord, open my eyes and my heart
so I can see what is right in front of me.**

The members of the Council were amazed to see how bold Peter and John were and to learn that they were ordinary men of no education.... "What shall we do with these men?" they asked. "Everyone in Jerusalem knows that this extraordinary miracle has been performed by them, and we cannot deny it. But to keep this matter from spreading any further among the people, let us warn these men never again to speak to anyone in the name of Jesus...."

Peter and John answered them, "You yourselves judge which is right in God's sight – to obey you or to obey God. For we cannot stop speaking of what we ourselves have seen and heard." So the Council warned them even more strongly and then set them free.

Acts 4: 13-21

> "...they were ordinary men of no education."

Expert witnesses

I once worked at a radio station that had an index system of phone numbers of experts who could talk credibly on any given topic. Radio producers believe their listeners like the authoritative charm of articulate experts, especially those with good credentials.

This list proved especially useful in the early hours of the morning when news items tend to be "bagged." I remember being overwhelmed by the experts' levels of knowledge about topics I had never even considered!

But, in today's reading, along come Peter and John, tipping all of that "expert" logic on its head. No degrees, no credentials of any kind. Just their own lived experience and raw, unbending faith. And they confound those who *think* they know.

**Dear God, help me to see, and to live,
an authentic witness to your love.**

Acts 4: 32-35; Ps 118; 1 Jn 5: 1-6; Jn 20: 19-31

As the date of each Olympic games draws near, runners carry a flaming torch to the site of the events. As privileged as these torch bearers are, Christians have a much greater privilege. We carry the resurrection torch to all peoples, giving them fullness of life.

The first and second readings remind us that if we are to be good torch bearers, we must be closely united to one another. As

Luke puts it in Acts, "The whole group of those who believed were of one heart and soul." The second reading tells us, "We know that we love the children of God, when we love God and obey his commandments."

In the gospel, John tells us how the risen Jesus first appeared to his disciples and said to them, "As the Father has sent me, so I send you." When Jesus appeared a second time, he said to Thomas, "Do not doubt but believe." Thomas responded, "My Lord and my God!" Thomas came to a deep belief, challenging us to do the same.

Before the 2012 Summer Olympics begin, torch bearers will run from Athens to London. But as Christians, we always bear the resurrection torch. We must continue to hold it high for all to see: the light of Christ is needed in order that the world might live.

**Lord, let me be a beacon of light,
leading others to your love.**

Jesus said, "I am telling you the truth: no one can see the kingdom of God without being born again."

"How can a grown man be born again?" Nicodemus asked. "He certainly cannot enter his mother's womb and be born a second time!" "I am telling you the truth," replied Jesus, "that no one can enter the kingdom of God without being born of water and the Spirit. A person is born physically of human parents, but is born spiritually of the Spirit. Do not be surprised because I tell you that you must all be born again. The wind blows wherever it wishes; you hear the sound it makes, but you do not know where it comes from or where it is going. It is like that with everyone who is born of the Spirit."

John 3: 1-8

> "...without being born again."

Reborn each day

I remember when my friend Mary was "born again." It was a dramatic event for her and did bring about a dramatic change in her life. A couple of months later, however, the drama had died down, and she was back to "normal," with little mention of the event or its implications.

When I look at my own life, I feel like I've been born again... and again... and again. In fact, I feel like I'm reborn every morning as I get up and ask God to help me through this day.

Bob Dylan said, "Whoever is not in the process of being born is in the process of dying." For me, being born again isn't a one-time event – it's a never-ending process.

**Lord, with each new day, let me be born again
– in faith, hope and love.**

" I tell you that you must all be born again. The wind blows wherever it wishes; you hear the sound it makes, but you do not know where it comes from or where it is going. It is like that with everyone who is born of the Spirit."

How can this be?" asked Nicodemus.... Jesus answered, "I am telling you the truth: we speak of what we know and report what we have seen, yet none of you is willing to accept our message. You do not believe me when I tell you about the things of this world; how will you ever believe me, then, when I tell you about the things of heaven? And no one has ever gone up to heaven except the son of Man, who came down from heaven."

John 3: 7-15

> "The wind blows wherever it wishes..."

The Spirit's presence

Who Has Seen the Wind? The title of this well-known novel by W. O. Mitchell captures the elusive yet compelling search for life's meaning that often absorbs our attention.

I can't "see" the wind, but I can observe its effects. I can't "know" the wind – hold it within my grasp to examine it – but I can feel its presence.

God's Spirit is just as elusive *and* just as real as the wind. I've seen God's Spirit when my children were born, when death visited our family, and in the concern friends have shown us in our time of need. I've known the Spirit's presence as I struggle to live a life of integrity and justice. An unseen God? Yes, but a God who is as close to me as the wind.

**Loving Spirit, guide my words and actions
when I cannot see clearly the way to go.**

will always thank the Lord;
I will never stop praising him.
I will praise him for what he has done;
may all who are oppressed listen and be glad!
Proclaim with me the Lord's greatness;
let us praise his name together!
I prayed to the Lord, and he answered me;
he freed me from all my fears....
The helpless call to him, and he answers;
he saves them from all their troubles.
His angel guards those who honour the Lord
and rescues them from danger.
Find out for yourself how good the Lord is.   *Psalm 34: 1-8*

> "Find out for yourself how good the Lord is."

Goodness and mystery

When I was a boy, I believed that God's goodness would be shown by dramatic or miraculous actions. Heavenly choirs would sing as an angel swooped down and rescued me from some near disaster.

As I got older, my imagination became less literal. God's goodness would be revealed through good things happening. The righteous would benefit from their actions. Love would be returned to the loving.

But now I know that the loving are not always loved; the good suffer; justice is repaid with indifference – God's goodness is seen in mystery and paradox. God is found at the heart of suffering. In the moment of bleak emptiness, God is present. How is this so? I don't know. It just is.

**Lord, thank you for revealing yourself to me
in so many ways.**

They brought the apostles in, made them stand before the Council, and the High Priest questioned them. "We gave you strict orders not to teach in the name of this man," he said; "but see what you have done! You have spread your teaching all over Jerusalem, and you want to make us responsible for his death!"

Peter and the other apostles answered, "We must obey God, not men. The God of our ancestors raised Jesus from death, after you had killed him by nailing him to a cross. God raised him to his right side as Leader and Saviour, to give the people of Israel the opportunity to repent and have their sins forgiven. We are witnesses to these things – we and the Holy Spirit, who is God's gift to those who obey him."

Acts 5: 27-33

> "We are witnesses to these things…"

Good news

Michael, who has severe cerebral palsy, does not speak in words. He needs a wheelchair to get around. But this has not prevented him from being part of a liturgical dance group at L'Arche Daybreak called "The Spirit Movers." That is where Michael shines! When his dance partner, Steve, whirls him around, Michael has a smile that lights up the whole room. His joy is irrepressible.

When Michael and Steve go places, people sometimes look at Michael critically, as if he doesn't have a right to be there – especially if he makes noises. But Steve insists that Michael participate. He knows Michael has something to say – "good news" to share that cannot be stifled.

**O Holy Spirit, give me the courage
to speak up for what I know to be true.**

Jesus asked Philip, "Where can we buy enough food to feed all these people? Philip answered, "For everyone to have even a little, it would take more than two hundred silver coins to buy enough bread." Then Andrew said, "There is a boy here who has five loaves of barley bread and two fish. But they will certainly not be enough for all these people."

"Make the people sit down," Jesus told them.... He took the bread, gave thanks to God, and distributed it to the people who were sitting there. He did the same with the fish, and they all had as much as they wanted. When they were all full, he said, "Gather the pieces left over." So they gathered them all and filled twelve baskets with the pieces left over from the five barley loaves which the people had eaten.

John 6: 1-15

"There is a boy here who has five loaves..."

Not much to offer

My brother and sister-in-law got married 20 years ago. Each doubted that they were lovable enough, or that they had enough to offer the other. Yet with that wonderfully foolish bravery that lovers have, the question was asked and the answer was Yes!

Since then they have brought forth three children; as well, they have made their home into a place of welcome for many beyond their own family.

Perhaps they each felt a bit like Andrew, who mentions that there are a few loaves and fishes available, but then immediately feels foolish for having suggested it. This simple and innocent offering, made with many doubts, is transformed by Jesus into abundance, enough for everyone with plenty to spare. This is the miracle of love.

Lord, I don't feel I have much to offer. But take it: you can work miracles with it.

Whu evening came, Jesus' disciples went down to the lake, got into a boat, and went back across the lake toward Capernaum. Night came on, and Jesus still had not come to them. By then a strong wind was blowing and stirring up the water.

The disciples had rowed about three or four miles when they saw Jesus walking on the water, coming near the boat, and they were terrified. "Don't be afraid," Jesus told them, "it is I!" Then they willingly took him into the boat, and immediately the boat reached land at the place they were heading for.

John 6: 16-21

> "…a strong wind was blowing and stirring up the water."

Between two shores

Years ago, five of us had to cross ten miles of lake in a small, open boat. It was windy but the fellow taking us thought it'd be OK. "Besides," he said, "if I waited every time it was rough, I'd never go anywhere." By the time we got to the other side, we were bailing and even he was very glad to have made it.

Life isn't always safe. If I stay on shore, there's no risk, but I'll never get where I need to go. It's that middle, turbulent part that's scary: when I'm between two shores, like the disciples that night.

Maybe miracles don't happen today, but help does come – a phone call, a word of encouragement – and I know I'm not alone.

Lord, when life is most stormy, let me feel your presence coming across the water to help me.

Acts 3: 13-15, 17-19; Ps 4; 1 Jn 2: 1-5; Lk 24: 35-48

I f asked to name significant persons in our lives, I suspect most of us would include a teacher on the list. That special teacher probably challenged and encouraged us, teaching life lessons along with the course material. Good teachers build confidence as well as a desire to make a difference in the world.

Jesus was the pre-eminent teacher whose words challenged and inspired all who would listen. Through his parables, he opened the eyes of many. Even after his death, Jesus appeared to the disciples and "opened their minds to understand the Scriptures." He taught his disciples about suffering, death and living a life of self-sacrificing love. "You are witnesses," he proclaimed. Witnesses that love is stronger than death, that suffering and death are not the final word. Jesus appeared to the disciples after his death to offer them peace.

Jesus continues to offer us peace, challenging us to go and teach all nations. We are the disciples left with the responsibility to proclaim the good news, to reach out in the compassion of Jesus. His appearance to the disciples 2,000 years ago brought with it a message to each of us. We, too, are sent to carry on his mission of proclaiming the good news, reaching out to the poor, being healers in a fractured world and modelling his forgiveness that brings peace.

**Jesus, continue to teach me. I have so much to learn.
And help me teach others your way of love.**

Next day the crowd that had stayed on the other side of the lake realized that there had been only one boat there. They knew that Jesus had not gone in it with his disciples, but that they had left without him. Other boats, which were from Tiberias, came to shore.... When the crowd saw that Jesus was not there, they got into those boats and went to Capernaum, looking for him.

When the people found Jesus on the other side of the lake, they said, "Teacher, when did you get here?" Jesus answered, "I am telling you the truth: you are looking for me because you ate the bread and had all you wanted, not because you understood my miracles. Do not work for food that spoils; instead, work for the food that lasts for eternal life."

John 6: 22-29

> "...work for the food that lasts..."

Food that lasts

I have to admit that there are times when I eat for the wrong reasons. Even though I'm not hungry, I fill myself with "food that spoils." Trying to fill an emptiness that exists within me. Trying to convince myself that these "small indulgences" will make me happy. Trying to silence an inner voice that cries out to be heard.

Fearful, I turn away from Jesus' challenge to "work for the food that lasts for eternal life."

When I *have* chosen to listen to that inner voice, it has shown me hurts that need healing. And it has shown me how love can heal those hurts, making my emptiness less frightening.

**Dearest Lord, out of fear I turn from your truth.
Give me the courage to be still, to listen,
and to allow your love to heal the hurt in my heart.**

"What miracle will you perform so that we may see it and believe you? What will you do? Our ancestors ate manna in the desert, just as the scripture says, 'He gave them bread from heaven to eat.'"

"I am telling you the truth," Jesus said. "What Moses gave you was not the bread from heaven; it is my Father who gives you the real bread from heaven. For the bread that God gives is he who comes down from heaven and gives life to the world."

"Sir," they asked him, "give us this bread always." "I am the bread of life," Jesus told them. "Those who come to me will never be hungry; those who believe in me will never be thirsty."

John 6: 30-35

> "Those who come to me will never be hungry..."

Bread of life

Breadmaking has always seemed like honest work to me. When I was at home with my young children, I used to enjoy plunging my fists into the dough, kneading it into our family's loaves. The smell of freshly baked bread was as welcome as the first warm days of spring.

When Jesus says he is the "bread of life," he speaks not about bread that satisfies physical hunger, but about feeding us with God's own life. In a sense, my fresh bread fed both body and spirit. My children felt God's tender care for them in our warm Nova Scotia kitchen, and in the taste of homemade bread.

Yet Jesus is the true bread of life. Through him I know God's love, and can share it with others.

**O God, show me how to be life-giving
in my encounters with others today.**

O Lord, I will always sing of your constant love;
I will proclaim your faithfulness forever.
I know that your love will last for all time,
that your faithfulness is as permanent as the sky....
The heavens sing of the wonderful things you do;
the holy ones sing of your faithfulness, Lord.
No one in heaven is like you, Lord;
none of the heavenly beings is your equal....
How happy are the people who worship you with songs,
who live in the light of your kindness!
Because of you they rejoice all day long,
and they praise you for your goodness.   *Psalm 89: 1-2, 5-6, 15-16*

"How happy are the people who worship you..."

Smelling the roses

I simply cannot be as busy as I think I am!

So often I feel pressed for time and do not fully experience whatever I am doing. I am trying to change that mindset.

Last summer, while taking a morning walk, I smelled something beautiful. Rather than pass by unthinkingly, I forced myself to stop and find the source – a wild patch of rugosa roses. I made a promise to myself: whenever I walked that way, I would stop, look and literally "smell the roses."

The first week or two, I would rush by them and have to go back. By the end of the summer, though, I was looking forward to that moment of prayer and praise – contemplating the last brave blooms and the hardy hips.

Teach me to be attentive, Lord.
Teach me to sing your praises.

An Ethiopian eunuch, who was an important official… was on his way home. As he rode along, he was reading from the book of the prophet Isaiah. The Holy Spirit said to Philip, "Go over to that carriage and stay close to it." Philip ran over and heard him reading from the book of the prophet Isaiah. He asked him, "Do you understand what you are reading…?" …Then Philip…told him the Good News about Jesus. As they travelled down the road, they came to a place where there was some water, and the official said, "Here is some water. What is to keep me from being baptized?"

The official ordered the carriage to stop, and both Philip and the official went down into the water, and Philip baptized him. When they came up out of the water, the Spirit of the Lord took Philip away.   *Acts 8: 26-40*

> "What is to keep me from being baptized?"

Time to act

April marks two important anniversaries in the life of Martin Luther King, Jr. – his famous "Letter from Birmingham Jail" in 1963, and his death in 1968.

King was arrested in Birmingham, Alabama, for participating in a non-violent protest against racial segregation. After his arrest, several local clergymen published a letter in the city's newspaper criticizing King's "impatience" and suggesting that segregation would take care of itself "in time." King penned a response that would become a classic in the literature of non-violence.

In his letter, King wrote, "Time itself is neutral. We must use time creatively, in the knowledge that the time is always ripe to do good." In his own way, King is like the eunuch who, upon seeing water, knew it was the moment to act.

God, help me see – and seize – the moment today.

P raise the Lord, all nations!
Praise him, all peoples!
     God's love for us is strong,
and his faithfulness is eternal.
Praise the Lord!

Psalm 117: 1-2

> **"God's love for us is strong..."**

Praise the Lord!

At times, when God seems distant and uncaring, the idea of giving praise seems so strange. But then, when I see a magnificent sunset, praising God suddenly makes all the sense in the world.

The idea of praising God is clearest to me when I see the most precious of all creation: human beings. When a baby wraps her hand around my finger, or when I visit someone in the hospital who is calmly battling to stay alive, I know there is a God.

When a person faces their inevitable return to the Creator with a deep sense of serenity, I know that God's love for us is strong. My doubts are not gone forever – but for those few minutes, my faith is strengthened.

O God, at times you seem so distant. Help me to look, and to see you in the people around me.

am telling you the truth: if you do not eat the flesh of the Son of Man and drink his blood, you will not have life in yourselves." Many of his followers heard this and said, "This teaching is too hard." Without being told, Jesus knew that they were grumbling about this, so he said, "Does this make you want to give up? Suppose that you should see the Son of Man go back up to the place where he was before? What gives life is God's Spirit; human power is of no use at all. The words I have spoken to you bring God's life-giving Spirit…. No people can come to me unless the Father makes it possible for them to do so."

John 6: 53, 60-69

"What gives life is God's Spirit."

Fed by love

No wonder the disciples were troubled! Could Jesus really want to turn them into cannibals? Were they supposed to gnaw on Jesus' bones? I have an advantage: I know about the Last Supper where Jesus took bread and wine and said, "*This* is my body…. *This* is my blood."

My own trouble is different. I'm often left gnawing on the human shortcomings of those who preside at the table of the Lord – and those who gather around it. Even telling myself that I have failings, too, doesn't help. I keep looking for perfectly wise and loving people.

From now on, I want to focus on something else: on the way God uses ordinary, flawed means – bread, wine, human beings – to lead me to eternal life.

Lord, nourish me with your body and blood, with your word, and with the love of friends and family.

Acts 4: 7-12; Ps 118; 1 Jn 3: 1-2; Jn 10: 11-18

Before starting college, David worked for a few months at a detox centre. The hours were long and the pay minimum wage. David was basically a janitor: cleaning toilets, looking after supplies and attending to a multitude of chores. But he liked the other staff members and was cheerful and friendly with the clients who were struggling with the pain of withdrawal.

David went to college and returned the next summer to the detox centre. He was given more responsibility and even started sitting in on some of the group counselling sessions. At the end of the summer, he went back to school and switched his major to social work.

After graduation, David got a full-time job working at the centre. The pay is still low and there is some shift work, but David is happy; he knows he is helping to make a difference in people's lives. David is making sacrifices for his chosen vocation, but he wouldn't see it that way; he is joyful knowing he has found his true vocation.

In today's gospel, Jesus is seen as the dedicated shepherd, the leader of his flock, ready to sacrifice all for them. What defines true Christian leadership? In the readings, Jesus points to himself as the model. What have we done to follow in his footsteps? What sacrifices have we made?

Perhaps in finding our own vocation we might find that the joy outweighs the sacrifice.

**Lord, lead me to my true calling and give me the courage
I need to pursue it each and every day.**

Jesus said, "I am telling you the truth: the man who does not enter the sheep pen by the gate, but climbs in some other way, is a thief and a robber. The man who goes in through the gate is the shepherd of the sheep. The gatekeeper opens the gate for him; the sheep hear his voice as he calls his own sheep by name, and he leads them out. When he has brought them out, he goes ahead of them, and the sheep follow him, because they know his voice. They will not follow someone else; instead, they will run away from such a person, because they do not know his voice."

John 10: 1-10

> "...a thief and a robber."

A culture of thieves

Some evenings I like to sit in front of the television and flip from station to station. It's a bad habit. I don't watch much of anything. I just sit in limbo, catching glimpses and fragments of different images and voices. In no time at all, I notice that an hour has stolen away.

I am like the sheep that don't have enough sense to recognize the voice that calls them to a restful place. I am so easily misled by the thieves of this culture.

How can I hear Jesus' voice when I give attention to so many other voices? I would like to change this habit. With more quiet time I might hear and recognize Jesus' voice at the end of the day.

Jesus, help me make time to hear your voice each day.

S ome of the believers who were scattered by the persecution that took place when Stephen was killed went as far as Phoenicia, Cyprus, and Antioch, telling the message to Jews only. But other believers, who were from Cyprus and Cyrene, went to Antioch and proclaimed the message to Gentiles also, telling them the Good News about the Lord Jesus. The Lord's power was with them, and a great number of people believed and turned to the Lord.

The news about this reached the church in Jerusalem, so they sent Barnabas to Antioch.... Then Barnabas went to Tarsus to look for Saul. When he found him, he took him to Antioch, and for a whole year the two met with the people of the church and taught a large group. It was at Antioch that the believers were first called Christians.

Acts 11: 19-26

> "...and a great number of people believed..."

Unexpected growth

Every winter, we fill our bird feeder with sunflower seeds. Birds are messy eaters: their busy beaks scatter shells – and a few uncracked seeds – all over our deck and patio. We sweep up what we can to put in the garbage or, being environmentally conscious, in the compost. But every spring, an unplanned crop of sunflowers pops up between the patio stones and in nearby flowerbeds.

The stoning of Stephen launched a wave of persecution that scattered the faithful throughout the eastern Mediterranean. It was supposed to sweep up this new, unsettling Jewish splinter group and dump them in the garbage can of history.

But something unexpected happened. Sunflowers popped up all over. And some of them took a new name – Christian.

**God, show me how my painful experiences
can turn into seeds for new growth.**

Jesus said, "Whoever believes in me believes not only in me but also in him who sent me. Whoever sees me sees also him who sent me. I have come into the world as light, so that everyone who believes in me should not remain in the darkness. If people hear my message and do not obey it, I will not judge them. I came, not to judge the world, but to save it. Those who reject me and do not accept my message have one who will judge them. The words I have spoken will be their judge on the last day! This is true, because I have not spoken on my own authority, but the Father who sent me has commanded me what I must say and speak. And I know that his command brings eternal life."

John 12: 44-50

> ## "I have come into the world as light…"

Light and life

Every night, when my children were very young, I'd go to their rooms and look in on them before going to bed. And every night, my visit to my youngest son's room was the same. He'd be fast asleep, but every single light would be on, giving off enough illumination for a plane to land!

He never said he was afraid of the dark, and he didn't seem afraid of the dark, but clearly he needed lots of light in order to feel secure enough to fall asleep.

I never said anything to him about the lights, but as I turned them all off, I used to smile to myself, happy that he could so directly and easily address his anxieties and worries.

My own darkness has always been far more resistant.

**Lord, as I wander about in darkness,
show me your light and guide me home.**

Holy clearly the sky reveals God's glory!
How plainly it shows what he has done!
Each day announces it to the following day;
each night repeats it to the next.
No speech or words are used,
no sound is heard;
yet their message goes out to all the world
and is heard to the ends of the earth.
God made a home in the sky for the sun.

Psalm 19: 1-4

> "How clearly the sky reveals God's glory!"

God's glory

The sky speaks, in a special way, to people who live on the prairies, to sailors and to anyone lucky enough to have some outdoor open space. Sunrises and sunsets that range from the tranquil to the wildly melodramatic. Deep velvet night skies packed with glittering jewels in motion. Richly textured sunlit clouds that invite the imagination to stroll on their tops like great mountains. Low, raking sunlight casting a deep magenta glow, and sharp shadows under retreating black clouds. And sundogs, comets and breathtaking moon appearances – all here for a brief moment, and then gone.

"Come, look!" we say. And in a moment, it has vanished and a new wonder is on its way. God's glory? How can it be anything else?

**My God, you write across the heavens with such beauty.
I love your style.**

"Do not be worried and upset," Jesus told them. "Believe in God and believe also in me. There are many rooms in my Father's house, and I am going to prepare a place for you. I would not tell you this if it were not so. And after I go and prepare a place for you, I will come back and take you to myself, so that you will be where I am. You know the way that leads to the place where I am going."

Thomas said to him, "Lord, we do not know where you are going; so how can we know the way to get there?" Jesus answered him, "I am the way, the truth and the life; no one goes to the Father except by me."

John 14: 1-6

> "...so how can we know the way to get there?"

Favourite apostle

Thomas gets my vote for favourite apostle. He never goes with the flow. He doesn't nod his head in agreement to fit in with the others. He doesn't mind looking like an idiot if he doesn't understand something. He voices the obvious question that everyone is thinking, but no one wants to ask.

Jesus never seems exasperated by Thomas. He takes Thomas' question seriously and gives him a serious answer. I think he's secretly glad that at least one of the twelve isn't a sheep.

I wish I were more like Thomas. All too often I hang back, not wanting to appear foolish. But if I don't step forward and say, "Lord, which way should I go?" how will I ever find the room that is prepared for me?

Thomas, teach me your determination to find the truth.

"For a long time I have been with you all; yet you do not know me, Philip? Do you not believe that I am in the Father and the Father is in me? The words that I have spoken to you," Jesus said to his disciples, "do not come from me. The Father, who remains in me, does his own work. Believe me when I say that I am in the Father and the Father is in me. If not, believe because of the things I do. I am telling you the truth: those who believe in me will do what I do – yes, they will do even greater things, because I am going to the Father. And I will do whatever you ask for in my name, so that the Father's glory will be shown through the Son. If you ask me for anything in my name, I will do it."

John 14: 7-14

> "…those who believe in me will do what I do…"

Echoing Jesus

My son has started going to a *dojo*, a traditional martial arts school. Because he is a beginner, many of the exercises he does are incomplete. They train a particular set of muscles or a specific instinctive move. The goal – after months of practice – will be to put the muscles, movements and awareness together so that when the *sensei* (teacher) says, "Do what I do," Ben will be able to echo the art of the sensei with his own body.

In today's reading, Jesus says that we believe less with our minds than with our whole being. We believe by *doing* as Jesus does – by investing our lives in love.

My goal is to echo the art of Jesus with my own body.

God, make me a willing and eager student of your art.

Acts 9: 26-31; Ps 22; 1 Jn 3: 18-24; Jn 15: 1-8

Vineyards were never a part of my experience as I was growing up. Maybe that's why I could never relate to the image of Jesus as the true vine.

Then I had the opportunity to live in a wine-growing area. I saw the process up close from beginning to end. Finally I understood! I came in autumn and saw the full harvest first. There were thick bunches of plump, juicy grapes suspended from lush vines that extended out as far as I could see. After the grapes were collected, the branches were cut down and burned. The fields strewn with stumps appeared too barren to ever produce again. They rested all winter until, come spring, tiny buds emerged and the process began again. The vine, rooted in rich soil, held the promise of life, the kind of life Jesus describes in the gospel.

Jesus is the vine – he remains the same, yesterday, today and forever. We are the branches – we come and go on this earth. The fruit we bear is offered to a hungry and thirsty world. We participate in the mission of Jesus, and when our mission is fulfilled, we let go and yield to those who follow us.

As we come together at eucharist, we draw our sustenance from the Vine. We pray together the prayer of the One who invites us to the banquet: "Take this, all of you, and drink from it."

**Lord Jesus, help me to stay rooted in your truth
and your love.**

When the crowds saw what Paul had done… they wanted to offer sacrifice to the apostles. When Barnabas and Paul heard what they were about to do, they tore their clothes and ran into the middle of the crowd, shouting, "Why are you doing this? We ourselves are only human beings like you! We are here to announce the Good News, to turn you away from these worthless things to the living God, who made heaven, earth, sea and all that is in them…. He has always given evidence of his existence by the good things he does: he gives you rain from heaven and crops at the right times; he gives you food and fills your hearts with happiness." Even with these words the apostles could hardly keep the crowd from offering a sacrifice to them.

Acts 14: 5-18

"…and fills your hearts with happiness."

Everyday miracles

The picture is vivid: people running around filled with zeal but missing the point; the two disciples trying in vain to be heard. What would happen when the miracles stopped? When life returned to normal – with sickness, hard work and those grey days?

On talk shows, people clamour for the latest weight-loss or pop psychology guru. I've seen friends follow this or that trend that has "changed their life." It doesn't usually last very long.

What remains are the miracles of everyday life: the smile of a baby, the first crocuses, the world in a water droplet seen through a microscope. Seeing people living Jesus' commandment to love their neighbour as themselves. I must look around and see that the kingdom of God is at hand.

**Lord, let me hear your message,
your real message, and live it.**

"Peace is what I leave with you; it is my own peace that I give you. I do not give it as the world does. Do not be worried and upset; do not be afraid. You heard me say to you, 'I am leaving, but I will come back to you.' If you loved me, you would be glad that I am going to the Father; for he is greater than I. I have told you this now before it all happens, so that when it does happen, you will believe. I cannot talk with you much longer, because the ruler of this world is coming. He has no power over me, but the world must know that I love the Father; that is why I do everything as he commands me."

John 14: 27-31

> "...it is my own peace that I give you."

"Pre-emptive" love

With so much talk of war in the news, who knows what state our world will be in by the time this reflection is published?

I am uneasy at how the word "peace" creeps into political speeches these days – often right next to "national security" and "pre-emptive strike" and "our way of life." This is peace as the world seeks it. And my government seems to believe that peace is really possible on these terms.

In reality, such peace – today, as in Jesus' time – means protecting the prosperity of a few from the desires of the many. Jesus identifies peace with "pre-emptive" love, and security with a "way of life" marked by humble service. Not everyone who promises peace has Jesus' meaning in mind.

Dear Jesus, do not let me be deceived by worldly claims of peace. Keep me attuned to your peace instead.

I was glad when they said to me,
"Let us go to the Lord's house."
And now we are here,
standing inside the gates of Jerusalem!
Jerusalem is a city restored
in beautiful order and harmony.
This is where the tribes come,
the tribes of Israel,
to give thanks to the Lord
according to his command.
Here the kings of Israel
sat to judge their people.

Psalm 122: 1-5

> "…in beautiful order and harmony."

God's house

"Time to get ready for church," I said, as we chatted together in our garden. "Why do we have to go to church?" asked my then five-year-old son. "Well, it's where we get together to say thank you to God," I explained. "But we can say thank you to God here!" he promptly replied.

Now that my children are teenagers, I struggle even more to get them to go to church. How I wish they were "glad… to go to the Lord's house." At times I, too, struggle with going to church. Where I seek "beautiful order and harmony," often I experience ugly squabbles and division.

These days we're trying to strike a balance between giving thanks to God in our daily lives *and* in the house of the Lord.

Lord, I often seek order and harmony. Help me to recognize your presence in the messiness of everyday life.

The apostles and the elders met together to consider the conversion of the Gentiles. After a long debate Peter stood up and said, "God, who knows the thoughts of everyone, showed his approval of the Gentiles by giving the Holy Spirit to them, just as he had to us. He made no difference between us and them; he forgave their sins because they believed. So then, why do you now want to put God to the test by laying a load on the backs of the believers which neither our ancestors nor we ourselves were able to carry? No! We believe and are saved by the grace of the Lord Jesus, just as they are." The whole group was silent as they heard Barnabas and Paul report all the miracles and wonders that God had performed through them among the Gentiles.

Acts 15: 7-21

> "He made no difference between us and them..."

Finding fault

One of my children tends to get "under my skin" more than the others. I'm quick to tell him how he is too judgmental, too impulsive or too critical. I label and categorize his behaviour; I tell him how he needs to change.

I cringe when I think about some of the things I've said. If I'm honest with myself, I must admit that many of the criticisms I level at my son are, in fact, a reflection of what I see in myself.

It's easy to find faults in my children. Then I don't have to look at my own limitations. It's much harder to pause in silence, to look and to discover "all the miracles and wonders" that God is performing in our family.

**Lord, before I point the finger, may I remember
to pause and look in the mirror first.**

have complete confidence, O God;
I will sing and praise you!
Wake up, my soul!
Wake up, my harp and lyre!
I will wake up the sun.
I will thank you, O Lord, among the nations.
I will praise you among the peoples.
Your constant love reaches the heavens;
your faithfulness touches the skies.
Show your greatness in the sky, O God,
and your glory over all the earth.

Psalm 57: 7-11

"I have complete confidence, O God."

True confidence

When asked, "How are you?" I usually reply, "Fine!" – even when it's not entirely true.

I remember teaching a girl, a leader in our school. She was near the top of the honour roll and had lots of friends. She was, by all appearances, the "perfect" student. One day after class, she told me she felt worthless. "It's all an act," she said. "If people only knew what a phony I am." She lived in fear of people finding out the "truth."

At times I feel the same way this young girl felt. I marvel at the confidence expressed in today's reading. How I'd like to believe in myself, and in God's love, so I could say with such enthusiasm, "I will wake up the sun!"

**Dear God, give me confidence in myself –
even when I feel I have very little to be confident about.**

The churches were made stronger in the faith and grew in numbers every day.

Paul and Timothy travelled through the region of Phrygia and Galatia because the Holy Spirit did not let them preach the message in the province of Asia. When they reached the border of Mysia, they tried to go into the province of Bithynia, but the Spirit of Jesus did not allow them. So they travelled right on through Mysia and went to Troas. That night Paul had a vision in which he saw a Macedonian standing and begging him, "Come over to Macedonia and help us!" As soon as Paul had this vision, we got ready to leave for Macedonia, because we decided that God had called us to preach the Good News to the people there.

Acts 16: 1-10

"Come over…and help us!"

Open to God

"Oh, come on!" I groaned as I slammed my fist against the dash and turned the ignition key yet another time. "Come on!!!" Sound familiar? When a car is flooded with fuel, you can turn the key till the cows come home, and it just won't start. It can't! Conditions in the engine aren't right.

Oddly enough, I've noticed that my experience of God is much the same. Without the right conditions inside me, it's pointless for God to try to reach me. I'm not open. I won't respond.

But when I have taken the time to prepare my heart and call, "Come over and help me!" the results can seem miraculous. God's love can heal even long-lingering hurts and sadness.

Loving God, give me the courage to examine my own life, in anticipation of your healing touch.

Acts 10: 25-26, 34-35, 44-48; Ps 98; 1 Jn 4: 7-10; Jn 15: 9-17

I n today's gospel Jesus uses the words "command" and "commandment" five times, urging his followers – including us – to obey his commandments.

"Command" is not a word that inspires a great response. It brings to mind thoughts of power and control, of being told what to do, of not being free. In our society, where the operating assumption is

that we are all equal, being given a command makes us bristle. It makes us feel that we are not being treated as responsible adults. Yet even our children don't like being told what to do. How many parents have heard, "You're not the boss of me!" when they ask their children to do something?

When someone says to us, "I want you to obey my commands," we naturally expect to be given a list of things to do and not do. But, as he often does, Jesus confuses our expectations. He says that obeying his commands is a mark of friendship, not servitude; obeying his commands is something that causes joy, not resentment; his commands are not a series of restrictions or regulations to be mindlessly followed, but one guiding principle that requires deep thought and reflection before being obeyed.

Jesus may be asking us to follow his commandments, but his challenge can be met only by those wise enough to understand what true obedience means.

Lord, I find it hard to obey.
Open my heart to follow you with love.

There was a meeting of the believers, about a hundred and twenty in all, and Peter stood up to speak. "My friends, someone must join us as a witness to the resurrection of the Lord Jesus. He must be one of the men who were in our group during the whole time that the Lord Jesus travelled about with us...."

So they proposed two men: Joseph, who was called Barsabbas, and Matthias. Then they prayed, "Lord, you know the thoughts of everyone, so show us which of these two you have chosen to serve as an apostle in the place of Judas, who left to go to the place where he belongs." Then they drew lots to choose between the two men, and the one chosen was Matthias, who was added to the group of eleven apostles.   *Acts 1: 15-17, 20-26*

"Then they drew lots..."

Choose and move on

Sometimes I get paralyzed about a decision. Should I leave a job that's driving me crazy? Do I need to change the way I deal with my spouse? my child? my friend?

When the disciples were faced with a difficult decision, they used their heads to think things through and came up with two candidates. Then they opened their hearts in prayer. But they still didn't have a decision. Finally they did something shocking. They drew lots. They gambled.

When I've gathered all the information I can get, when I've prayed over my decision and still can't make up my mind, maybe I should follow the disciples' example. Maybe I should say one last prayer, flip a coin and get on with my life.

Lord, when I have a decision to make, help me to balance the need for caution with the need for action.

"Now I am going to him who sent me, yet none of you asks me where I am going. And now that I have told you, your hearts are full of sadness. But I am telling you the truth: it is better for you that I go away, because if I do not go, the Helper will not come to you. But if I do go away, then I will send him to you. And when he comes, he will prove to the people of the world that they are wrong about sin, because they do not believe in me; they are wrong about what is right, because I am going to the Father and you will not see me any more; and they are wrong about judgment, because the ruler of this world has already been judged."

John 16: 5-11

> "...they are wrong about what is right..."

Choosing what is right

Jesus promised to send the Helper to us. But why, in our day, does it seem so difficult to hear this voice? Can we really say we know what's wrong and what's right?

I open the newspaper and read of regions in Africa where doctors don't even have Aspirin to relieve the pain of children who have cancer. I see pictures of the most affluent countries in the world where some people have no choice but to make the streets their home. I see articles that defame and expose our political leaders – and they, in turn, say, "I'll take the publicity."

And at times, my own moral choices are so complex, so unclear. How difficult to hear the Helper. How hard to listen.

Spirit of God, help me to hear your voice telling me what's right. Give me the strength to follow.

" I have much more to tell you, but now it would be too much for you to bear. When, however, the Spirit comes, who reveals the truth about God, he will lead you into all the truth. He will not speak on his own authority, but he will speak of what he hears and will tell you of things to come. He will give me glory, because he will take what I say and tell it to you. All that my Father has is mine; that is why I said that the Spirit will take what I give him and tell it to you."

John 16: 12-15

> "...he will lead you into all the truth."

Live the question

When my husband was diagnosed with terminal cancer, a close friend asked, "Where is your God of love?" Now, years later, I can say with deep conviction that God has never been far from me.

Within the pain and the loss, the confusion, the searching for inner peace (and outer stability!), I have discovered new truths about myself, others and God. It hasn't been easy. I've wanted to "know," to have the answers to my many questions... now! But each new question has kept me straining to discover God's Spirit, to be open to the "things to come."

I know there won't be black-and-white answers to my questions. But when I live the questions, I discover the many vibrant colours that life has to offer.

Lord, help me to "be patient toward all that is unsolved in my heart and help me to try to love the questions themselves." (Rainer Maria Rilke)

" n a little while you will not see me any more, and then a little while later you will see me." Some of his disciples asked among themselves, "What does this mean? He tells us that in a little while we will not see him, and then a little while later we will see him. What does this 'a little while' mean? We don't know what he is talking about!"

Jesus knew that they wanted to question him, so he said, "I said, 'In a little while you will not see me, and then a little while later you will see me.' I am telling you the truth: you will cry and weep, but the world will be glad; you will be sad, but your sadness will turn into gladness."

John 16: 16-20

"...a little while later you will see me."

Darkness and light

Sometimes I get discouraged, bogged down, frazzled. I begin to wonder if life has meaning. My sense of God's loving presence fades to grey. But I have a promise: Jesus says, "A little while later you will see me."

If I look back over the years, I see that periods of grey have alternated with periods of brightness, when life had meaning and direction. At other times, life looks very black: I lose a job, a home, a loved one.

But in the midst of my anguish, I remember the promise: impossible as it may seem, these dark times will come to an end. "A little while later you will see me.... You will cry and weep; you will be sad, but your sadness will turn into gladness."

Lord, help me to hang on through the darkest hours until I see your light again.

" I am telling you the truth: you will cry and weep, but the world will be glad; you will be sad, but your sadness will turn into gladness. When a woman is about to give birth, she is sad because her hour of suffering has come; but when the baby is born, she forgets her suffering, because she is happy that a baby has been born into the world. That is how it is with you: now you are sad, but I will see you again, and your hearts will be filled with gladness, the kind of gladness that no one can take away from you.

"When that day comes, you will not ask me for anything. I am telling you the truth: the Father will give you whatever you ask of him in my name."

John 16: 20-23

> "...her hour of suffering has come..."

No gain without pain

I'm almost jealous. As a man, I have never given birth to a child. I have held our newborn children in my arms; I have comforted them in the dark hours of the night; I have marvelled at their fragile perfection.

But I've missed a significant learning about life. Women know that the birth of anything new always comes as a painful experience. There's no way of easing into a new life. Rather, at some point, the new life takes over. It tears you apart. It demands to be born. And you cannot stay as you were.

That's as true for spiritual birth as for physical birth. It's a hard lesson for a man to learn.

Lord, I usually try to avoid pain.
Help me to see it instead as a gateway to new life.

C lap your hands for joy, all peoples!
Praise God with loud songs!
The Lord, the Most High, is to be feared;
he is a great king, ruling over all the world....
God is king over all the world;
praise him with songs!
God sits on his sacred throne;
he rules over the nations.
The rulers of the nations assemble
with the people of the God of Abraham.
More powerful than all armies is he;
he rules supreme.

Psalm 47: 1-2, 7-9

> "...he rules supreme."

Hope for the hopeless

At times, I am overcome by the state of the world. I cringe when I hear the latest news of conflict, war, terrorist attacks and misguided judgment. How can we extricate ourselves from the mess we're in? How can we learn to love one another? We seem to be past the point of no return – with our zero tolerance, our prejudices and our inability to listen to one another.

When I feel this way, I remind myself that humans do not have the last word. God does: "More powerful than all armies is he; he rules supreme." These words give me hope. And although I can't see my way clear through the various wars and injustices, I take comfort in the knowledge that God can.

Lord, help me hold on to hope when conflict surrounds me.

Acts 1: 1-11; Ps 47; Eph 1: 17-23 or Eph 4: 1-13; Mk 16: 15-20

With their Lord's ascension, the disciples had a decision to make: would they, through their own ministry, continue to proclaim the life, death and resurrection of Jesus, or would the story stop with them? The crucifixion of the One in whom they had put their hope had been devastating. Yet now, the risen Lord appeared before them, laying out the appropriate actions for apostles (those *sent*), so that the next stage of Jesus' mission might be accomplished.

We know that, despite their weaknesses, the apostles succeeded in this task, for we also have become witnesses to Christ Jesus. Called by God and formed in the Holy Spirit, we are a people who proclaim Jesus' victory over death. The Spirit, principle of unity, makes us witnesses to this one faith. Amazingly, the Spirit's diverse gifts to individuals do not compete with each other, but bind the community together in peace.

This requires every effort on our part, however, since we know very well our capacity to cause division. We are not always humble, gentle or patient with each other. Nor do we always bear with one another in love.

We give thanks, then, for today's new opportunity to give thanks for God's faithful love for humanity and for the presence of Jesus with us always in the eucharist. Sent forth as apostles, we eagerly tell others that the promise of salvation has been fulfilled.

**Lord, help me to keep sharing with others
the good news of your love for us.**

The disciples said to Jesus, "Now you are speaking plainly, without using figures of speech. We know now that you know everything; you do not need to have someone ask you questions. This makes us believe that you came from God."

Jesus answered them, "Do you believe now? The time is coming, and is already here, when all of you will be scattered, each of you to your own home, and I will be left all alone. But I am not really alone, because the Father is with me. I have told you this so that you will have peace by being united to me. The world will make you suffer. But be brave! I have defeated the world!"

John 16: 29-33

> **"Do you believe now?"**

Believing in myself

While studying lithography, a labour-intensive printmaking method, I took copious notes and asked questions ad nauseam. I was fine doing the work – as long as the instructor was nearby and I knew I could ask for help if I needed it.

One day, as I arrived at the studio to do a major project, I found that I'd left my notes behind. Horrified and anxious, I pleaded for a deferral. But the instructor smiled knowingly and said, "This is probably the best thing that could happen." To my surprise, as I calmed down, I got involved in the work and discovered that I had internalized the process and didn't need my notes after all!

Like the disciples, I needed reassurance – and a little push.

**God, help me to trust all you have taught me
as I move into new experiences.**

Y ou caused abundant rain to fall
and restored your worn-out land;
your people made their home there;
in your goodness you provided for the poor....
Praise the Lord,
who carries our burdens day after day;
he is the God who saves us.
Our God is a God who saves;
he is the Lord, our Lord,
who rescues us from death.

Psalm 68: 9-10, 19-20

"...who carries our burdens day after day..."

A heavy load

One afternoon, on our way home from school, my daughter felt over-whelmed. It had not been a good day in Grade 1. Small woes had plagued her all day: a spilled juice box in her knapsack, a scraped knee at recess, a lost library book.... She poured out her troubles as we walked home together. As she struggled with her knapsack, she reached her breaking point. Dropping it on the ground, she burst into tears.

Usually when my daughter balks at carrying her bag, I launch into the lecture about "responsibility." That day I picked up her bag without saying a word. Her hand slipped into mine and we continued on our way.

How easy it was for me to lighten her load! How often I forget that God offers to do the same for me.

**God, I know you will help me carry my burdens
today and every day.**

Holy Father! Keep them safe by the power of your name, the name you gave me, so that they may be one just as you and I are one. While I was with them, I kept them safe by the power of your name, the name you gave me…. And now I am coming to you, and I say these things in the world so that they might have my joy in their hearts in all its fullness…. Just as I do not belong to the world, they do not belong to the world. Dedicate them to yourself by means of the truth; your word is truth. I sent them into the world, just as you sent me into the world. And for their sake I dedicate myself to you, in order that they, too, may be truly dedicated to you."

John 17: 11-19

> "Keep them safe by the power of your name…"

The power of a name

One of our wedding prayers asked that, in our marriage, we be kept safe in the meaning – "the power" – of our names: that Margaret would always find herself to be a "precious pearl," and that I, David, would always know myself to be "beloved."

The power of God's name can be sensed in its meaning: "I will be who I will be." It is the name God revealed to Moses in the burning bush, and it carries the promise of both freedom and surprise: who can limit or even anticipate God?

When Jesus prays, "Keep them safe by the power of your name," he is asking that the disciples – including me – remain willing to be surprised by God's capacity to bring freedom where it is not yet.

God, keep me safe in your name. Let my words and actions show others your ability to surprise and to set free.

" I pray that they may all be one. Father! May they be in us, just as you are in me and I am in you. May they be one, so that the world will believe that you sent me. I gave them the same glory you gave me, so that they may be one, just as you and I are one: I am in them and you in me, so that they may be completely one, in order that the world may know that you sent me and that you love them as you love me.

"Father! You have given them to me, and I want them to be with me where I am, so that they may see my glory, the glory you gave me; for you loved me before the world was made."

John 17: 20-26

> "I pray that they may all be one."

United in love

Today's reading is a complicated expression of Jesus' deepest desire for us to know the intimacy with God that Jesus himself knew: an intimacy to be shared with one another, as well.

But yesterday, after reading the newspaper, I simply couldn't imagine the caring relationship Jesus describes. I lay my head on the table, in despair over the state of our world.

That night, when I went out, a friend put my three-year-old to bed. At four in the morning, my daughter awoke and called for me. I picked her up and she threw her arms around me, saying, "You came back!" We stood by the window in the dark, holding each other – a moment of paradise. I think I got a glimpse of what Jesus meant.

**God, help me to keep my senses alert
for the signs of your love around me.**

After they had eaten, Jesus said to Simon Peter, "Simon son of John, do you love me more than these others do?"

"Yes, Lord," he answered, "you know that I love you." Jesus said to him, "Take care of my lambs." A second time Jesus said to him, "Simon son of John, do you love me?"

"Yes, Lord," he answered, "you know that I love you." Jesus said to him, "Take care of my sheep." A third time Jesus said, "Simon son of John, do you love me?" Peter became sad because Jesus asked him the third time, "Do you love me?" and so he said to him, "Lord, you know everything; you know that I love you!" Jesus said to him, "Take care of my sheep…." Then Jesus said to him, "Follow me!"

John 21: 15-19

> "A third time Jesus said, 'Do you love me?'"

Three times

Threes have an amazing power. I teach English to would-be writers and editors. Three examples are enough to convince anyone, I tell them – additional examples become overkill. Three characteristics will give readers a thumbnail sketch of any character. The most basic English sentence has three elements: subject, verb, object.

In religion, we have the Holy Trinity: Father, Son and Holy Spirit. At Christmas, the "three wise men" came from the east to see Jesus. In the wilderness, Jesus faced three temptations.

And here, in this passage, Jesus asked Simon Peter three times, "Do you love me?" Perhaps he wanted three questions to balance the three times Peter denied knowing Jesus in the high priest's courtyard.

The rule of three must have worked. Peter got a second chance. He didn't need a third one.

**Dear God, I wish I had only denied you three times.
Thank you for giving me so many second chances.**

The Lord is in his holy temple;
he has his throne in heaven.
He watches people everywhere
and knows what they are doing.
He examines the good
and the wicked alike;
the lawless he hates with all his heart.
The Lord is righteous
and loves good deeds;
those who do them will live
in his presence.

Psalm 11: 4, 5, 7

> "The Lord is righteous and loves good deeds."

Too quick to judge

I like to think that my list of "good guys" and "bad guys" matches God's list exactly. The "wicked" include all the usual suspects: murderers, thieves, rapists, and anyone who happens to annoy me that day.

And it goes without saying that I'm one of the "righteous." It's reassuring to think of God, "up there," looking down angrily on all those evil folks.

When I lapse into this kind of self-righteous, simplistic thinking, it's usually because I feel threatened or uncertain. I'm looking for easy answers to baffling moral questions. My ego doesn't much like the truth: that only God is in the position to judge the good and the bad.

Only God truly knows what is in another's heart.

Today, Lord, heal my hard, judgmental heart.

Acts 2: 1-11; Ps 104; I Cor 12: 3-7, 12-13 or Gal 5: 16-25; Jn 15: 26-27, 16: 12-15

When Cardinal Roncalli became Pope John XXIII in 1958, no one expected any changes in the Church. This proved to be a total misreading of how good the Spirit is at surprising God's people. The surprise came when good Pope John, moved by the Spirit, called an ecumenical council, the first to take place in almost a century. The Church, he believed, was ripe for nothing less than "a new Pentecost."

The first Christian Pentecost, too, came as total surprise. It was already a great day for devout Jews to gather in Jerusalem and com-

memorate the wondrous gift of Torah and covenant on Mount Sinai. But no one expected a sudden rush of wind to blow down from heaven or tongues of fire to rest upon a small group of fearful Galileans, making them bold proclaimers of the gospel of Christ.

More than 40 years after the completion of Vatican II, many of us still yearn for a new Pentecost to take place in our Church. We feel the need for "a wind of change" so that the gospel of Christ may be proclaimed to the world with more passion and meaning. Why should we wait for the initiative to come from somewhere else? We are called to "live by the Spirit" and bear the fruits that can change the face of the world.

Loving God, send the wind of change to blow through our hearts and our lives as we seek to follow you.

A man knelt before [Jesus] and asked, "What must I do to receive eternal life?" … Jesus looked straight at him with love and said, "You need only one thing. Go and sell all you have and give the money to the poor, and you will have riches in heaven; then come and follow me." When the man heard this, gloom spread over his face, and he went away sad, because he was very rich.

Jesus said, "It is much harder for a rich person to enter the kingdom of God than for a camel to go through the eye of a needle."

At this the disciples were completely amazed: "Who, then, can be saved?" Jesus looked straight at them and answered, "This is impossible for human beings but not for God; everything is possible for God."

Mark 10: 17-27

> "Jesus looked straight at him with love…"

The challenge

I often feel like that rich young man in today's reading. I say I want to follow Jesus and, to show my good intentions, I make some dramatic gestures. But then the thought of Jesus looking "straight at me with love" reminds me of all I still cling to, all I don't *really* want to give up.

At different times in my life, I've clung to money, an unhealthy relationship, the habit of self-pity. Could I really give up everything to which my heart secretly clings?

However often I turn away, with gloom spread over my face, I know that Jesus waits for me – to let go and to follow him. When I finally do, I'll realize how poor I really was.

Jesus, look straight at me with love: show me what I cling to, and help me to let it go and follow you.

P eter spoke up, "Look, we have left everything and followed you." "Yes," Jesus said to them, "and I tell you that those who leave home or brothers or sisters or mother or father or children or fields for me and for the gospel, will receive much more in this present age. They will receive a hundred times more houses, brothers, sisters, mothers, children, and fields – and persecutions as well; and in the age to come they will receive eternal life. But many who are now first will be last, and many who are now last will be first."

Mark 10: 28-31

> "...and many who are now last will be first."

Reasonable, or not?

The reaction of those who heard Jesus speak must have been surprise: "The last will be first? That just isn't logical."

A while ago, my daughter desperately needed new running shoes, so we went shopping. But when we got to the store, Katie suggested we wait until the next paycheque. Why? So I could buy her younger brother a much needed and totally awesome new winter jacket that was on sale, half-price. Katie knew how thrilled Kevin would be.

I recounted this beautiful story to a relative, who then insisted on sending a cheque to Katie for shoes. Katie purchased shoes far superior to anything we could have afforded. Thinking of that experience, I was reminded of today's reading: it no longer seemed so illogical after all!

**Lord, grant that I may trust you enough
to put the needs of others before my own.**

James and John came to Jesus. "Teacher, when you sit on your throne in your glorious kingdom, we want you to let us sit with you…." Jesus said, "You don't know what you are asking for. Can you drink the cup of suffering that I must drink?" "We can," they answered.

Jesus said, "You will indeed drink the cup I must drink…. But I do not have the right to choose who will sit at my right and my left. It is God who will give these places to those for whom he has prepared them…. If one of you wants to be great, you must be the servant of the rest…. For even the Son of Man did not come to be served; he came to serve and to give his life to redeem many people."

Mark 10: 32-45

> "…you must be the servant of the rest…"

Servant-leader

I have worked for many bosses in my life, and most have liked the sense of power they had over their employees. For them, this "power over others" seemed to be one of the perks of the job.

Once, however, I did work for a man who really took the gospel seriously. I will always remember him saying, "Power has only one real purpose: service. If power is not used to help others, then that power is wasted."

I was raised to believe status was partly determined by how many people you had "under you." What a radical idea to suggest that the boss is there to help and serve! I am challenged to look at how I use my power to serve others – at work and at home.

**Dear God, teach me a spirit of service
– both at work and at home.**

Love must be completely sincere. Hate what is evil, hold on to what is good. Love one another warmly as Christians, and be eager to show respect for one another. Work hard and do not be lazy. Serve the Lord with a heart full of devotion. Let your hope keep you joyful, be patient in your troubles, and pray at all times. Share your belongings with your needy fellow Christians, and open your homes to strangers.

Ask God to bless those who persecute you – yes, ask him to bless, not to curse. Be happy with those who are happy, weep with those who weep. Have the same concern for everyone. Do not be proud, but accept humble duties. Do not think of yourselves as wise.

Romans 12: 9-16

> "Work hard and do not be lazy."

Work as holy

From this list of Christian principles, I am drawn to the ones about *work*. The sacred nature of work is a tenet of the Shaker community, a religious sect that no longer exists. Because I live in the area where Mother Ann Lee first established the Shakers, I've learned about them through many local initiatives set up to preserve their heritage.

I recently attended a performance by a local group that plays Shaker music. The violinist explained that the Shakers played as hard as they worked, enjoying music and often dancing far into the night. They sought balance and order in what they produced and how they produced it.

To them, work was a meeting of the human and divine. Their motto was "Put your hands to work, and your hearts to God."

**Lord, help me to savour my daily tasks
and to share them with you.**

S ay to all the nations, "The Lord is king!
The earth is set firmly in place and cannot be moved;
he will judge the peoples with justice."
Be glad, earth and sky!
Roar, sea, and every creature in you;
be glad, fields, and everything in you!
The trees in the woods will shout for joy
when the Lord comes to rule the earth.
He will rule the peoples of the world
with justice and fairness.

Psalm 96: 10-13

"…with justice and fairness."

Are we all human?

A few years ago I attended a presentation by retired General Roméo Dallaire, who was head of the United Nations Forces in Rwanda in the 1990s.

I was struck by his passion and compassion as he described his experiences, telling us how the world community failed to come to the aid of those being killed. He asked us repeatedly, "Are all humans human, or do some count more than others?" He challenged us, who are living in one of the wealthiest countries in the world, to consider our global perspective. Do we care enough to get involved?

Today's reading both reassures and challenges me. While God will rule with justice and fairness, what does God think of how we treat others now?

**God of justice, forgive us our trespasses.
May your kingdom come.**

As Jesus was walking in the Temple, the chief priests, the teachers of the Law, and the elders came to him and asked him, "What right do you have to do these things? Who gave you such right?"

Jesus answered them, "I will ask you just one question, and if you give me an answer, I will tell you what right I have to do these things. Tell me, where did John's right to baptize come from: was it from God or from human beings?"

They started to argue among themselves: "What shall we say? If we answer, 'From God,' he will say, 'Why, then, did you not believe John?' But if we say, 'From human beings…'" So their answer to Jesus was, "We don't know."

Mark 11: 27-33

"What right do you have to do these things?"

Winning and losing

I hate playing chess! Playing with my older brother always made me anxious. I felt the game was not about the pieces on the board but about reading the other person's mind. At least with poker you can't see the other person's cards and they can't see yours. In chess the only thing you can hide is your intentions.

Today's reading reminds me of the way some people treat human relationships like a chess game. Someone is going to get "caught," so one must always be on the defensive. Jesus realizes the chief priests are out to "catch" him, so he does the wise thing: he walks away from the game – a game that's not about the truth, but about winning and losing.

Lord, give me the grace to be open and trusting in my relationships – even when others are not so with me.

Deut 4: 32-34, 39-40; Ps 33; Rom 8: 14-17; Mt 28: 16-20

The last verses of Matthew's gospel describe a scene that is both enigmatic and comforting. The eleven disciples have gone to the mountain to which Jesus had directed them. "When they saw him, they worshipped him; but some doubted." Even in this last privileged encounter with the risen Christ, their struggle of faith and commitment continues. Worship and doubt coexist in the first disciples and in all who follow them.

It is precisely out of this awkward tension between worship and doubt that Jesus sends the eleven to the nations. The word "disciple" itself means one who learns: in this case, to be in a relationship with Jesus that is ongoing and evolving. The risen Christ calls these eleven teachers to invite others into their struggling company as he promises to be with them even to the end of the age. Baptism – a life-transforming plunge into a mysterious relationship with the Father, Son and Spirit – follows on accepting discipleship, giving further witness to the way Matthew understands the process of faith.

Trinity Sunday invites believers to reflection and commitment – to a conscious and ever-deepening relationship with the Father through, with and in the Son, who, in the presence and power of the Spirit, remains to the end of the age.

As awkward as the coexistence of worship and doubt might feel in our life of faith, it is not only normal, it is life-giving.

Lord Jesus, help me to see that my doubts can lead me into a deeper relationship with you.

"Once there was a man who planted a vineyard, put a fence around it, dug a hole for the wine press, and built a watchtower. Then he rented the vineyard to tenants and left home on a trip. When the time came to gather the grapes, he sent a slave to the tenants to receive from them his share of the harvest. The tenants grabbed the slave, beat him, and sent him back without a thing. Then the owner sent another slave; the tenants beat him over the head and treated him shamefully. The owner sent another slave, and they killed him; and they treated many others the same way, beating some and killing others. Last of all, then, he sent his son to the tenants.... But those tenants said to one another, 'This is the owner's son. Come on, let's kill him, and his property will be ours!'"

Mark 12: 1-12

> "...they treated many others the same way..."

Doing what's right

I get the point... I think. I could write about how many times I've been the tenants in today's reading: how many times I avoided "paying up." How many times I didn't do what's right.

But, to be honest, when I read and reread this story, I always think, "What would it be like to be one of this guy's slaves?" You know, you're slave number 19, thinking, "Oh no, I'm next." I mean, wouldn't you send the police, or go together for safety?

But life's like that, isn't it? Sometimes you have to go in, knowing you're going to get clobbered. Sometimes it's not easy to follow the master's orders. It's not easy to do your job, to do what's right.

**Lord, let me go in and do what's right,
even when it costs.**

Some Pharisees and some members of Herod's party were sent to Jesus to trap him with questions. They came to him and said, "Teacher, we know that you tell the truth, without worrying about what people think. You pay no attention to anyone's status, but teach the truth about God's will for people. Tell us, is it against our Law to pay taxes to the Roman Emperor? Should we pay them or not?"

But Jesus saw through their trick and answered, "Why are you trying to trap me? Bring a silver coin, and let me see it." They brought him one, and he asked, "Whose face and name are these?" "The Emperor's," they answered. So Jesus said, "Well, then, pay to the Emperor what belongs to the Emperor, and pay to God what belongs to God."

Mark 12: 13-17

> "...pay to God what belongs to God."

Paying the emperor

The question the Pharisees asked, while not sincere, was fairly straightforward. Jesus' answer to their question was both sincere and straightforward: Pay those you owe what they are due.

Sometimes life is not so straightforward. I'm a middle-aged guy with a family, and often there's just not enough money, time and energy to go around. There are simply too many emperors! What do I owe my employer? How many times must I volunteer at the school? And my kids' needs...? After all, they won't be with me forever. And, oh yeah, take some "quality" time for yourself. Right!

I have a good life. A great life! It's just hard sometimes to know what belongs to the emperor, and how much I should be paying.

**God, may I have the wisdom to know
how much I can truly give.**

S ome Sadducees said, "Teacher, Moses wrote this law for us: 'If a man dies and leaves a wife but no children, that man's brother must marry the widow....' Once there were seven brothers; the oldest got married and died without having children. Then the second one married the woman, and he also died without having children.... All seven brothers married the woman and died without having children. Last of all, the woman died. Now, when all the dead rise to life on the day of resurrection, whose wife will she be?"

Jesus answered them, "When the dead rise to life, they will be like the angels in heaven and will not marry. Now, as for the dead being raised... it is written that God is the God of the living, not of the dead."

Mark 12: 18-27

"...the God of the living, not of the dead."

A God who frees

I recently spent an afternoon with a notary, a lawyer and a property developer. It was a simple matter of positioning two parking spaces, but insults were flung, threats were uttered, and papers were thrown across the table. Our law binds us with words that seem cast in stone, and we use legal arguments to try to disable each other.

The Sadducees applied these same legal tools to the question of the resurrection. In the situation they described, there would be adultery, or polygamy, in heaven! Instead of answering their question, Jesus shifts the talk from death to life. Our legal tools, necessary for sorting out parking spaces, cannot pin down God or God's creatures. Instead, God liberates us from all that keeps us in the tomb.

Lord, I cannot pin you down.
Help me embrace my life without calculation.

A teacher of the Law came to Jesus with a question: "Which commandment is the most important of all?"

Jesus replied, "The most important one is this: 'Listen, Israel! The Lord our God is the only Lord. Love the Lord your God with all your heart, with all your soul, with all your mind, and with all your strength.' The second most important commandment is this: 'Love your neighbour as you love yourself.' There is no other commandment more important than these two."

The teacher of the Law said to Jesus, "Well done, Teacher! It is true, as you say, that only the Lord is God and that there is no other god.... And it is more important to obey these two commandments than to offer on the altar animals and other sacrifices to God."

Mark 12: 28-34

> "Love your neighbour as you love yourself."

As you love yourself

The car became airborne on the last hill. It took hours to get Mary out of the wreck. After six months of reconstructive surgery and physiotherapy, she landed in my class unable to remember anything of that drug- and alcohol-filled night.

I had known Mary as a child – the perfect straight-A student who never disappointed anyone. After the accident, she went back to her life of drinking and drugs. One day I finally asked her, "Why?" She said she'd spent her whole life loving and pleasing others. She had never learned to love herself.

Jesus seems to assume that his comparison will be understood: "Love your neighbour as you love yourself." For some, love of neighbour is easier than love of self.

God, may I love myself enough to truly love others.

But you have followed my teaching, my conduct, and my purpose in life; you have observed my faith, my patience, my love, my endurance, my persecutions and my sufferings.... But the Lord rescued me from them all. Everyone who wants to live a godly life in union with Christ Jesus will be persecuted; and evil persons and impostors will keep on going from bad to worse, deceiving others and being deceived themselves. But as for you, continue in the truths that you were taught and firmly believe.... All Scripture is inspired by God and is useful for teaching the truth, rebuking error, correcting faults, and giving instruction for right living, so that the person who serves God may be fully qualified and equipped to do every kind of good deed.

2 Timothy 3: 10-17

> "...continue in the truths that you were taught..."

Tough advice

Paul's advice to a young man, Timothy, is penned at a dark time. Timothy is being persecuted, but he is also deflated by what he sees around him, especially in his own church. He has few friends, and some of the people he once trusted have not only deserted him, they have turned on him.

So Paul writes to his young apprentice, urging him to hang on. He then shares some advice, the fruit of his own experience. You will, he says, be persecuted for the faith. But don't lose sight of "the truth." There is no kind of good deed that you can say no to. And don't worry, he continues, whether the time is right or not. Just say it. Just do it.

Lord, give me the strength to remain loyal, not to my own biased assumptions, but to you alone.

All day long I praise you
and proclaim your glory.
Do not reject me now that I am old;
do not abandon me now that I am feeble....
I will always put my hope in you;
I will praise you more and more.
I will tell of your goodness....
I will go in the strength of the Lord God;
I will proclaim your goodness, yours alone.
You have taught me ever since I was young,
and I still tell of your wonderful acts....
I will praise your faithfulness, my God.
On my harp I will play hymns to you,
the Holy One of Israel.

Psalm 71: 8-9, 14-17, 22

"You have taught me ever since I was young..."

My whole life long

I'm not old, but I'm older than I used to be. As the years go by and life experiences accumulate, I'm beginning to see a pattern – to see mountains and valleys in my personal story of faith.

When I was a child, faith shaped our family and our social life. During adolescence and young adulthood, when I thought I was in charge of my life, faith played a lesser role. Now that I am a parent and have hit a few potholes along the way, I rely on God more and more to get me through the hard times. And I take time to praise and thank God for the good times.

Now, more than ever, I see God's faithfulness at work in my life each and every day – my whole life long.

**Lord, I praise you for your faithfulness to me
– in good times and in hard times.**

Ex 24: 3-8; Ps 116; Heb 9: 11-15; Mk 14: 12-16, 22-26

Two words echo through today's readings: covenant and blood. The two go together. Moses dashed blood on the people of the original covenant. Jesus shed his blood for the people of a new covenant and he gives the people of the new covenant his blood to drink. Today's readings celebrate this gift – this blood of the new covenant that Jesus has given us – and call on us to ponder and appreciate it.

A covenant is a special type of agreement. Consider this: if I make a contract with someone, I do not have to pay them if they do not do the work, and they do not have to do the work if I do not pay them. Not so with a covenant. Even if one side does not honour the covenant, the other side is still bound to keep it.

God makes covenants, not contracts. No matter how often the people break the covenant, God remains faithful. Through Jesus, we have an eternal covenant with God. In every celebration of the eucharist this covenant is renewed. When we share in the body and blood of Christ we renew our promise to live as members of Christ's body. To share the precious blood of the Lamb of God is an awesome and privileged act. We who are called to his supper rejoice at this gift.

Lord, your covenant with us is sacred.
Help me to honour it always.

"Go and preach, 'The kingdom of heaven is near!' Heal the sick, bring the dead back to life, heal those who suffer from dreaded skin diseases, and drive out demons. You have received without paying, so give without being paid. Do not carry any gold, silver, or copper money in your pockets; do not carry a beggar's bag for the trip or an extra shirt or shoes or a walking stick. Workers should be given what they need.

"When you come to a town or village, go in and look for someone who is willing to welcome you.... When you go into a house, say, 'Peace be with you.' If the people in that house welcome you, let your greeting of peace remain; but if they do not welcome you, then take back your greeting."

Matthew 10: 7-13

> "...so give without being paid."

Small acts of kindness

My thirteen-year-old son and I watched the movie *Gandhi* the other night. I wondered to myself: Does my son have any role models who do good, for reasons other than money? He seems to be growing up in such a selfish, materialistic world.

A couple of days later, my son started French tutorials with a high school student named John. I knew John had already fulfilled his volunteer requirements for graduation, but when I insisted that he take money for the tutoring, he steadfastly refused. I pushed the money into his hand, but he wouldn't take it. "It's OK. I enjoy doing this," he said.

My son learned something important that day: acts of service and sacrifice can be most powerful when they're small.

**Lord, let me do some small kindness today,
expecting nothing in return.**

"You are like salt for the whole human race. But if salt loses its saltiness, there is no way to make it salty again. It has become worthless, so it is thrown out and people trample on it.

"You are like light for the whole world. A city built on a hill cannot be hid. No one lights a lamp and puts it under a bowl; instead it is put on the lampstand, where it gives light for everyone in the house. In the same way your light must shine before people, so that they will see the good things you do and praise your Father in heaven."

Matthew 5: 13-16

"But if salt loses its saltiness…"

Thinking metaphorically

My friend John takes things literally. He has never seen salt lose its saltiness – though he wishes sometimes it would, such as when the city works crews spread it on the streets in winter and it rots the bottom of his car. So he treats these words as meaningless.

I tell him, "Don't ask whether it can happen – ask what it would be like if it could happen. If salt could lose its saltiness. Or if paint lost its colour. If food lost its taste. If springs lost their bounce. If light bulbs lost their light. They'd become useless. You'd throw them out."

John has trouble thinking metaphorically. But sometimes, it's the only way to understand the Bible's message for us.

God, help me to nurture whatever it is that makes me what I am, so that I don't become useless to you.

Protect me, O God; I trust in you for safety.
I say to the Lord, "You are my Lord;
   all the good things I have come from you...."
Those who rush to other gods
bring many troubles on themselves.
I will not take part in their sacrifices;
I will not worship their gods.
You, Lord, are all I have,
and you give me all I need;
my future is in your hands....
I am always aware of the Lord's presence;
he is near, and nothing can shake me....
You will show me the path that leads to life;
your presence fills me with joy
and brings me pleasure forever.   *Psalm 16: 1-2, 5, 8, 11*

"I am always aware of the Lord's presence..."

Where's Waldo?

At the end of the day, my daughter coaxes me into a game of *Where's Waldo?* She loves to sit with the big book on her lap, its pages open to the chaos of characters hiding the ever-smiling Waldo.

I get impatient: there are dishes to put away, lunches to make and garbage to put out. I half-heartedly skim over the pages. She always finds Waldo before I do. I wonder if it is because she *believes*. She never tires of searching for him.

It dawns on me that God is like Waldo in my life: ever-present, hiding among the chaos. Perhaps the secret is to delight in the searching. God's presence will be revealed when I take the time to look.

God, I know you are with me.
Help me feel your presence today.

"You have heard that people were told in the past, 'Do not commit murder; anyone who does will be brought to trial.' But now I tell you: if you are angry with your brother you will be brought to trial, if you call your brother 'You good-for-nothing!' you will be brought before the Council, and if you call your brother a worthless fool you will be in danger of going to the fire of hell. So if you are about to offer your gift to God at the altar and there you remember that your brother has something against you, leave your gift there in front of the altar, go at once and make peace with your brother, and then come back and offer your gift to God."

Matthew 5: 20-26

"…and make peace with your brother…"

Saying "I'm sorry"

Some time ago, two mothers won the Nobel Prize for their efforts to bring peace to Northern Ireland. It's not surprising that they were mothers. Maybe it was all those years of telling their children, "Go and say you're sorry."

I think of childhood fights in the sandbox when my mother would say to me, "Go and tell Johnny you're sorry." I remember thinking, "But I'm not sorry." It was so hard to say, and so much harder to mean.

It's hard for husbands to say "I'm sorry" to their wives. It's hard for parents to say it to children. It's hard to say it at work; it's hard to say it at home. And it's hard when, as in so many places, the ghosts of loved ones hover close by, listening.

**Dear God, help me to forgive others.
Help me to work for peace in our world today.**

The Lord says, "When Israel was a child, I loved him and called him out of Egypt as my son.... Yet I was the one who taught Israel to walk.... I drew them to me with affection and love. I picked them up and held them to my cheek; I bent down to them and fed them....

"How can I give you up, Israel? How can I abandon you? Could I ever destroy you as I did Admah, or treat you as I did Zeboiim? My heart will not let me do it! My love for you is too strong. I will not punish you in my anger; I will not destroy Israel again. For I am God and not a mere human being. I, the Holy One, am with you. I will not come to you in anger."

Hosea 11: 1-4, 8-9

> "I was the one who taught Israel to walk."

A tender and caring love

I love this passage. Most of the Bible portrays fathers as distant autocrats and rulers of the household. Hosea reveals a father's tender and loving side.

Helping a child learn to walk is such a satisfying accomplishment! Recently, our granddaughter took her first steps. At first, we had to hold her hand. Then she launched out on her own. Her face showed a wild joy, an ecstasy. As her confidence grew, she went from tentative steps to a trot to a gallop. In a single weekend, she taught herself three different ways of going down stairs: backwards, facing frontwards on her rear, and standing up holding the handrail.

As I read Hosea's words, I can identify with him, and with his love.

Tenderly and gently, you taught me to take my first tentative steps in faith. Thank you!

Every year the parents of Jesus went to Jerusalem for the Passover Festival. When Jesus was twelve years old, they went to the festival as usual. When the festival was over, they started back home, but the boy Jesus stayed in Jerusalem. His parents did not know this; they thought that he was with the group, so they travelled a whole day and then started looking for him among their relatives and friends....

On the third day they found him in the Temple, sitting with the Jewish teachers, listening to them and asking questions.... His mother said to him, "Son, why have you done this to us? Your father and I have been terribly worried...." He answered them, "Why did you have to look for me? Didn't you know that I had to be in my Father's house?".

Luke 2: 41-51

"...they found him in the Temple..."

Anxious and worried

When I was four years old, I went to stay with my aunt on her farm. In spite of her watchful eye, I wandered off. You can imagine her horror when she saw my footprints in the snow lead toward a hole in the river ice! I can still see her ashen face when she found me safe at a neighbour's house.

The young people in my family may fail to phone when I have reason to worry about them; they may adopt attitudes and ideas I find repugnant. When that happens, I need to remember the story of the adolescent Jesus and his terrified parents, and even my own childhood experience.

I'm not the first person to spend anxious hours or days worrying about the children I love.

**Lord, help me to find peace
when I'm anxious about the ones I love.**

Ezek 17: 22-24; Ps 92; 2 Cor 5: 6-10; Mk 4: 26-34

I f a small farmer in Puerto Rico wants a fence that will last, a strong limb from a roble tree will do the job. The branch, once placed in a post hole along a fence line, will come alive in the moist tropical soil. New growth will soon appear on the seemingly dead post. It will grow into a sturdy tree that will resist rot and decay.

Life can be held in a piece of wood or the most insignificant seed. The Bible offers us parables: the cedar twig spoken of by the prophet Ezekiel, the grain of wheat and the mus-  tard seed in Mark's gospel. They show us that the kingdom of God can come alive from the most insignificant of things.

Performing a simple act of kindness to a stranger, standing up to give witness against an injustice, or handing a warm bowl of soup to a hungry person may be the small act that plants the seed of the kingdom in another person's heart. Christianity itself took root from a small community of women and men fearfully huddled together in the upper room after the crucifixion. Jesus, their teacher, was seen by the authorities as just an itinerant preacher from Galilee whose teachings caused them trouble. Today, Christians account for a full third of the world's population. Confidently scattering its seeds, we know the kingdom grows around us.

Lord, help me to spread the good news of your kingdom, one small seed at a time.

"You have heard that it was said, 'An eye for an eye, and a tooth for a tooth.' But now I tell you: do not take revenge on someone who wrongs you. If anyone slaps you on the right cheek, let him slap your left cheek too. And if someone takes you to court to sue you for your shirt, let him have your coat as well. And if one of the occupation troops forces you to carry his pack one mile, carry it two miles. When someone asks you for something, give it to him; when someone wants to borrow something, lend it to him."

Matthew 5: 38-42

> "Do not take revenge on someone who wrongs you."

A peaceful response

Over the centuries, Christians have wrestled with this passage. How difficult it is to live!

But we see how Gandhi, a devout Hindu, used it as the basis for his life stance of non-violence. Martin Luther King also used it to develop his political platform of civil disobedience. What enormous reserves of love it must take not to retaliate when faced with physical violence.

I don't have anyone physically compelling me to do things. But what about the grudging way I take on chores? When criticized, why do I fire back with angry words? What patience and humility this passage asks of me – to move out of my self-centredness and to try to see the other person more clearly!

Dear Lord, give me the courage to live with peace and goodwill throughout this day.

You have heard that it was said, 'Love your friends, hate your enemies.' But now I tell you: love your enemies and pray for those who persecute you, so that you may become the children of your Father in heaven. For he makes his sun to shine on bad and good people alike, and gives rain to those who do good and to those who do evil. Why should God reward you if you love only the people who love you? Even the tax collectors do that! And if you speak only to your friends, have you done anything out of the ordinary? Even the pagans do that! You must be perfect – just as your Father in heaven is perfect."

Matthew 5: 43-48

"…have you done anything out of the ordinary?"

Jealousy

My mother was a wise woman. When I was young, she used to warn me never to compare myself to others. There would always be someone better off and someone worse off than me, she'd say, and making those distinctions would only cause trouble.

The older I get, the more truth I see in her words. Jealousy is one of those sins we acknowledge, but don't really talk about. While I can admit that I lack love for a certain person, I have a hard time admitting that I am jealous of them.

But what, more than jealousy, can undermine my ability to love others? What, if not jealousy, makes me second guess a God who rewards those I think less than worthy?

Dear Lord, heal my heart so I can love with the purity and intensity you desire.

"Make certain you do not perform your religious duties in public.... When you give something to a needy person, do it in such a way that even your closest friend will not know about it....

"When you pray, do not be like the hypocrites! They love to pray in the houses of worship and on the street corners, so that everyone will see them.... But when you pray, go to your room, close the door, and pray to your Father, who is unseen. And your Father, who sees what you do in private, will reward you."

Matthew 6: 1-6, 16-18

"When you pray, go to your room..."

An unseen God?

One grey afternoon, the house is silent all around me. In the quiet twilight I reflect on the activities of my day. One special moment stands out: a long-distance telephone call to a friend. She cheered me up when I was gloomy, changing the day from sad to glad for me.

Now, quietly grateful for my friend's kind words, I read Jesus' words about prayer. In the silent stillness of my empty house, deep in the privacy of my heart and my mind, I am newly conscious of my blessings, humbly grateful for God's presence all around me.

An unseen God? Yes, but a presence as real, as alive, as immediate as my unseen friend on the other end of the telephone.

O unseen God, hear my prayer: when you look into my heart, may you find gratitude and peace dwelling there.

Whten you pray, do not use a lot of meaningless words. Your Father already knows what you need before you ask him. This, then, is how you should pray: 'Our Father in heaven: May your holy name be honoured; may your Kingdom come; may your will be done on earth as it is in heaven. Give us today the food we need. Forgive us the wrongs we have done, as we forgive the wrongs that others have done to us. Do not bring us to hard testing, but keep us safe from the Evil One.'

"If you forgive others the wrongs they have done to you, your Father in heaven will also forgive you. But if you do not forgive others, then your Father will not forgive the wrongs you have done."

Matthew 6: 7-15

> "Forgive others the wrongs they have done."

Forgiving myself

How do I know I have been forgiven? Do I wait until I die or do I experience God's forgiveness here and now? I think of the times when I've held on to my anger, to the wrongs that were done to me. I see how that anger remained inside, working away, hurting me more than it hurt the "transgressor."

A country song goes, "A heart stained in anger grows weak and grows bitter. You become your own prisoner...." If I judge harshly, I judge not only others, but myself also.

So God's forgiveness begins here, with forgiving myself. When I forgive others, I experience in a real way that I, too, am forgivable. In the words of William Shakespeare, "The quality of mercy is twice blessed."

Dear God, help me to forgive.
May I not remain a prisoner of my anger.

"Do not store up riches for yourselves here on earth, where moths and rust destroy, and robbers break in and steal. Instead, store up riches for yourselves in heaven, where moths and rust cannot destroy, and robbers cannot break in and steal. For your heart will always be where your riches are.

"The eyes are like a lamp for the body. If your eyes are sound, your whole body will be full of light; but if your eyes are no good, your body will be in darkness. So if the light in you is darkness, how terribly dark it will be!"

Matthew 6: 19-23

> "…your heart will always be where your riches are."

Hands to hold

We had gathered as an extended family to share a meal. As we prepared to give thanks for our food, my dad invited us to join hands (rather than fold them, as is our usual custom). As soon as we said "Amen," and even before we could release our hands, three-year-old Susanna announced to me, with the thrill of genuine discovery, "Look, Dad, there's just enough hands for everyone to hold one!"

Much more than elementary math prompted her insight. With simple eloquence, Susanna named the treasure of the day: the gift of being present to one another.

And naming it so exuberantly, we heard in Susanna's wonder what Jesus might mean when he says, "The kingdom of God is at hand."

Jesus, help me recognize the true treasures in my life, and take hold of them.

"You cannot be a slave of two masters; you will hate one and love the other; you will be loyal to one and despise the other. You cannot serve both God and money....

"Look how the wild flowers grow: they do not work or make clothes for themselves. But I tell you that not even King Solomon with all his wealth had clothes as beautiful as one of these flowers.... Won't [God] be all the more sure to clothe you?

"So do not start worrying: 'Where will my food come from? or my drink? or my clothes?' Your Father in heaven knows that you need all these things. Instead, be concerned above everything else with the kingdom of God and with what he requires of you, and he will provide you with all these other things. So do not worry about tomorrow."

Matthew 6: 24-34

> "So do not worry about tomorrow."

Trust in God

I have spent too much of my life worrying about money. I have been broke and in debt several times – a fact I'm not proud of. I have lain awake many nights worrying about how I was going to make ends meet, how I was going to get out of the current crisis.

After all these years of struggling financially, I've begun to realize one thing – I'm still here! These financial crises did not destroy me. My family has had food, clothing and shelter – however humble or simple.

I think that today's reading is true. God takes care of us – in so many ways. There's a twelve-step-program saying that goes: "If you worry, you do not trust. If you trust, you do not worry."

I trust in you, my God. Let my worry be replaced with even greater trust.

Isa 49: 1-6; Ps 139; Acts 12: 22-26; Lk 1: 57-66, 80

He was God's gift to an elderly couple, Elizabeth and Zechariah. "His name is John," wrote Zechariah on a tablet. All the neighbours were amazed. The birth of John showed all the marks of divine purpose. The signs pointed to someone specially called and chosen by God for a great mission. As a prophet like none other, John the Baptist would move many hearts in Israel to repentance, preparing them for Jesus, the long-awaited Messiah.

How many of us have ever thought of our baptism in Christ as a vocation to be a prophetic sign of God's love in the "wilderness" of modern society? It may seem a bit frightening in the face of the glaring issues of our day. Yet our baptism intrinsically links us to Jesus' mission to be the Light of God's salvation "to the ends of the earth."

What can we learn from John? Paul shows us in today's reading from Acts that John's first quality is humility. Though clearly a prophet, he rejects any suggestion of being himself the Messiah. Humble service to others is key to living our baptismal vocation. Second is to ponder the meaning of being called and chosen by God. This implies that God truly trusts us and needs our participation. Can we in turn trust God enough to help us do our part, without letting our fears, our ego or other distractions get in the way of our witnessing to the Reign of God?

Lord, keep me humble – your humble servant.

Y ou have rejected us, God, and defeated us;
  you have been angry with us – but now turn back to us.
  You have made the land tremble, and you have cut it open;
now heal its wounds, because it is falling apart.
You have made your people suffer greatly;
  we stagger around as though we were drunk....
Save us by your might; answer our prayer,
  so that the people you love may be rescued....
Have you really rejected us?
Aren't you going to march out with our armies?
Help us against the enemy;
  human help is worthless.

Psalm 60: 1-2, 3, 5, 10-11

"...now heal its wounds..."

The courage to hope

This psalm is striking in the way it weaves its way between despair
and hope.

How painful to hear the voice behind this lament – a voice I
recognize. This is the voice of the wound that never seems to heal.
It is the voice that trembles as it tries to move past rejection to find
the courage to ask for healing. It is the child asking to draw closer
to a parent who doesn't understand. It is the parent trying to carve
out some common ground with a teenager who lives a culture and a
world away. It is the voice that speaks with a fierce but fragile hope.

I can only imagine that God hears this voice, and responds with
compassion.

**Loving God, hear the prayers of all those
who need healing.**

"Do not give what is holy to dogs – they will only turn and attack you. Do not throw your pearls in front of pigs – they will only trample them underfoot.

"Do for others what you want them to do for you: this is the meaning of the Law of Moses and of the teachings of the prophets.

"Go in through the narrow gate, because the gate to hell is wide and the road that leads to it is easy, and there are many who travel it. But the gate to life is narrow and the way that leads to it is hard, and there are few people who find it."

Matthew 7: 6, 12-14

> "But the gate to life is narrow…"

To go beyond

As a child, I loved to walk by the sea. My beloved seashore, though, was definitely not easy terrain. Breathtaking beauty, rugged cliffs and frightening drops were all connected by the narrowest of paths that clung precariously to the rocks. Many days I felt unsafe walking there, and would turn back at a point called "Devil's Gulch."

But one day I was possessed with a wild courage that drew me beyond that impasse. I was staggered by the most glorious vista I'd ever seen! I encountered a holy scene of beauty that was seared onto my heart forever.

Since then, I've longed many times for the return of that same wild courage. It's the courage I need to go beyond the wide, easy path today.

**May I step beyond my fears today,
O God, and trust you will see me through.**

Be on your guard against false prophets; they come to you looking like sheep on the outside, but on the inside they are really like wild wolves. You will know them by what they do. Thorn bushes do not bear grapes, and briers do not bear figs. A healthy tree bears good fruit, but a poor tree bears bad fruit. A healthy tree cannot bear bad fruit, and a poor tree cannot bear good fruit. And any tree that does not bear good fruit is cut down and thrown in the fire. So then, you will know the false prophets by what they do."

Matthew 7: 15-20

> "You will know them by what they do."

Know by what I do

I talked to a teen the other day. He'd had a lot of troubles for a person his age. I could see it in his face, and in the way he looked at me when I started talking to him. Waiting. Waiting for the con.

When I asked him what was up, he said, "Well, people either say they like you and never prove it, or tell you they don't and always prove it. You just have to watch long enough."

Well, I hope the longer he watches, the better I look. I hope I'm not just another false prophet, another person who proves to him that nobody's there for the long haul. It's not by what I say that I'll prove myself. It's by what I do.

**Lord, if I'm to be known for what I do,
help me do what's right and good.**

"Not everyone who calls me 'Lord, Lord' will enter the kingdom of heaven, but only those who do what my Father in heaven wants them to do....

"So then, anyone who hears these words of mine and obeys them is like a wise man who built his house on rock. The rain poured down, the rivers flooded over, and the wind blew hard against that house. But it did not fall, because it was built on rock.

"But anyone who hears these words of mine and does not obey them is like a foolish man who built his house on sand. The rain poured down, the rivers flooded over, the wind blew hard against that house, and it fell. And what a terrible fall that was!"

Matthew 7: 21-29

> "...and it did not fall, because it was built on rock."

A supporting love

My mother was a woman of deep faith. Widowed at 29, with two small children, and living in a strange country, she kept our family together and in our own home.

At times Mother did not know where the money would come from, but she always prayed and worked hard to make ends meet. Through the years, her hard work and faith in God were rewarded. She retired comfortably and gave generously to others in need.

As the older child, I shared my mother's fears about paying the bills, and about an uncertain future. Over the years, I've struggled with anxiety. Now I turn to my mother's source of consolation, confident that God will support me with loving care.

**O God, when I am lonely and afraid,
help me to recognize your presence in my life.**

As for me, the hour has come for me to be sacrificed; the time is here for me to leave this life. I have done my best in the race, I have run the full distance, and I have kept the faith. And now there is waiting for me the victory prize of being put right with God, which the Lord, the righteous Judge, will give me on that Day....

But the Lord stayed with me and gave me strength, so that I was able to proclaim the full message for all the Gentiles to hear; and I was rescued from being sentenced to death. And the Lord will rescue me from all evil and take me safely into his heavenly kingdom. To him be the glory forever and ever! Amen.

2 Timothy 4: 6-8, 17-18

> ## "I have done my best...."

Keeping the faith

My friend Tom is dying of prostate cancer. He knows his time is limited. He's not famous, but he has done a great deal in his 80 years: working as a missionary in Angola, a teacher in adult education programs, an administrator for a group of Aboriginal churches, the director of a publishing house. He has lived through his wife's death from cancer. Now he faces his own death with courage.

I find Tom deeply moving. Just as, for the same reasons, I find Paul's letter to Timothy moving. In many ways, this is Paul's Last Will and Testament. Soon, he will go out from his prison cell to his death. And he looks back, and is grateful. He has done his best; he has kept the faith.

When my time comes, God, may I look back without regrets, and look forward with confidence.

My eyes are worn out with weeping; my soul is in anguish.
I am exhausted with grief at the destruction of my people.
Children and babies are fainting in the streets of the city.
Hungry and thirsty, they cry to their mothers;
They fall in the streets as though they were wounded,
And slowly die in their mothers' arms.
O Jerusalem, beloved Jerusalem, what can I say?
How can I comfort you? No one has ever suffered like this.
Your disaster is boundless as the ocean; there is no possible hope....
All through the night get up again and again to cry out to the Lord;
Pour out your heart and beg him for mercy on your children –
Children starving to death on every street corner!

Lamentations 2: 2, 10-14, 18-19

"Let your tears flow like rivers…"

Light in the dark

I feel torn about choosing to write on this passage. People want something uplifting – right? But then I consider our world: how different are things today? So many countries experience war and poverty. Even within the so-called developed world, there's great wealth alongside destitution. And spiritual poverty – I look at the values that television is selling my children. Today, one of my students started on anti-depressants again. "It's too much," he says.

But then, I hear Clara Hughes, after winning her 5000-metre Olympic speed skating race, saying that sport and play can give so much to the world. She has, I learn, given all her savings to "Right to Play," a charity for Third World children.

Find the light in the darkness. Find the hope. For the New Jerusalem.

Dear God, when I despair, show me reason to hope.

Wis I: I3-I5, 2: 23-24; Ps 30; 2 Cor 8: 7, 9, I3-I5; Mk 5: 2I-43

We often express gratitude for our faith. Today's readings invite us to reflect on how profoundly that faith influences our view of the world and our actions.

Creation is holy, the Wisdom writer suggests – "wholesome." And we, made "in the image" of God's "own eternity," are infused with the divine. We are in constant relationship with a God of wonder who transforms us, heals us, turning our "mourning into dancing." "Do not fear, only believe," says Jesus to an anxious father. A woman isolated through illness hears, "Your faith has made you well; go in peace." Faith, Jesus says, is everything: it allows the seemingly impossible.

Holiness. Relationship. Healing. Transformation. All seem connected in the vision of faith fashioned in today's readings. A faith grounded in beauty and wonder challenges us to treat each other and the earth as precious. A faith enlivened by the Holy Spirit invites our participation in the mission of Jesus, God who embraced our humanity.

With Jesus, we are invited to build the kingdom through loving encounter. Faith invites us to consider possibilities: to act in hope affirming the holy, the wondrous; to commit to the seemingly impossible as agents of transformation in our time and place.

At the heart of our faith we meet God, who urges us to recognize the holiness that is, while working toward what might be.

**Loving God, teach me to live my faith actively,
as I help to build your kingdom.**

When Jesus noticed the crowd around him, he ordered his disciples to go to the other side of the lake. A teacher of the Law came to him. "Teacher," he said, "I am ready to go with you wherever you go."

Jesus answered him, "Foxes have holes, and birds have nests, but the Son of Man has no place to lie down and rest."

Another man, who was a disciple, said, "Sir, first let me go back and bury my father."

"Follow me," Jesus answered, "and let the dead bury their own dead."

Matthew 8: 18-22

> "Let the dead bury their own dead."

The living dead

Pretty sharp remarks… and from Jesus, a man of such empathy. Think of someone whose father has just died, and consider his answer.

Maybe Jesus was tired: tired of people not understanding. But he sure made it clear – what a big step it was to follow him.

I'm not a scholar, but I think "the dead" are the people Jesus saw mired in a dead-end way of thinking about spiritual life. I wonder how he'd respond today were he to see what has become of his message.

Are we "the dead" Jesus spoke of? We claim to be virtuous because we follow all the rules – but often die to his great commandment of love. Are we "the dead"?

Dear God, keep me alive, and help me to keep growing.

So then, you Gentiles are not foreigners or strangers any longer; you are now citizens together with God's people and members of the family of God. You, too, are built upon the foundation laid by the apostles and prophets, the cornerstone being Christ Jesus himself. He is the one who holds the whole building together and makes it grow into a sacred temple dedicated to the Lord. In union with him, you too are being built together with all the others into a place where God lives through his Spirit.

Ephesians 2: 19-22

> "...not foreigners or strangers any longer..."

No longer strangers

Ancient hatreds are rekindled for political gain. People leave their countries as new boundaries are drawn, boundaries intended to include and to exclude.

Two people I know, one a Muslim and the other a Christian, have been through this. One of them is young, and Canada has become home. The other is old enough to know that she may never feel "at home" again. Her children will, and that is enough for her. Both have told me they love this country. "Here I can pray in my way, without fear." As they speak, I see tears in their eyes.

Today's reading strikes a chord in me as we, the children of the conquerors and the conquered – the old and the new – are still trying to live together. Trying to become "us," not "us and them."

Lord, help me share my world
with my brothers and sisters.

Make it your aim to do what is right, not what is evil, so that you may live. Then the Lord God Almighty really will be with you, as you claim he is. Hate what is evil, love what is right, and see that justice prevails in the courts. Perhaps the Lord will be merciful to the people of this nation who are still left alive....

The Lord says, "I hate your religious festivals; I cannot stand them! When you bring me burnt offerings and grain offerings, I will not accept them; I will not accept the animals you have fattened to bring me as offerings. Stop your noisy songs; I do not want to listen to your harps. Instead, let justice flow like a stream, and righteousness like a river that never goes dry." *Amos 5: 14-15, 21-24*

"I hate your religious festivals…"

True worship

The little church I attend is in trouble. Attendance is dropping. Church school consists of three families. Half our annual income comes from people over the age of 70, and they're starting to die off or move away.

Obviously, what we're doing is not attracting new people. Yet whenever we attempt something new, the pressure grows to go back to the old ways, whatever they were.

Contemporary worship? "It doesn't feel reverent." Contemporary music? "Why don't we sing any of the good old hymns anymore?" Midweek services? "We'll split into two congregations. We must stay together." Project words on a screen? "I can't see them from the back."

I suspect that if Amos – or Jesus – wandered into a worship service today, he'd fall asleep at best, or at worst, walk out in disgust.

**Help me set aside my preconceptions, God,
and worship as you want to be worshipped.**

Some people brought Jesus a paralyzed man, lying on a bed. When Jesus saw how much faith they had, he said to the paralyzed man, "Courage, my son! Your sins are forgiven."

Then some teachers of the Law said to themselves, "This man is speaking blasphemy!" Jesus perceived what they were thinking, and so he said, "Why are you thinking such evil things? Is it easier to say, 'Your sins are forgiven,' or to say, 'Get up and walk'? I will prove to you, then, that the Son of Man has authority on earth to forgive sins." So he said to the paralyzed man, "Get up, pick up your bed, and go home!"

The man got up and went home. When the people saw it, they were afraid, and praised God for giving such authority to people.

Matthew 9: 1-8

"Courage... your sins are forgiven."

Healing life's hurts

Usually I'm a very healthy, energetic person. But for the past few weeks, I've been sick: unable to work, to care for my family, to go for a walk, even. At the risk of sounding ungrateful, if Jesus were to stand before me and say, "Your sins are forgiven," I think I'd ask him to reconsider. Couldn't he restore my physical health instead?

My body has forced me to take notice of what's happening at other levels – within my heart and my soul. Physical limitations have given me the opportunity to look at my life: at truths that I've not wanted, or taken the time, to consider.

Indeed, Jesus offers to heal me where I most need healing. It's just that in my busyness, I don't always recognize it.

Lord, help me to seek healing at all levels of my being: body, mind, heart and soul.

Jesus left that place, and as he walked along, he saw a tax collector, named Matthew, sitting in his office. He said to him, "Follow me." Matthew got up and followed him.

While Jesus was having a meal in Matthew's house, many tax collectors and other outcasts came and joined Jesus and his disciples at the table. Some Pharisees saw this and asked his disciples, "Why does your teacher eat with such people?"

Jesus heard them and answered, "People who are well do not need a doctor, but only those who are sick. Go and find out what is meant by the scripture that says: 'It is kindness that I want, not animal sacrifices.' I have not come to call respectable people, but outcasts."

Matthew 9: 9-13

> "It is kindness that I want..."

Wanted: kindness

I feel that Jesus is talking to me directly. While I may not offer dead birds or animals on an altar, I am aware of the times when my words and actions, while socially acceptable, are empty. They lack kindness.

I think of how I routinely speak to my children in an angry and frustrated way. I may be "right" in insisting that their chores be done, that they don't use "bad" language, that they learn "good" manners. But all of that is empty, meaningless, if my words lack kindness. In my striving to do what is "right," I need to be reminded that I stand in need of Jesus' loving acceptance. In that love I find the strength to be kind to others, especially those who are vulnerable.

Dear God, help me when I do what is "right," but with the "wrong" spirit in my heart.

I am listening to what the Lord God is saying;
he promises peace to us, his own people....
Love and faithfulness will meet;
righteousness and peace will embrace.
Human loyalty will reach up from the earth,
and God's righteousness will look down from heaven.
The Lord will make us prosperous,
and our land will produce rich harvests.
Righteousness will go before the Lord
and prepare the path for him.

Psalm 85: 8, 10-13

"...righteousness and peace will embrace."

Love and faithfulness

I have a notebook in which I record various quotes and comments. It's an eclectic, wide-ranging collection of sayings from novelists, playwrights, composers, theologians and the occasional poet. When this leather-bound notebook is full, I replace the pages and keep the written sheets in a box.

Leafing through my notebook, I come across a biblical quotation. It's from today's psalm. I have always been mesmerized by the idea that when God and humankind reach toward one another – when loyalty and righteousness combine – we will meet.

I guess I have some justice work to do!

**O God, I long for the moment
when love and faithfulness will meet.**

Ezek 2: 3-5; Ps 123; 2 Cor 12: 7-10; Mk 6: 1-6

"Impudent and stubborn," the heavenly voice railed against the people of Israel. Go among this nation "who have rebelled against me," said the Lord God. Ezekiel heard; he obeyed. The people would know that there had been "a Prophet among them."

Ezekiel's call to prophesy came in the sixth century before Christ. The world this prophet knew had been turned upside down, with thousands of Israelites forced into exile. Eventually, a rebellion against foreign rule among those remaining in their homeland led to the fall of Jerusalem and the destruction of the first Temple in 587 B.C.

Ezekiel offered hope to the exiles. If they were faithful, if they witnessed to their beliefs even as strangers in a strange land, Israel would be restored.

Our world today is constantly in turmoil. Do we hear the prophetic voices calling out to us? Now, as in Ezekiel's time, they offer the hope of salvation. Has our impudent and stubborn refusal to consider the changes needed to heal a broken and bleeding world deafened us to the prophets' entreaties?

Jesus is always among us. Here in this place, now in this time, his call is as clear as it was two millennia ago in his hometown of Nazareth. Surrounded by his brothers, sisters and neighbours, he spoke to the gathering. Teaching in his hometown synagogue, he offered hope. He offered salvation. They chose not to listen. What do we choose?

**Dear Lord, open my ears and my heart
to your life-giving word.**

A Jewish official knelt before Jesus, and said, "My daughter has just died; but come and place your hands on her, and she will live."

Jesus got up and followed him. A woman who had suffered from severe bleeding for twelve years came up behind Jesus and touched the edge of his cloak. She said to herself, "If only I touch his cloak, I will get well." Jesus turned around and saw her, and said, "Courage, my daughter! Your faith has made you well." At that very moment the woman became well.

Then Jesus went into the official's house. He said, "The little girl is not dead – she is only sleeping!" As soon as the people had been put out, Jesus went into the girl's room and took hold of her hand, and she got up. *Matthew 9:18-26*

> "Courage, my daughter! Your faith has made you well."

Courage to change

Why the warning to have courage now? Surely this is a courageous woman! Though unclean, she dares to reach out and touch Jesus. She believes that simple contact will heal her. But perhaps even greater courage is needed to walk away – healed!

Many things in my life need healing: from major hurts to minor habits. But do I have any idea what letting go of them will really involve? Am I committed to living the new life Jesus wants to create in me?

Sometimes I choose to go on living with the familiar – unhealthy as it may be. It seems easier than risking the unknown. At other times, even when people around me scoff at the possibilities, I grasp the hand that offers new life.

**Jesus, today I ask for the courage
to take one small step in the direction of new life.**

Why should the nations ask us,
"Where is your God?"
Our God is in heaven;
he does whatever he wishes.
Their gods are made of silver and gold,
formed by human hands...
May all who made them
and who trust in them
become like the idols they have made.
Trust in the Lord, you people of Israel.
He helps you and protects you.

Psalm 115: 3-10

> "...become like the idols they have made."

Powerful gods

We think of ourselves as far more theologically advanced than the people for whom the psalmist wrote. Their gods were visible but powerless. Our gods are invisible but enormously powerful.

It's true that our gods are still made of silver and gold, but they no longer have actual body parts. Yet they see and touch us all the time and are never, ever silent.

A trip to their temple shows how clearly they see our secret hopes and fears and how they reach out to us with their soft and soothing words: "Buy me and you will be loveable." "Own me and you will never be alone." "Worship me and I will take care of you." And we who trust them have become like them – things to be bought and sold.

Lord, our gods are powerful gods.
Help me to keep my trust in you.

The people of Israel were like a grapevine that was full of grapes. The more prosperous they were, the more altars they built. The more productive their land was, the more beautiful they made the sacred stone pillars they worship. The people whose hearts are deceitful must now suffer for their sins. God will break down their altars and destroy their sacred pillars.

These people will soon be saying, "We have no king because we did not fear the Lord...." I said, "Plow new ground for yourselves, plant righteousness, and reap the blessings that your devotion to me will produce. It is time for you to turn to me, your Lord, and I will come and pour out blessings upon you."

Hosea 10: 1-3, 7-8, 12

> "The more prosperous they were..."

True security

I am a member of the richest society in the entire history of humanity. For me, prosperity is a given. Most of the time I don't even think about it.

Yet, in my quiet moments, I understand the failing of the people of Israel only too well. Like them, I forget that this prosperity is not of my doing. The altars before which I bow down – an ever-rising standard of living, secure pensions, more and more entertainment – are as fragile as the sacred stone pillars the Israelites foolishly worshipped.

When the wealth ends – as it does for each of us, if only at death – where will I find my security? What will my foundation be then?

**Lord, help me remember that
you are my only sure foundation.**

"Go and preach, 'The kingdom of heaven is near!' Heal the sick, bring the dead back to life, heal those who suffer from dreaded skin diseases, and drive out demons. You have received without paying, so give without being paid. Do not carry any gold, silver or copper money in your pockets; do not carry a beggar's bag for the trip or an extra shirt or shoes or a walking stick. Workers should be given what they need.

"When you come to a town or village, go in and look for someone who is willing to welcome you, and stay with him until you leave that place…. And if some home or town will not welcome you or listen to you, then leave that place and shake the dust off your feet."

Matthew.10: 7-15

> "…do not carry a beggar's bag for the trip…"

An unseen love

Memories flash before me as I think of Jesus walking among the disciples, straightening a robe, brushing off a shoulder, worried as he watches them go off to a future they cannot see.

Thirty years ago, my mother brushed me off and sent me away to college. I remember her watching from the window, receding in the distance as I ventured off into the world. Twenty years later, I watched my son go off alone to his friend's fourth birthday party.

As God watches us go to find our joys and sorrows, struggling and stumbling on our way, does he worry? Does God, like me and my mother before me, like Jesus with his disciples, send his love along – unseen but always there to help me through?

**God, as I go out into the world,
let me always be aware of your presence.**

B e merciful to me, O God,
because of your constant love.
Because of your great mercy
wipe away my sins!
Wash away all my evil
and make me clean from my sin!
Sincerity and truth are what you require;
fill my mind with your wisdom.
Remove my sin, and I will be clean;
wash me, and I will be whiter than snow.
Create a pure heart in me, O God,
and put a new and loyal spirit in me.
Do not banish me from your presence;
do not take your holy spirit away from me.

Psalm 51: 1-2, 6-7, 10-12, 15

"Create a pure heart in me, O God…"

Healing the heart

I spent years trying to "fix" my life. I felt hopelessly flawed, damaged beyond repair. I tried to heal painful childhood memories and bitter resentments through "self-help" and "self-improvement." But the more books I bought, the more workshops I attended, the more therapists I saw, the more confused I became.

Later I realized that only the grace of God could help me. And, to accept that grace, all I really needed was humility. This humility meant not thinking less of myself, but thinking of myself less.

As grace transformed my sense of humiliation into humility, I came to rely less upon my "self" and more upon God. That's when my healing really began.

God, grant me the humility to accept your healing grace.

"Whatever is now covered up will be uncovered, and every secret will be made known. What I am telling you in the dark you must repeat in broad daylight, and what you have heard in private you must announce from the housetops. Do not be afraid of those who kill the body but cannot kill the soul; rather be afraid of God, who can destroy both body and soul in hell. For only a penny you can buy two sparrows, yet not one sparrow falls to the ground without your Father's consent. As for you, even the hairs of your head have all been counted. So do not be afraid; you are worth much more than many sparrows!

"Those who declare publicly that they belong to me, I will do the same for them before my Father in heaven."   *Matthew 10: 24-33*

"So do not be afraid..."

Precious in God's eyes

A few years after the event, some friends and family members of those killed in the World Trade Center on September 11, 2001, travelled to Iraq to meet and pray with Iraqi people who also had lost loved ones through violence. This gesture put a human face on a people and a country on whom public fear had been projected. The two groups discovered their common humanity and compassion for one another.

This action – of moving toward that which we fear – reminds me of how I used to be afraid of people with disabilities. But when I came to know several such people personally, in fact I discovered a treasure.

In today's reading, Jesus tells us, "Do not be afraid." He invites us to discover that each human life, like the sparrow, is precious in God's eyes.

**Lord, help me to move beyond my fears
to discover the worth of each person.**

Amos 7: 12-15; Ps 85; Eph 1: 3-14; Mk 6: 7-13

In only seven verses, we hear a message that will take us our whole lives to comprehend. Jesus assigns the task: proclaim the need for repentance and offer the gift of healing. He offers clear instructions: go with a partner, carry only a walking stick, and be prepared to "shake off the dust."

Most of us would not venture on a journey with only a walking stick. Perhaps this message is encouraging us to own only what we truly need and to share with others what we no longer require.

In Jesus' day, it was common practice to "shake the dust" from one's sandals when leaving foreign territory, a symbolic act of separating oneself from the beliefs and practices of that community. It can be difficult to know when we are called to be accepting and understanding, and when we must take a stand for what we believe.

Recall that Jesus sent no one out alone. While there are times when we may stand alone as we carry out our part of Jesus' mission, we always need others for support and encouragement. We are grateful for those who understand our mission and who assist us faithfully and courageously in carrying it out. Today, as we pray, listen to sacred scripture, and share the eucharist with one another, we acknowledge our deep need for companions and our call to be a support to others.

Lord Jesus, help me to figure out what I need on this journey of faith and to find support in my fellow travellers.

"Do not think that I have come to bring peace to the world. No, I did not come to bring peace, but a sword. I came to set sons against their fathers, daughters against their mothers, daughters-in-law against their mothers-in-law; your worst enemies will be the members of your own family.

"Those who love their father or mother more than me are not fit to be my disciples; those who love their son or daughter more than me are not fit to be my disciples. Those who do not take up their cross and follow in my steps are not fit to be my disciples. Those who try to gain their own life will lose it; but those who lose their life for my sake will gain it."

Matthew 10: 34 – 11: 1

> "I did not come to bring peace, but a sword."

Honesty and peace

Here Jesus says, "I did not come to bring peace…." But didn't he also say, "I leave you peace. My peace I give you"? I want peace in my life, but perhaps the peace I seek is not what Jesus means by "peace."

I remember an argument I had with my mother. Up to that moment I had always avoided conflict with her. But this time there was no avoiding it. It wasn't easy: I didn't know how to tell her what I felt or all that I held deep in my heart.

However, with time, my mother and I have come to know a deep peace, deeper than I ever imagined possible. Jesus' kind of peace challenges me to speak with honesty – especially when it seems too hard.

God, give me the courage to speak with honesty.
Help me trust that honesty is the only pathway to peace.

The people in the towns where Jesus had performed most of his miracles did not turn from their sins, so he reproached those towns. "How terrible it will be for you, Chorazin... [and] Bethsaida! If the miracles which were performed in you had been performed in Tyre and Sidon, the people there would have long ago put on sackcloth and sprinkled ashes on themselves, to show that they had turned from their sins! I assure you that on Judgment Day God will show more mercy to the people of Tyre and Sidon than to you! And as for you, Capernaum... if the miracles which were performed in you had been performed in Sodom, it would still be in existence today! You can be sure that on Judgment Day God will show more mercy to Sodom than to you!"

Matthew 11: 20-24

"If the miracles which were performed in you..."

A call to change

I cringe when Jesus sounds so angry. I'd rather he pray serenely, bless the children, teach the crowds, work a miracle – do the sorts of things he does in popular pictures. I imagine the people of Chorazin and Bethsaida felt the same way.

Jesus is angry because, even after he went about doing good, the people still refused to repent – just as I hesitate to make any radical changes in my life. I still measure out my commitment to him on a day-to-day basis.

It's easy to say I just don't like the image of an angry Jesus. It's a lot more honest to say that my discomfort is with his anger and what it implies about me. I could, this very moment, repent. Will I?

**Jesus, help me to take my focus off your anger
and to put it on my repentance.**

At that time Jesus said, "Father, Lord of heaven and earth! I thank you because you have shown to the unlearned what you have hidden from the wise and learned. Yes, Father, this was how you were pleased to have it happen. My Father has given me all things. No one knows the Son except the Father, and no one knows the Father except the Son and those to whom the Son chooses to reveal him."

Matthew 11: 25-27

> "...you have shown to the unlearned..."

A loving parent

The little boy had probably become too rowdy for the folks inside the church. His dad had him on his knee on a bench outside and was showing him one of the most ancient of rituals: "Here is the church and here is the steeple. Open the doors and see all the people!" The boy's stubby little fingers had some difficulty in opening up to "show all the people." He whooped with joy when he was able to do it for the first time.

As I watched, I recalled similar times spent with my father, and I was reminded of how aware Christ was of that kind of tender care. And I said a quiet prayer for the children who do not have a kind and loving parent.

Lord, help all parents and children as they negotiate the difficult passages involved in their relationships.

Come to me, all of you who are tired from carrying heavy loads, and I will give you rest. Take my yoke and put it on you, and learn from me, because I am gentle and humble in spirit; and you will find rest. For the yoke I will give you is easy, and the load I will put on you is light."

Matthew 11: 28-30

> "...the load I will put on you is light."

A lighter load

I try to imagine the people listening to Jesus: bodies aching from work, or eyes weary from studying the law. Has the load of living ever been light – for anyone?

Are they listening to Jesus at the end of their day, the sun beating down on them? Or is it late, and they're bathed in the light of the moon?

I remember a night, and the moon in my window. My wife and one child sick; I'm wearily pacing the floor with the other child. Feeling the load. Then, looking up at the moon, thinking, "In 30 years, what would I pay to be here, holding this child, having this moment again?" And my load became lighter: duty became joy, obligation became a gift.

It's funny how love changes things.

Lord, let me accept what is sent to me as gift.
Help me realize that my load is light.

Jesus was walking through some wheat fields on a Sabbath. His disciples were hungry, so they began to pick heads of wheat and eat the grain. When the Pharisees saw this, they said to Jesus, "Look, it is against our Law for your disciples to do this on the Sabbath!"

Jesus answered, "Have you never read what David did that time when he and his men were hungry? He went into the house of God, and he and his men ate the bread offered to God, even though it was against the Law for them to eat it…. I tell you that there is something here greater than the Temple. The scripture says, 'It is kindness that I want, not animal sacrifices.' If you really knew what this means, you would not condemn people who are not guilty."

Matthew 12: 1-8

> "It's kindness that I want, not animal sacrifices."

Breaking the rules

As a teacher, I struggle every day with the issue of *rules*. Rules provide structure and order – essential things when there are 1,500 teenagers in the same building!

On the other hand, I am dealing with human beings – and the rules can get in the way of compassion and understanding.

The Pharisees wanted to adopt a "zero tolerance" approach. As parenting guru Barbara Coloroso has said, "Zero tolerance means zero thinking." And zero compassion.

How many times have I been the exception to the rule? I must allow others the same dignity. The spirit of the law is, indeed, more important than the letter. When faced with a choice between a person's needs and the rules, I'll go with the person.

**Lord, give me the wisdom to put people first,
and to show compassion in applying rules.**

The Pharisees made plans to kill Jesus. When Jesus heard about the plot against him, he went away from that place; and large crowds followed him. He healed all the sick and gave them orders not to tell others about him. He did this so as to make come true what God had said through the prophet Isaiah: "Here is my servant, whom I have chosen, the one I love, and with whom I am pleased. I will send my Spirit upon him, and he will announce my judgment to the nations. He will not argue or shout, or make loud speeches in the streets. He will not break off a bent reed, nor put out a flickering lamp. He will persist until he causes justice to triumph, and on him all peoples will put their hope."

Matthew 12: 14-21

> "He will persist until he causes justice to triumph…"

A persistent love

The neighbourhood bully preys on the misfit. An aggressive, powerful nation overtakes one that is defenceless and peace-loving. There is a vicious streak within us that finds expression whenever we trample on the vulnerable in an attempt to strengthen ourselves. We are all capable of it at some level – manipulating our family with angry moods, gossiping to defame our neighbour, buying "cheap" and perpetuating economic exploitation of others.

Jesus is clear that this is not his way. He does not despise or reject us for our weakness. Neither does he take advantage of us, forcing us to follow him. Patiently, persistently, he confronts us with his truth until our love ignites and we freely place our hope in him.

Do we do the same for one another?

**Lord, fill me with your strength when I am weak.
And help me bring your patient love to others
when they are weak.**

Jer 23: 1-6; Ps 23; Eph 2: 13-18; Mk 6: 30-34

Shepherds don't get much time off. It's a job that requires steady energy and commitment. Sheep need to be watched constantly. Without a watchful eye, they can get themselves into tight spots and don't always have the sense to get themselves out. Where one misguided sheep goes, others are likely to follow.

Being a shepherd is a hard and lonely job in many ways – even a lowly job. And yet, what a responsibility it is to be a shepherd. For sheep provide wool and milk and meat – things that keep people warm and fed. Caring well for the sheep helps to keep them and the community healthy and safe.

It is easy to see Jesus as a shepherd. He gathers us around him. He protects us, cares for us, saves us from our own stubbornness and foolishness. He makes us lie down in green pastures. He restores our soul. He prepares a table for us.

In accepting to be our shepherd, Jesus gave up a lot: time with his friends and family, time alone, time to rest. Ultimately, he gave up his life. Each time we gather as a community for the eucharist, we remember his incredible gift of himself and we are thankful. We know that with the Lord as our shepherd, there is nothing we shall want. All we need to do is to listen to his voice and follow him.

Lord, I want to follow you.
Keep me safe as I walk each day on this path.

Listen to the Lord's case against Israel. Arise, O Lord, and present your case.... The Lord says, "My people, what have I done to you? How have I been a burden to you? Answer me...."

What shall I bring to the Lord, the God of heaven, when I come to worship him? Shall I bring the best calves to burn as offerings to him? Will the Lord be pleased if I bring him thousands of sheep or endless streams of olive oil? Shall I offer him my first-born child to pay for my sins? No, the Lord has told us what is good. What he requires of us is this: to do what is just, to show constant love, and to live in humble fellowship with our God.

Micah 6: 1-4, 6-8

> "...to do what is just, to show constant love..."

Understanding why...

When I first started editing, I studied all the rules of punctuation and grammar. Unfortunately, there were – and still are – endless rules about commas. I discovered that no rule can cover every possible eventuality. Not in punctuation. Not in life.

One day, a younger but wiser fellow editor did for me what the prophet Micah did for the Jews' 613 laws that covered everything from slavery to washing their hands. Micah cut through the details, and gave the people simple principles to follow.

The editor told me that my job was just to help the reader. That principle didn't tell me what to do, or how to do it. But it helped me understand why I was doing it.

Cutting through the conflicting pressures of daily duties isn't easy, God. Share with me your wisdom.

Jesus was still talking to the people when his mother and brothers arrived. They stood outside, asking to speak with him....
Jesus answered, "Who is my mother? Who are my brothers?" ...
Whoever does what my Father in heaven wants is my brother, my sister, and my mother."

Matthew 12: 46, 48, 50

"Who is my mother?"

Family ties

What shocking words – so naked and so harsh! I know Jesus is making a point about the urgency of his mission, and the importance of our response. But such roughness is hard to understand.

I'm a father, and this story makes me feel for Jesus' mother. Why had she come? What did she want to say to him?

Maybe she hadn't seen her son for a long time and wanted to give him a greeting. Perhaps she was worried and wanted to reassure herself that he was all right. Maybe there was important family news to share. We're not told. And we're not told what happened when she heard his response. But I can guess.

We mothers and fathers need special strength sometimes.
Lord, give us that strength.

Yet we who have this spiritual treasure are like common clay pots, in order to show that the supreme power belongs to God, not to us. We are often troubled, but not crushed; sometimes in doubt, but never in despair; there are many enemies, but we are never without a friend; and though badly hurt at times, we are not destroyed. At all times we carry in our mortal bodies the death of Jesus, so that his life also may be seen in our bodies. Throughout our lives we are always in danger of death for Jesus' sake, in order that his life may be seen in this mortal body of ours. This means that death is at work in us, but life is at work in you.

2 Corinthians 4: 7-15

"We are often troubled, but not crushed…"

Hope in the darkness

As I write this reflection, we live on a knife-edge between fear and hope. The daughter of good friends, a childhood friend of our oldest son, lies in a hospital, her future unknown.

She was rushed there after coming home from a party and collapsing in the doorway. The drugs found in her system have taken her far away. She doesn't know who she or anyone else is – and no one can say whether she will ever come back.

Her mother asks for prayers and her family and friends wait in anguish. And I hope that Paul is right, and that this good family, so deeply hurt, is not crushed and destroyed, and has a Friend to help them.

**Lord, show your friendship to those in crisis.
Give them the strength they need to make their way
through this dark time.**

As for you, how fortunate you are! Your eyes see and your ears hear. I assure you that many prophets and many of God's people wanted very much to see what you see, but they could not, and to hear what you hear, but they did not."

Matthew 13: 16-17

"God's people wanted very much to see…"

Look again

A few years ago my husband gave me one of those optical illusion plaques. The image looks like scrambled lines, but apparently if you stare at it long enough a three-dimensional figure will appear.

Many of our friends have stood before it oohing and ahhhing in amazement. I have never seen anything but squiggly lines. But something in me says, "Keep trying!"

It's that way with the parables for me. Some of them evade me; many frustrate me. But every once in a while I will read or hear a commentary that sheds some light on the parable's message, and I am encouraged to look again.

God, I can't always see what is right in front of me. Open my eyes!

Those who hear the message about the kingdom but do not understand it are like the seeds that fell along the path. The Evil One comes and snatches away what was sown in them. The seeds that fell on rocky ground stand for those who receive the message gladly as soon as they hear it. But it does not sink deep into them, and they don't last long. So when trouble or persecution comes because of the message, they give up at once. The seeds that fell among thorn bushes stand for those who hear the message; but the worries about this life and the love for riches choke the message, and they don't bear fruit. And the seeds sown in the good soil stand for those who hear the message and understand it: they bear fruit."

Matthew 13: 18-23

> "Those who hear the message about the kingdom…"

Life's thorn bushes

In a way, I'm like all those soil conditions – my struggles taking different forms at different times. *Hearing but not understanding* – how often am I in a situation just not knowing what to do? *Seeds on rocky ground that don't sink deep* – while I may agree with this passage, when parents start to dissect my son's soccer coach, do I say, "Let the one who is without sin…"?

But it's *the thorn bushes* most of all – in the rough and tumble of everyday life, it's hard to keep focused on what is true and important. Concerns about school closures, layoffs and how to pay for the repairs to the bathroom close in, choking me. They are like the thorn bushes, and every day I must hack them down to keep them at bay.

Lord, may I be fertile ground for your love.

"The kingdom of heaven is like this. A man sowed good seed in his field. One night, when everyone was asleep, an enemy came and sowed weeds among the wheat and went away. When the plants grew and the heads of grain began to form, then the weeds showed up. The man's servants said, 'Sir, where did the weeds come from?' 'It was some enemy who did this,' he answered. 'Do you want us to go and pull up the weeds?' they asked him. 'No,' he answered, 'because as you gather the weeds you might pull up some of the wheat along with them. Let the wheat and the weeds both grow together until harvest. Then I will tell the harvest workers to pull up the weeds first, tie them in bundles and burn them, and then to gather in the wheat and put it in my barn.'"

Matthew 13: 24-30

> "...then the weeds showed up."

Identifying the weeds

Year one: in late spring, I weed my young garden. I am, at the time, a rank beginner. Hmm, this looks "weedish" – out you come. As summer progresses, much of what I planted is gone.

Year two: I've learned. I wait a few days, until I'm sure they're weeds. Up they come... and with them, many plants I want! Their roots still tiny; they come together in clumps of sod. As summer progresses, most of what I planted is gone.

Life! What are weeds? What are plants? Even when you think you know, how do you untangle them? With plants you can wait until you're sure. In life? Not so clear; sometimes you have to choose. And if you're wrong, you need faith that you can plant again.

God, give me eyes to see.
Help me untangle the weeds from the wheat.

2 Kgs 4: 42-44; Ps 145; Eph 4: 1-6; Jn 6: 1-15

I t's hard to believe, but the statistics are just as shocking as they are terrible: in our day and age, some 800 million people still suffer from malnutrition or starvation, and 18,000 children die from hunger *every day*. How can hunger remain such a glaring plague, when our society claims unparalleled living standards and unmatched technological sophistication?

In biblical times, people struggled with famine and starvation, We hear the prophets speak about the unequal distribution of wealth and food. Prophets like Amos, Isaiah and Jeremiah were quick not only to denounce such inequality and inequity, but also to propose alternatives based on commitment to social justice and compassion for the poor. They did more than talk: the prophet Elisha multiplied loaves, as did Jesus, for the starving crowds.

Through these prophets, we learn that God is a life-giving God who cares for hungering crowds. And when God gives, he always gives overabundantly: "They shall eat and have some left." Whether through his prophet Elisha or through his beloved son, Jesus, God always provides more than we need, for he wants us to be restored to our dignity as human beings and to fullness of life. We who are privileged to have all the food we need and more can make a difference by sharing with those in need.

**God of abundance, help me to find creative ways
to share your bounty with others.**

Jesus told another parable: "The kingdom of heaven is like this. A man takes a mustard seed and sows it in his field. It is the smallest of all seeds, but when it grows up, it is the biggest of all plants. It becomes a tree, so that birds come and make their nests in its branches."

Jesus told them still another parable: "The kingdom of heaven is like this. A woman takes some yeast and mixes it with a bushel of flour until the whole batch of dough rises."

Jesus used parables to tell all these things to the crowds; he would not say a thing to them without using a parable. He did this to make come true what the prophet had said, "I will use parables when I speak to them; I will tell them things unknown since the creation of the world."

Matthew 13: 31-35

"…he would not say a thing to them without using a parable."

The storyteller syndrome

Dave Jones is a brilliant teacher. He's won many awards. One of his students even praised him on a television commercial.

One day he told me his secret: "Never give them the answers," he said. "Give them the exercise. Give them the experience. But they'll remember the point much better if they come up with it themselves."

Dave didn't realize it, but he was copying the Jewish rabbinical method. That was their technique, too. In response to a question, the rabbis told a story. If the hearers remained puzzled, they told another story. And another. Until a little light went on, and they got it.

That's why Jesus told so many parables. He was waiting for that "Aha!" moment to dawn.

Lord, tell me the old, old stories – and maybe someday I'll understand their intent a little better.

" The man who sowed the good seed is the Son of Man; the field is the world; the good seed is the people who belong to the kingdom; the weeds are the people who belong to the Evil One; and the enemy who sowed the weeds is the Devil. The harvest is the end of the age, and the harvest workers are angels. Just as the weeds are gathered up and burned in the fire, so the same thing will happen at the end of the age; the Son of Man will send out his angels to gather up out of his kingdom all those who cause people to sin and all others who do evil things, and they will throw them into the fiery furnace.... Then God's people will shine like the sun in their Father's kingdom."

Matthew 13: 36-43

> "The harvest is the end of the age..."

Leave the weeds

Community life is often messy. There are always "weeds" in it: people who I feel don't quite belong. They think differently than I do or take up too much space. I'm tempted to think, "If only that person wasn't here, the community would be perfect."

The problem is that my judgments are not always reliable. Often that irritating person has something vital to contribute: something that I can't or am not willing to see at the time.

Jesus tells me it is dangerous to judge. I might be damaging some of the wheat in trying to pull out what I consider to be weeds. I am a much better community member if I can refrain from judging, and instead encourage the wheat to grow, even when it seems to be weedy.

**Lord, help me to be non-judgmental of those
with whom I live and work.**

"The kingdom of heaven is like this. A man happens to find treasure hidden in a field. He covers it up again, and is so happy that he goes and sells everything he has, and then goes back and buys that field.

"Also, the kingdom of heaven is like this. A man is looking for fine pearls, and when he finds one that is unusually fine, he goes and sells everything he has, and buys that pearl."

Matthew 13: 44-46

"...sells everything he has, and buys that pearl."

Mindfulness

A colleague of mine commented that she rarely, if ever, sees me sitting still or empty-handed. As we talked, I kept photocopying, sorting and stapling... and I had to agree with her. Like so many people these days, I'm into "multi-tasking." I feel obliged to cram as much as possible into my day, and often end up juggling too much.

I can't imagine acting like the man in this parable. Rarely do I concentrate on one thing. The thought of enthusiastically and joyfully putting all of my resources toward one goal seems almost foolish.

What if I focused on doing one thing in an effort to bring more peace and harmony to my world? Who knows what wonderful things might happen!

God, help me approach this day
with a focused heart and a glad hand.

The Lord said to me, "Go down to the potter's house, where I will give you my message." So I went there and saw the potter working at his wheel. Whenever a piece of pottery turned out imperfect, he would take the clay and make it into something else.

Then the Lord said to me, "Don't I have the right to do with you people of Israel what the potter did with the clay? You are in my hands just like clay in the potter's hands."

Jeremiah 18: 1-6

"...like clay in the potter's hands."

Clay with attitude

When I read this text, I can't help but smile and picture myself as clay – clay with attitude! I've been a seminary student, a restaurant worker, a forklift driver, a husband and a graduate student. Right now I'm a single parent/college professor.

It seems that God has started over with me not once, but several times. I don't think that means I keep "getting it wrong." Rather, I see my life as an active, ongoing dialogue with the Potter.

So, as "clay with attitude," my goal is not to work at "getting it right" once and for all. Instead, I need to look for and recognize the Potter's touch in the very ebb and flow of my life's journey.

Potter God, let me see the changes in my life as the dance between my living clay and your loving touch.

W hen Jesus finished telling these parables, he left that place and went back to his hometown. He taught in the synagogue, and those who heard him were amazed. "Where did he get such wisdom?" they asked. "And what about his miracles? Isn't he the carpenter's son? Isn't Mary his mother, and aren't James, Joseph, Simon, and Judas his brothers? Aren't all his sisters living here? Where did he get all this?" And so they rejected him.

Jesus said to them, "A prophet is respected everywhere except in his hometown and by his own family." Because they did not have faith, he did not perform many miracles there.

Matthew 13: 54-58

> "Where did he get such wisdom?"

Seeing the truth

Not so long ago, a dear friend of mine died. The services at both the funeral home and the church were filled to overflowing. Friends, neighbours and colleagues came to express their deep sorrow at his passing and to share with one another stories of his life among them. To my surprise, my friend's family was unprepared for this response and exclaimed, "We're overwhelmed! We thought no one would be here."

How sad that they did not know their son and brother as the trusted confidant, respected colleague, committed parent, caring friend and neighbour that so many had come to know and love.

How sad that, holding onto old familiar views of them, I miss discovering who my own family members and friends have become.

**Lord, help me to love others –
not as they were, but as they are.**

S ave me from sinking in the mud;
keep me safe from my enemies,
safe from the deep water.
Don't let the flood come over me;
don't let me drown in the depths
or sink into the grave....
But I am in pain and despair;
lift me up, O God, and save me!
I will praise God with a song;
I will proclaim his greatness by giving him thanks....
When the oppressed see this, they will be glad;
those who worship God will be encouraged.

Psalm 69: 14-15, 29-30, 32-33

"I will praise God with a song..."

A gift of praise

As I step outside to call my family in for supper, I hear my daughter singing to herself in the garden. I spot her tiny back hunched down among the hostas, and hear her voice as it drifts upon the dappled glow of evening. Deep in concentration, she is unaware of my presence. What is she up to?

I take a breath to call her, but catch myself before I break the spell of her singing. Edging closer, I can just make out her words: "Thank you. Thank you. Thank you for the flowers."

Her voice continues, rising and falling. Soon it is lost among the chimes swaying on our cherry tree. I smile. I am sure God has heard this pure gift of praise.

**God, may I always remember to give you thanks
and praise – even when the demands of life
threaten to overwhelm me.**

Ex 16: 2-4, 12-15, 31; Ps 78; Eph 4: 17, 20-24; Jn 6: 24-35

I n today's gospel, the people are pursuing Jesus because he gave them bread to eat. Jesus challenges them to work for bread that will last. His point is that we can become preoccupied with having enough things – and some to spare; when this happens, our spiritual nature, our deepest selves, can become malnourished or even starved.

We need to be attentive to what will sustain us in that deep place where God dwells. In addition to sharing in the eucharist in a caring community, this spiritual food may include quiet times away from television and computer – time in nature, time of reflection, prayer or spiritual reading, time with family or friends where our spirits are replenished.

I once heard Jean Vanier speaking to a young person. He urged her to find the space to get in touch with her deepest desires, for it is through our deepest desires, he explained, that God calls us. In a spiritually malnourished state, we live in what Paul calls "the futility of [our] minds," always trying to figure out in our heads how to get what we feel we need. When we attend to our relationship with God, our minds become clearer, our values truer, our decisions simpler and more just, and we ourselves more whole and happier human beings.

**God of endless peace, help me to find the space
to be with you so I can discover my deepest desires.**

We have not depended on made-up stories in making known to you the mighty coming of our Lord Jesus Christ. With our own eyes we saw his greatness. We were there when he was given honour and glory by God the Father, when the voice came to him from the Supreme Glory, saying, "This is my own dear Son, with whom I am pleased!" We ourselves heard this voice coming from heaven, when we were with him on the holy mountain.

So we are even more confident of the message proclaimed by the prophets. You will do well to pay attention to it, because it is like a lamp shining in a dark place until the Day dawns and the light of the morning star shines in your hearts.

2 Peter 1: 16-19

"...it is like a lamp shining in a dark place..."

Dark times

It's all very well for Peter to tell us he has seen Jesus with his own eyes and has heard God's voice proclaiming Jesus as the Son. It's easy to have faith in something you have witnessed for yourself. But it takes faith – sometimes a huge amount of faith – to believe in something, or someone, we cannot see or touch.

Faith is a tricky thing – elusive at certain times, a beacon at others. When I find it, I am comforted; when it vanishes, I am lost.

Losing faith for me is like wandering in a pitch-black space. I don't know where to turn to get home again. If only I could remember that Jesus is beside me, ready to hand me a lamp to show me the way!

**Lord, when I am stumbling in the dark,
offer me the light of faith once more.**

The boat was far out in the lake, tossed about by the waves.... Between three and six o'clock in the morning Jesus came to the disciples, walking on the water. When they saw him, they were terrified. "It's a ghost!" they screamed. Jesus spoke to them at once. "Courage!" he said. "It is I. Don't be afraid!"

Then Peter spoke up. "Lord, if it is really you, order me to come out on the water to you." "Come!" answered Jesus. So Peter got out of the boat and started walking on the water to Jesus. But when he noticed the strong wind, he was afraid and started to sink down in the water. "Save me, Lord!" he cried. Jesus reached out and grabbed hold of him and said, "What little faith you have! Why did you doubt?"

Matthew 14: 22-36

> "It is I. Don't be afraid!"

Peace amid the storm

In my enthusiasm, I tend to overcommit myself to a range of projects. Then I wake up in the middle of the night in a panic: "How am I ever going to do all this?" Like Peter sinking in the water, I feel overwhelmed and afraid.

Last week I had such an episode. Going for a walk with an old friend helped me realize that my fears were about myself: What if I fall apart, have a breakdown? My friend offered me peace and perspective.

I remembered the importance of the projects waiting for me, and the work involved. I'm better off not thinking about the impossibility of it all, but remembering that I can do it – with the help of Jesus.

**Jesus, when I am overwhelmed and afraid,
help me to keep my eyes on you.**

A Canaanite woman came to Jesus. "Son of David!" she cried out. "Have mercy on me, sir! My daughter has a demon and is in a terrible condition...." His disciples came to him and begged him, "Send her away! She is following us and making all this noise!" Then Jesus replied, "I have been sent only to the lost sheep of the people of Israel."

At this the woman came and fell at his feet. "Help me, sir!" she said. Jesus answered, "It isn't right to take the children's food and throw it to the dogs."

"That's true, sir," she answered, "but even the dogs eat the leftovers that fall from their masters' table." Jesus answered her, "You are a woman of great faith! What you want will be done for you." And at that very moment her daughter was healed.   *Matthew 15:21-28*

> "...the woman came and fell at his feet."

Parental love

I know this Canaanite woman. She's one of the other parents I've met in hospital emergency rooms waiting anxiously with a sick child. She's one of the parents I've talked to whose heart has bled when their child was hurt or disappointed or who failed at something important. She's one of the parents I've been humbled to see live uncomplainingly and even joyfully with a child who has been given enormous challenges in life.

She is as ordinary and familiar as any parent – and as heroic. Twelve angry men blocking her way? Not a problem. The Son of God brushing her off? A minor setback.

Is there anything as powerful as the love of parents for their children? Not that I've seen.

**Loving God, continue to support and inspire all parents
as they care for the needs of their children.**

Jesus asked his disciples, "Who do people say the Son of Man is?"
"Some say John the Baptist," they answered. "Others say Elijah, while others say Jeremiah or some other prophet."

"What about you?" he asked them. "Who do you say I am?" Simon Peter answered, "You are the Messiah, the Son of the living God."

"Good for you, Simon son of John!" answered Jesus. "For this truth did not come to you from any human being, but it was given to you directly by my Father in heaven. And so I tell you, Peter: you are a rock, and on this rock foundation I will build my church, and not even death will ever be able to overcome it. I will give you the keys of the kingdom of heaven."

Matthew 16: 13-23

> "...on this rock foundation..."

Doing God's work

When Peter gets it right, Jesus praises him, When he gets it wrong, Jesus reprimands him. Peter never stops trying: he doesn't rest on his laurels after success, and he doesn't fall apart after his failures.

Jesus doesn't call Peter "a rock" because he's never wrong. Rather, Jesus recognizes in Peter his unfaltering love for God and his willingness to keep going.

Like Peter, I don't need to be perfect to do God's work. I admit it feels good to be praised and it feels lousy to fail. And both boasting and wallowing in self-pity are seductive in their own ways. It's only when I dig more deeply that I find the love and resilience I need to carry on doing God's work.

God, give me strength to do your work.

Remember that the person who plants few seeds will have a small crop; the one who plants many seeds will have a large crop. You should each give, then, as you have decided, not with regret or out of a sense of duty; for God loves the one who gives gladly. And God is able to give you more than you need, so that you will always have all you need for yourselves and more than enough for every good cause....

And God, who supplies seed for the sower and bread to eat, will also supply you with all the seed you need and will make it grow and produce a rich harvest from your generosity.

2 Corinthians 9: 6-10

> "...you will always have all you need..."

Giving gladly

I am tired. Tired of being a single parent for so long. Tired of being the only one responsible for the needs – physical, social and emotional – of my children. Tired of giving. I am so tired that at times I feel I can't give anymore.

Today's reading reminds me that God has promised to give me more than I need. So I'll always have all I need – for myself, and "more than enough for every good cause." I tend to forget that promise, and try to do it all on my own. No wonder I run out of steam!

Turning to God doesn't change the day-to-day reality of my life. But it does give me a sense of peace, knowing someone is there who cares.

Lord, remind me that you are there
and have promised to supply my every need, and more.

A man came to Jesus and said, "Sir, have mercy on my son! He is an epileptic and has such terrible attacks.... I brought him to your disciples, but they could not heal him."

Jesus answered, "How unbelieving and wrong you people are! ... How long do I have to put up with you? Bring the boy here to me!" Jesus gave a command to the demon, and it went out of the boy, and at that very moment he was healed.

Then the disciples asked Jesus, "Why couldn't we drive the demon out?" "It was because you do not have enough faith," answered Jesus. "I assure you that if you have faith as big as a mustard seed, you can say to this hill, 'Go from here to there!' and it will go. You could do anything!"

Matthew 17: 14-20

> "You could do anything!"

Faith and hope

The computer breaks down, the babysitting arrangements fall through, the bills need paying, a deadline looms. And I miss my daughter growing up... as my face is anxiously glued to the computer screen.

In trying to balance loving my daughter and running my own business, I often get furiously impatient with myself, as Jesus does when his disciples fail to heal this sick man. But he's not asking them to be stronger, better qualified or more organized. He's simply asking them to have more faith.

When I remember to ask God for what I need, I see my own frustrations and failures in a different light. The possibilities of what I can do – with just a tiny seed of faith – fill me with hope instead of disappointment.

Lord, teach me to exchange my impatience with myself for a mustard seed of faith in you.

1 Kgs 19: 4-8; Ps 34; Eph 4: 30 – 5.2; Jn 6: 41-51

"It is enough." Words of the prophet whispered in a plea, choked, gasped out between anguished sobs. "It is enough!" we, too, echo from our valley of tears. Like Paul in his world, we also are filled to the breaking point with the bitterness, wrath, anger, wrangling, slander, malice, grief, sorrow and sadness we know too well. "It is enough. Take us away from this."

"Do not complain among yourselves," says Jesus. "Listen! Learn and believe."

"But really, Lord! Bread that came down from heaven? Living bread?" Our exasperated astonishment cannot be masked.

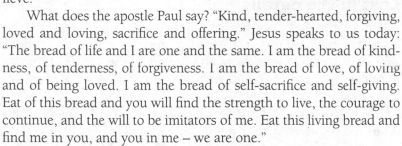

"Yes," he says. "Listen! Learn and believe."

What does the apostle Paul say? "Kind, tender-hearted, forgiving, loved and loving, sacrifice and offering." Jesus speaks to us today: "The bread of life and I are one and the same. I am the bread of kindness, of tenderness, of forgiveness. I am the bread of love, of loving and of being loved. I am the bread of self-sacrifice and self-giving. Eat of this bread and you will find the strength to live, the courage to continue, and the will to be imitators of me. Eat this living bread and find me in you, and you in me – we are one."

"It is enough!" Not a bone-weary plea of exasperation, but rather the joy-filled exclamation of our hearts made flesh and our minds newly enlightened: "It is enough, Lord, for nothing more can be given!"

Lord, give me this living bread,
which fills and sustains me.

Jesus said, "The Son of Man is about to be handed over to those who will kill him; but three days later he will be raised to life...."

The collectors of the Temple tax came to Peter and asked, "Does your teacher pay the Temple tax?" "Of course," Peter answered.... Jesus spoke up, "Simon, who pays duties or taxes to the kings of this world? The citizens of the country or the foreigners?" "The foreigners," answered Peter. "Well, then," replied Jesus, "that means that the citizens don't have to pay. But we don't want to offend these people. So go to the lake and drop in a line. Pull up the first fish you hook, and in its mouth you will find a coin worth enough for my Temple tax and yours. Take it and pay them our taxes."

Matthew 17: 22-27

> "Who pays duties or taxes to the kings of this world?"

Lost in the details

When I started my own business, I received a lot of advice about taxes. The language was very mundane and uninspiring: "This decision leads to that... but avoid that by doing this...." Launching a business calls for dreams and ambitions that can be eclipsed by dry tax manuals.

Today's reading captures a similar tension. Jesus predicts his death and resurrection, and a little later he and the disciples end up discussing who pays what tax. And there's the additional jolt about a mysterious coin to be found in the mouth of a fish. Everyday concerns and inexplicable mystery vie for the disciples' attention.

How like my life today, where the demands of my business and family jostle for attention, threatening to eclipse Jesus' presence in my life.

God, never let me get so wrapped up in the details of my daily obligations that I leave no space for you in my life.

The disciples came to Jesus, asking, "Who is the greatest in the kingdom of heaven?" So Jesus called a child to come and stand in front of them, and said, "I assure you that unless you change and become like children, you will never enter the kingdom of heaven. The greatest in the kingdom of heaven is the one who humbles himself and becomes like this child. And whoever welcomes in my name one such child as this, welcomes me....

"See that you don't despise any of these little ones. Their angels in heaven, I tell you, are always in the presence of my Father in heaven...."

Matthew 18: 1-5, 10, 12-14

"Who is the greatest...?"

The wrong question

The wrong question will hardly ever get you to the right answer. My daughter once asked me, "Daddy, how many miles are there until Christmas?" It was a sincere question; she really wanted to know something. But I couldn't answer the question she asked: you can't measure time in miles.

Jesus uses a child – the epitome of humility – to make a similar point: you can't use greatness to measure *value* in the kingdom of God. Then he goes even further, telling his disciples the right word, the right category to measure the distance between here and the kingdom: welcome.

So, how many "welcomes" until the kingdom? As many as it takes until everyone is welcome. And with each one, we get a little closer.

**Jesus, teach me to welcome others
as freely as you welcome them.**

When Elizabeth heard Mary's greeting, the baby moved within her. Elizabeth was filled with the Holy Spirit and said, "You are the most blessed of all women, and blessed is the child you will bear...."

Mary said, "My heart praises the Lord; my soul is glad because of God my Saviour, for he has remembered me, his lowly servant! From now on all people will call me happy, because of the great things the Mighty God has done for me. His name is holy; from one generation to another he shows mercy to those who honour him. He has stretched out his mighty arm and scattered the proud with all their plans. He has brought down mighty kings from their thrones, and lifted up the lowly. He has filled the hungry with good things, and sent the rich away with empty hands."

Luke 1: 39-56

> "...and lifted up the lowly."

An open heart

Marie called with wonderful news: she was leaving for China to bring her new daughter home! When the question of names came up, I suggested Hannah, for Mary's Magnificat echoed the Song of Hannah found in the book of Samuel. Both these prayers of praise tell how God turns oppression upside down and thwarts the evil plans of the mighty and the powerful.

Here we have a tiny girl – classified as a burden by some in her society because of her sex – being lifted up into a loving embrace. And we have this woman, opening her heart and life to cherish and nourish all the promise the tiny girl carries. Each one playing her part in the great things God is doing in our midst. Magnificent!

**God, let my soul praise you,
and help me to turn the world right-side up.**

"Once there was a king who decided to check on his servants' accounts... one of them was brought in who owed him millions of dollars.... The servant fell on his knees before the king. 'Be patient with me,' he begged, 'and I will pay you everything!' The king felt sorry for him, so he forgave him the debt and let him go.

"The man went out and met one of his fellow servants who owed him a few dollars. 'Pay back what you owe me!' he said. His fellow servant begged him, 'Be patient with me, and I will pay you back!' But he refused.... When the other servants saw what had happened, they were very upset and went to the king and told him everything. So he called the servant in. 'You worthless slave!' he said. 'You should have had mercy on your fellow servant, just as I had mercy on you.'"

Matthew 18: 21 – 19: 1

"You should have had mercy..."

Bill collectors

Many stock traders, bill collectors, soldiers and political leaders behave as if the forgiving of debts – if left unchecked – would bring the world to a halt. The problem about debt is not the need to collect it; it is the need to *forgive* it.

Jesus calls me to forgive the debt of a relative or a neighbour – or the debt I feel is owed me by members of another religion, race or country. He calls me to forgive even the worst kind of debt: the debt of an enemy.

If I insist on collecting these debts, I am, says Jesus, heading for trouble. That is, unless I am so certain I am able to pay off all my own debts.

Lord, in gratitude I experience your mercy in my life – mercy that is meant to be spread around.

The Sovereign Lord says, "I will treat you the way you deserve, because you ignored your promises and broke the covenant. But I will honour the covenant I made with you when you were young, and I will make a covenant with you that will last forever. You will remember how you have acted, and be ashamed of it when you get your older sister and your younger sister back. I will let them be like daughters to you, even though this was not part of my covenant with you. I will renew my covenant with you, and you will know that I am the Lord...." The Sovereign Lord has spoken.

Ezekiel 16: 59-63

> "I will honour the covenant I made with you..."

Faithful love

I like this: the Sovereign Lord assesses the situation, applies consequences, but continues to forgive and remain committed to his covenant.

I'm a teacher. In my business, we have to deliver a message: "I'll treat you the way you deserve." Sometimes it's hard to remember the second part: "I will honour the covenant I made with you."

A covenant is not a contract – it's not *quid pro quo*. It doesn't give up. It doesn't say, "You've had your chance." Instead, it says, "I am committed to you. Even when you've given up on yourself."

What a wonderful model for relationships: I will be truthful, but I will forgive. And I will be there. Committed.

**Lord, make me mindful of my covenants.
Keep me faithful to them.**

Some people brought children to Jesus for him to place his hands on them and to pray for them, but the disciples scolded the people. Jesus said, "Let the children come to me and do not stop them, because the kingdom of heaven belongs to such as these."

He placed his hands on them, and then went away.

Matthew 19: 13-15

> "...the kingdom of heaven belongs to such as these."

Children

A line from a country song: "My old man is just another child that's grown old." As we all are – children growing old.

It's hard to remain a child. And glib to pretend that's what we are, for the child in us goes. Those mornings when we rush off to work after too little sleep. Those bills to pay. Those compromises made, where right and wrong are not as clear as they once were. All the pain of lost love, sick children, loved ones gone. As time, that thief, steals our childhood from us.

But, perhaps if I stop and listen to the wind. Give spontaneously. Say yes to an invitation without stopping to think it over. Live only today. Only right now. Laugh. Perhaps just for a moment, the kingdom can begin, right now.

Dear God, let me see your creation with a child's eyes.

Prov 9: 1-6; Ps 34; Eph 5: 15-20; Jn 6: 51-58

Wisdom has set a table and invited us to eat. Our invitation to the banquet demands that we replace immaturity with insight. That's a tall order! In the gospel, Jesus also sets a table; his menu consists of his body and blood. Many immature souls leave; it requires insight to accept this invitation.

As an immature child I used to strategically pick my communion line-up. I was "in love" with Father W – I *had* to receive communion from him. When he recognized me and smiled at me, my day brightened. I felt blessed and filled with happiness. Every Sunday, once communion stations were determined, I would weave my way around the church to be in Father W's "flock." I was and still am a determined soul.

Today I look back and wonder: was I really all that immature? At seven, I knew that receiving communion was about being recognized. Recognition brightened my day and lightened my step – I felt blessed. Were my immature antics founded on insight?

I bless my seven-year-old self. I implore her to continue to see God in Father W and all that surrounds her. I applaud her boldness and insist that she continue to weave her way through life both giving and receiving recognition and blessing. I am ready to come to the table... I recognize and embrace all that feeds me. I am in communion.

God of all goodness, help me to see you in everyone and everything around me.

Once a man came to Jesus. "Teacher, what good thing must I do to receive eternal life?" "There is only One who is good. Keep the commandments if you want to enter life." "What commandments?" he asked. Jesus answered, "Do not commit murder; do not commit adultery; do not steal; do not accuse anyone falsely; respect your father and your mother; and love your neighbour as you love yourself."

"I have obeyed all these commandments. What else do I need to do?" Jesus said to him, "If you want to be perfect, go and sell all you have and give the money to the poor, and you will have riches in heaven; then come and follow me."

When the young man heard this, he went away sad, because he was very rich.

Matthew 19: 16-22

"What else do I need to do?"

Rich in love

I lived much of my life believing that I could earn love and happiness by doing the "good" and "right" things. I applied this mathematical approach to my faith, too. I tried to win God's love and my own salvation. A capable "do-er" of many worthwhile things, I hoarded accounts of good deeds. I clung to my record as to an amassed fortune.

But over the years, failure, disappointment, loss and suffering pried me loose. Finally incapable of doing anything more on my own, I experienced God's love in the very depths of my being.

As I learn to be "who I am" for God and others, any good I do is but a joyful response to the rich gifts of love and life I have received.

Lord, fill me with your love, that I may share it with those whose paths will cross mine today.

Jesus said, "I assure you: it is much harder for a rich person to enter the kingdom of God than for a camel to go through the eye of a needle." When the disciples heard this, they were completely amazed. "Who, then, can be saved?" they asked. Jesus looked straight at them and answered, "This is impossible for human beings, but for God everything is possible."

Then Peter spoke up. "Look, we have left everything and followed you. What will we have?" Jesus said, "Everyone who has left houses or brothers or sisters or father or mother or children or fields for my sake, will receive a hundred times more and will be given eternal life. But many who now are first will be last, and many who now are last will be first."

Matthew 19: 23-30

> "...to go through the eye of a needle."

Wide and narrow

A woman who comes to our church stands out, and not just because she's very tall. She wears a nightgown with a petticoat over the top, a big square hat and a dramatically torn fur coat. She carries a jewel-encrusted gold handbag stuffed with loose bits of paper. She makes me feel like the most boring dresser in the world.

Conversations with her rush off in several directions at once, and sometimes she breaks into song mid-sentence. Just today she called to invite herself for supper, and I said no. Why did I do that? I can't phone her back – she has no phone.

One thing's sure: she may be large and flamboyant, but she'll fit through the eye of that needle long before I will.

Lord, help me see the essentials.
Narrow me down so I can fit through.

The Lord is my shepherd;
I have everything I need.
He lets me rest in fields of green grass
and leads me to quiet pools of fresh water.... ·
He guides me in the right paths,
as he has promised....
You prepare a banquet for me,
where all my enemies can see me;
you welcome me as an honoured guest
and fill my cup to the brim.
I know that your goodness and love
will be with me all my life;
and your house will be my home
as long as I live.

Psalm 23: 1-6

"I have everything I need."

A guiding hand

I always worry about whether I've made the right choices – about how to raise the kids, career moves, where to live.... The list goes on.

When I look back at our old photo albums and see the smiling faces, I realize that things were good – even when they did not go the way I planned.

At mid-life, I look back and begin to see a pattern. I realize that the Lord has been my shepherd, even though I didn't realize it at the time. And things that I thought were problems, even disasters, led me to places I would not otherwise have gone. In fact, my life is richer and more interesting when I step back and let God show me the way.

**Dear God, give me the humility to let go
and accept your guiding hand in my life.**

"The kingdom of heaven is like this. Once there was a king who prepared a wedding feast for his son. He sent his servants to tell the invited guests to come to the feast, but they did not want to come.... The king was very angry...; then he called his servants and said to them, 'My wedding feast is ready, but the people I invited did not deserve it. Now go to the main streets and invite to the feast as many people as you find.' So the servants went out into the streets and gathered all the people they could find, good and bad alike....

"The king went in to look at the guests and saw a man who was not wearing wedding clothes. 'Friend, how did you get in here without wedding clothes?'"

Matthew 22: 1-14

> "...but they did not want to come..."

Ready to party

The greatest party invitation they'd ever received – and they were all too busy to come.

Throughout the day I am pulled in a hundred directions, and they're all worthwhile: work, volunteer commitments, a friend in trouble. So when my gentle two-year-old invited me to play yesterday, I said, "I just have to..." and carried on with what I was doing. After several tries she became angry, and I realized I was turning down the most precious request of the day.

I sat down to play with her, but she sensed my mind was elsewhere – I wasn't "wearing wedding clothes." It was only when I let go of everything and gave her my full attention that she was satisfied... and we started to party.

**Give me the grace to recognize your invitation,
Lord, and to accept it with a joyful and undivided heart.**

P hilip found Nathanael and told him, "We have found the one whom Moses wrote about in the book of the Law and whom the prophets also wrote about. He is Jesus son of Joseph, from Nazareth." "Can anything good come from Nazareth?" Nathanael asked. "Come and see," answered Philip. When Jesus saw Nathanael coming to him, he said about him, "Here is a real Israelite; there is nothing false in him!" Nathanael asked him, "How do you know me?" Jesus answered, "I saw you when you were under the fig tree before Philip called you." "Teacher," answered Nathanael, "you are the Son of God! You are the King of Israel!" Jesus said, "Do you believe just because I told you I saw you when you were under the fig tree? You will see much greater things than this!"

John 1:45-51

"You will see much greater things than this!"

The bigger picture

So often I see events only in terms of how they affect me. When my child's school had to close, I worried about how I'd manage. When a bus strike loomed, I wondered how I'd get to work. When bad weather hit, I wondered how long I would have my mother-in-law in the house. The bigger issues – the needs of the school community, justice for bus workers, the trials others faced during the storm – were secondary.

I often respond to situations as Nathanael responded to Jesus. I'm interested when I'm part of the story, indifferent when I'm not. How many of the greater things do I miss when I respond to life in this way: when I fail to look past my own immediate interests?

**Jesus, help me look beyond my own concerns
to see the bigger picture today.**

The teachers of the Law and the Pharisees are the authorized interpreters of Moses' Law. So you must obey and follow everything they tell you to do; do not, however, imitate their actions, because they don't practise what they preach. They tie onto people's backs loads that are heavy and hard to carry yet they aren't willing even to lift a finger to help them carry those loads.... They love to be greeted with respect in the marketplaces and to have people call them 'Teacher.' You must not be called 'Teacher,' because you are all equal and have only one Teacher.... The greatest one among you must be your servant. Whoever makes himself great will be humbled, and whoever humbles himself will be made great."

Matthew 23: 1-12

"Whoever humbles himself will be made great."

Beyond my fears

I admit it – the stories about the Pharisees make me feel so *good*. How misguided they were, I think to myself. They couldn't see the forest for the trees!

But if I'm honest, I must acknowledge that sometimes I act like a Pharisee. When I think I'm better than others. When I don't practise what I preach. When I get so focused on following the rules that I can't leave room for a better way.

If I could let go… If I could be less rigid… If I could accept that I'm OK – with my strengths and weaknesses – and don't need to pretend that I'm better than I really am… Maybe then I'd get somewhere. Maybe then I'd see the forest in the middle of all those trees.

**Jesus, help me see beyond my fears and doubts
so I can be open to your presence.**

Josh 24: 1-2, 15-17, 18; Ps 34; Eph 4: 32 — 5: 2, 21-32; Jn 6: 53, 60-69

Faith is always a matter of choice. We choose to believe in other persons, in institutions, in values and causes. All our truly significant relationships and commitments arise out of such choices. This process of faith inevitably involves risk. To believe in nothing, however, is a form of death. To risk nothing is to die as a human being.

As their life unfolds, Joshua invites the tribes of Israel to choose faith and commitment to each other and to God. Their passage from slavery to freedom is well in the past and new generations need to make this story their own. As their leader, Joshua challenges them to reconsider their common history and recommit to their faith in a new land.

Peter, too, makes a choice for ongoing belief in a time of change and tension. He senses that wandering away from faith and commitment to Jesus would be wandering away from life itself. He boldly testifies to his intuition as he presumes to answer for the Twelve.

From an ancient past, these great biblical figures bear witness to the challenge of faith decisions in the face of changing circumstances. They also invite us to reflect on our need to continually choose faith in Jesus. As believers of all ages, we stand with Joshua and Peter as they experience the life-giving risk of embracing their own story as an ongoing adventure of faith and hope.

Loving God, it is scary to take risks.
Help me make my leap of faith!

"How terrible for you, teachers of the Law and Pharisees! You hypocrites! You lock the door to the kingdom of heaven in people's faces, but you yourselves don't go in, nor do you allow in those who are trying to enter!

"How terrible for you, teachers of the Law and Pharisees! You hypocrites! You sail the seas and cross whole countries to win one convert; and when you succeed, you make him twice as deserving of going to hell as you yourselves are!

"How terrible for you, blind guides! You teach, 'If someone swears by the Temple, he isn't bound by his vow; but if he swears by the gold in the Temple, he is bound.' Blind fools! Which is more important, the gold or the Temple which makes the gold holy?"

Matthew 23: 13-22

> "You hypocrites!"

Hypocrisy and humility

This is not the calm, cool and collected Jesus I'm used to hearing about in the gospels. He's on quite a roll here!

Hypocrisy is a hard one, because I'm as guilty of it as anyone. It's an occupational hazard for me as a parent and as a teacher who is in the business of "training" children.

Where I teach I've seen students suspended for swearing in class, and then have gone into the staff room only to hear teachers swearing! I've seen kids being "reamed out" in the hall for being late for class by a teacher who takes days off to catch up on marking.

There are days when I would love to scream "hypocrite!" – just as Jesus did. But instead, I think I'll work on practising what I preach.

**Lord, help me to practise what I preach
and remain humble about my own righteousness.**

"How terrible for you, teachers of the Law and Pharisees! You hypocrites! You give to God one tenth even of the seasoning herbs, such as mint, dill, and cumin, but you neglect to obey the really important teachings of the Law, such as justice and mercy and honesty. These you should practise, without neglecting the others. Blind guides! You strain a fly out of your drink, but swallow a camel!

"How terrible for you, teachers of the Law and Pharisees! You hypocrites! You clean the outside of your cup and plate, while the inside is full of what you have gotten by violence and selfishness. Blind Pharisee! Clean what is inside the cup first, and then the outside will be clean too!"

Matthew 23: 23-26

> "Clean what is inside the cup first…"

Pause before judging

Alex and I went to the same high school. He smoked too much, swore… that sort of thing. He was held up as an example to other students of how not to behave.

Late one night, a bunch of us were heading into an all-night café. On the sidewalk was a woman, a "working girl." She was a little drunk, probably having finished for the night. The remarks started – from the ones who were the "good" boys, I'm ashamed to admit. Alex, however, asked her, "Want a coffee?" She came in and he bought her a coffee and something to eat, and talked to her. When she left, he said, "Take care of yourself."

Whose cup was cleanest on the inside?

**God, may I remember to look within
before judging someone else.**

Lord, I have come to you for protection;
never let me be defeated!
Because you are righteous, help me and rescue me.
Listen to me and save me!
Be my secure shelter
and a strong fortress to protect me;
you are my refuge and defence.
Sovereign Lord, I put my hope in you;
I have trusted in you since I was young.
I have relied on you all my life;
you have protected me since the day I was born.
I will always praise you....
I will tell of your goodness....
You have taught me ever since I was young,
and I still tell of your wonderful acts.   *Psalm 71: 1-6, 15, 17*

"I put my hope in you."

Amazing grace

I waited nervously in the dentist's chair as he decided on the course of treatment. The pain was intense and I was feeling very anxious. Part of me wanted to flee.

Then I heard an old favourite song on the radio, playing quietly in the background. The warm, rich tones of the contralto calmed me, and I closed my eyes. I breathed deeply and repeated to myself, "God is with me," over and over again. I remembered the many times God had indeed been with me.

What followed seemed miraculous to me. I began to relax. Fear turned to trust. I felt I was in good hands. And when the dentist returned, I knew that whatever followed, all would be well.

**God, through all the seasons of my life,
you hold me gently in your arms. Thank you.**

From Paul, who was called by the will of God to be an apostle of Christ Jesus, and from our brother Sosthenes.

To the church of God that is in Corinth, to all who are called to be God's holy people, who belong to him in union with Christ Jesus, together with all people everywhere who worship our Lord Jesus Christ, their Lord and ours:

May God our Father and the Lord Jesus Christ give you grace and peace.

I always give thanks to my God for you because of the grace he has given you through Christ Jesus. For in union with Christ you have become rich in all things.... God is to be trusted, the God who called you to have fellowship with his Son Jesus Christ, our Lord.

1 Corinthians 1: 1-9

> "To the church of God that is in Corinth…"

The beauty of letters

Letter writing has become a lost art.

My mother was the letter writer in our family. Once a week, every week, she wrote to her two sisters in Ireland. Every second week, she wrote to her closest friends. And when she got letters from those sisters, those friends, she read them aloud to her own family.

Those letters took weeks to get delivered. But when we visited Ireland, even though we had been separated for years, we felt instantly in touch. We had already shared their successes and failures, their joys and sorrows.

Like Paul's letters, my mother's letters kept us in touch. Telephone calls may be more direct, and e-mail more instant, but we don't share ourselves the way we used to in letters.

Lord, thank you for letter writers like Paul. And thank you for those who had the wisdom to preserve those letters.

"Once there were ten young women who took their oil lamps and went out to meet the bridegroom. Five of them were foolish, and the other five were wise. The foolish ones took their lamps but did not take any extra oil with them, while the wise ones took containers full of oil for their lamps. The bridegroom was late in coming, so they began to nod and fall asleep. It was already midnight when the cry rang out, 'Here is the bridegroom! Come and meet him!' The ten young women woke up and trimmed their lamps. Then the foolish ones said to the wise ones, 'Let us have some of your oil, because our lamps are going out....'"

Jesus concluded, "Watch out, then, because you do not know the day or the hour."

Matthew 25: 1-13

> "...and did not take any extra oil with them..."

Packing the essentials

Packing my daughter's diaper bag for an outing is always a challenge. Let's see: diapers, a bib, extra clothing, a snack, water, a suitable toy that will distract her but not others. No matter how hard I try, it always seems that I forget an essential item. Like the foolish women, I think I am prepared, only to find that I've overlooked something really important.

How many times have I forgotten to put humour and understanding in the bag? How often have I found myself with enough wipes but not enough patience? Sometimes I am like the women who have lamps without enough oil.

Today I will try not to be distracted by unimportant details. I will remember to carry the essentials.

**Lord, help me to prepare for today's journey
with the things that are truly necessary.**

Saturday | SEPTEMBER 1

N ow remember what you were, my friends, when God called you. From the human point of view few of you were wise or powerful or of high social standing. God purposely chose what the world considers nonsense in order to shame the wise, and he chose what the world considers weak in order to shame the powerful. He chose what the world looks down on and despises and thinks is nothing, in order to destroy what the world thinks is important. This means that no one can boast in God's presence. But God has brought you into union with Christ Jesus, and God has made Christ to be our wisdom. By him, we are put right with God; we become God's holy people and are set free.

1 Corinthians 1: 26-31

> "…what the world considers weak…"

Strength in weakness

Back in the 1960s, Pauline Vanier thought her son Jean had gone crazy. He chose to leave a promising career in the Navy and move in with two men with developmental disabilities – the start of the international movement called L'Arche. Over time, she came to share her son's conviction that the lowly and despised in the world have much to teach us about God.

After the death of her husband, Governor General Georges Vanier, Pauline moved into a small house in the French village where L'Arche originated. Leaving behind years of wining and dining with kings, queens and presidents, Pauline found peace and joy in living with the "foolish" and weak. Affectionately called "Mammi," she was everyone's Great Lady until her death.

Jesus, give me the courage to meet your greatness in foolishness and weakness, in myself as well as others.

Deut 4: 1-2, 6-8; Ps 15; James 1: 17-18, 21-22, 27; Mk 7:.1-8, 14-15, 21-23

What would Jesus do? A few years ago that question became a popular slogan on bracelets and bumper stickers. Perhaps it can suggest a useful approach to today's readings about rules and laws.

Laws are a good and necessary component of human society. Thus, Moses exhorts his people to obey the "statutes and ordinances" of God's law. James points out that obedience to the letter of the law

is not enough, however, and he challenges his community to be "doers" and not merely "hearers" of God's word.

Mark's gospel shows what happens when the letter of the law is slavishly followed. The scribes and Pharisees criticize the disciples for their failure to observe the laws about hand washing. Elsewhere in the gospels, Jesus himself is often challenged for breaking the rules – healing on the Sabbath, for example, or ignoring barriers of class or gender. Here he reminds us that what is important is not what the rules dictate, but what is inside a person's heart.

Discipleship is never as straightforward as simply following the rules. For one thing, rules can be unjust, or too rigid, or discriminatory. Sometimes we are called to question such rules in order to serve God and our neighbour in generosity and truth.

So, what would Jesus do? Simply put, he would act according to the demands of justice and compassion, even if that meant disregarding the rules. Can we, his disciples, do any less?

Lord Jesus, help me to follow your rule of love.

Jesus went to Nazareth... and on the Sabbath he went as usual to the synagogue. He stood up to read the Scriptures and was handed the book of the prophet Isaiah. "The Spirit of the Lord is upon me, because he has chosen me to bring good news to the poor. He has sent me to proclaim liberty to the captives and recovery of sight to the blind, to set free the oppressed and announce that the time has come when the Lord will save his people." Jesus rolled up the scroll, gave it back to the attendant, and sat down. "This passage of scripture has come true today, as you heard it being read."

When the people heard this, they were filled with anger.

Luke 4: 16-30

> "He has sent me to proclaim liberty to captives."

True courage

Ever stood up for what was right, no matter what? Ever been possessed with the raw courage to speak out clearly about an act of injustice? I work in a high school where that courage is shown every day. Inevitably, when people gang up on someone who is weak, a voice will dare to speak up and say, "Hang on now. That isn't right!" It happens all the time.

Wow! Courage breaks through even in the face of the verbal assaults sure to follow! "Who are you to tell us what to do?" they'll scream. "You're just...." But the young prophet delivers the word, and its power is undeniable. No one can misunderstand the challenge.

Youth know the prophetic ways of Jesus. It's in their blood.

O God, create within me a heart of courage to speak your word today in a world that longs for truth.

Jesus went to Capernaum, a town in Galilee, where he taught the people…. In the synagogue was a man who had the spirit of an evil demon in him; he screamed out in a loud voice, "Ah! What do you want with us, Jesus of Nazareth? Are you here to destroy us? I know who you are: you are God's holy messenger!" Jesus ordered the spirit, "Be quiet and come out of the man!" The demon threw the man down in front of them and went out of him without doing him any harm. The people were all amazed and said to one another, "What kind of words are these? With authority and power this man gives orders to the evil spirits, and they come out!" And the report about Jesus spread everywhere in that region.

Luke 4: 31-37

> "…you are God's holy messenger!"

In the face of evil

What a life of torment and misery the man with the evil demon must have led! And yet Jesus had the power to drive out that evil force and make the man well.

Every day I see people on the streets tormented by their own demons: addictions, or mental illness, or crushing bad luck. I know that some of these street people also suffer from the effects of childhood abuse. Still, it's so difficult for me to face their pain – and their demands – that, to my shame, I sometimes cross the street hoping to avoid them.

I wonder how I could make a difference in the life of at least one of these abandoned people. How can I be "God's holy messenger," as Jesus was?

Lord, give me some of your wisdom, your strength, your power to drive out evil and heal its effects.

J esus left the synagogue and went to Simon's home. Simon's mother-in-law was sick with a high fever and they spoke to Jesus about her. He went and stood at her bedside and ordered the fever to leave her. The fever left her, and she got up at once and began to wait on them.

After sunset all who had friends who were sick with various diseases brought them to Jesus; he placed his hands on every one of them and healed them all.

Luke 4: 38-44

> "...she got up at once and began to wait on them."

A mother's love

Simon Peter's mother-in-law had a lot to put up with. First her daughter marries this none-too-bright fisherman. Then he quits his job to follow a mysterious, possibly dangerous, teacher. Then he brings home a bunch of the man's followers for dinner – while she is lying sick in bed!

But the mysterious teacher cures her. And she does what so many other mothers I know would do: she gets out of bed to pitch in and help with the meal.

I am amazed by people like that – people like my own mother. A little fatigue or a few aches and pains can't stop her. She'll arrive at my home for a visit carrying a suitcase full of groceries to cook my favourite meal.

**God, humble me and make me grateful
for generous men and women. Help me learn from them.**

Y ou should not fool yourself. If any of you think that you are wise by this world's standards, you should become a fool, in order to be really wise. For what this world considers to be wisdom is nonsense in God's sight. As the scripture says, "God traps the wise in their cleverness"; and another scripture says, "The Lord knows that the thoughts of the wise are worthless." No one, then, should boast about what human beings can do. Actually everything belongs to you: Paul, Apollos and Peter; this world, life and death, the present and the future – all these are yours, and you belong to Christ, and Christ belongs to God.

1 Corinthians 3: 18-23

"God traps the wise in their cleverness."

True wisdom

Jim wore his learning on his sleeve. He loved to go on about all the books he had read and would draw people into complicated philosophical debates that he would always "win" – usually by intimidating the other person.

At first, we were all very impressed by Jim's intelligence, and we all deferred to him. Over time, however, his attitude began to wear thin and some people began to question his sincerity.

It got to the point where Jim was regularly mocked behind his back. I felt very sorry for him, because I knew he just wanted what everyone wants – to be loved and accepted. He confused impressing people with being liked. He confused being smart with being a good friend.

Lord, teach me humility about my intelligence.
Let me always put the heart before the head.

S ome people said to Jesus, "The disciples of John fast frequently and offer prayers, and the disciples of the Pharisees do the same; but your disciples eat and drink."

Jesus answered, "Do you think you can make the guests at a wedding party go without food as long as the bridegroom is with them? Of course not! But the day will come when the bridegroom will be taken away from them, and then they will fast."

Jesus also told them this parable: "You don't... pour new wine into used wineskins, because the new wine will burst the skins, the wine will pour out, and the skins will be ruined. Instead, new wine must be poured into fresh wineskins! And you don't want new wine after drinking old wine."

Luke 5: 33-39

> "...the new wine will burst the skins..."

Room for the Spirit

In the Middle Ages, some churches in Europe were built with "Holy Spirit holes" – openings that were left in the roof to remind people that God's Spirit could move freely about, both within and beyond the church building. It was an architectural attempt to reflect the theological truth that God is like new wine: always in ferment, always expanding. God is free to move within – and beyond – our buildings, our worship, our best ideas.

Sometimes, when I look at the church today, I think it's time to put some Holy Spirit holes in our buildings again – and see whether that opens up a little breathing space in our imaginations, as well.

**Dear God, give me a faith with enough holes
for you to move around a bit.**

rely on your constant love;
I will be glad, because you will rescue me.
I will sing to you, O Lord,
because you have been good to me.

Psalm 13: 5-6

"I rely on your constant love…"

A child's trust

When my kids were very young, I was like a god to them.

Don't misunderstand. They certainly didn't think I was all-powerful or all-wise. No. Their belief in my god-like powers was about something else. When they looked at me, I could tell they were absolutely certain they were safe and that as long as I was there, nothing could go wrong.

It was unnerving. I knew very well my own weaknesses and the uncertainty of the world we live in. But it was deeply moving at the same time. I learned a lot about trust in those moments.

This simple prayer recalls those times, as I, too old to believe in certainty but too human not to long for it, try to put my faith in God.

**Lord, in my weakness and uncertainty,
help me trust in your never-ending goodness.**

Isa 35: 4-7; Ps 146; James 2: 1-5; Mk 7: 31-37

I t's early September. Summer is unofficially over, but the beautiful days of autumn are still to come. There is a sense of beginning with the start of the school year, yet little excitement for most people. In many ways, this is just another ordinary day.

For the deaf man in the gospel, it was almost certainly an ordinary day. He may not have known who Jesus was or that he was in the area. He did not seek healing or change. Like most of us, he was probably comfortable with the situation he knew. He did not expect to be touched by God or to have his life changed.

Yet God came to him, much as God comes to us, in the very ordinariness of life. And this man was given the ability to hear Jesus' words for himself and respond. He did not seek Jesus, but Jesus touched him because a few friends, a few ordinary people, wanted to help.

The second reading reminds us that we do not always find God where we expect. Often God is not in those people or circumstances we find immediately attractive. Often God is not necessarily where we think God ought to be. God comes to us in the common, the ordinary. We need only eyes to see and ears to hear, for the ordinary is a place of extraordinary blessing.

God of blessing, change my life.
Send me your healing touch.

Jesus went into a synagogue.... A man was there whose right hand was paralyzed. Some teachers of the Law and some Pharisees wanted a reason to accuse Jesus of doing wrong, so they watched him closely to see if he would heal on the Sabbath.... Jesus said to the man, "Stand up and come here to the front." The man got up and stood there. Then Jesus said to them, "I ask you: What does our Law allow us to do on the Sabbath? To help or to harm? To save someone's life or destroy it?" He looked around at them all; then he said to the man, "Stretch out your hand." He did so, and his hand became well again. They were filled with rage and began to discuss... what they could do to Jesus.

Luke 6: 6-11

> "To help or to harm?"

Pharisee mode

Some days I wake up to discover I'm in "Pharisee mode." The announcer on the radio is annoying, the editorials in the newspapers are stupid, the dumb cat invariably trips me on the stairs, and the toast ends up burnt. These are the days I find it painfully easy to see the things that are wrong with everything and everyone around me. Of course, I have done nothing to cause any of this!

Deep down I know I feel this way because I'm overtired or am worried about money, work or my parents' health. But falling headlong into this uncomfortable darkness can be paralyzing. That's when I need to stop, take a deep breath, and stretch out my withered hands and heart to God for healing.

Lord, before I criticize someone today, help me to stop and look at the fear or the hurt that lies within me.

J esus went up a hill to pray and spent the whole night there praying to God. When day came, he called his disciples to him and
chose twelve of them, whom he named apostles....

When Jesus had come down from the hill with the apostles, he
stood on a level place with a large number of his disciples. A large
crowd of people was there from all over Judea and from Jerusalem
and from the coast cities of Tyre and Sidon; they had come to hear
him and to be healed of their diseases. Those who were troubled by
evil spirits also came and were healed. All the people tried to touch
him, for power was going out from him and healing them all.

Luke 6: 12-19

> "Jesus went up a hill to pray..."

The sound of silence

When I was young, my life had a soundtrack to it. Bach for times
I wanted to think. Rock and roll for getting my energy moving. Bob
Dylan or Paul Simon for stirring me up. My friends were the same,
although they had different selections for their soundtracks.

Back then, I didn't care much for silence or solitude. They made
me jittery and uncomfortable. The thought of going to some deserted
place alone, and talking to God all night, would have sent me round
the bend.

Things are different now. I've learned I need the stillness and quiet
that Jesus found on that hill. Without them, I can't hear myself, let
alone God. And then how would I know how to live my life?

Lord, help me hear your voice in the stillness.

Jesus said, "Happy are you poor; the kingdom of God is yours! Happy are you who are hungry now; you will be filled! Happy are you who weep now; you will laugh! Happy are you when people hate you, reject you, insult you, and say that you are evil, all because of the Son of Man! Be glad when that happens and dance for joy, because a great reward is kept for you in heaven…

"But how terrible for you who are rich now; you have had your easy life! How terrible for you who are full now; you will go hungry! How terrible for you who laugh now; you will mourn and weep! How terrible when all people speak well of you; their ancestors said the very same things about the false prophets."

Luke 6: 20-26

> **"Happy are you who weep now…"**

A God who cares

How I wish that Jesus were kidding when he said these things! I keep trying to read them in a way that makes them easier to accept.

I don't like the thought of rejection, insults and slander. I don't like mourning and weeping, being poor or hungry. And yet, these are the experiences I am called to live. Experiences of lingering unemployment, grief over the loss of a loved one, or pain at being maligned … these carve out my internal capacity for joy, happiness and peace.

Such moments do prepare me to receive the kingdom. And oddly enough, they also contain the kingdom, as I experience an intimately caring God right by my side.

**God, grant me the courage to believe
that your presence transforms pain into new life.**

L ord, you have examined me and you know me.
You know everything I do;
from far away you understand all my thoughts.
You see me, whether I am working or resting;
you know all my actions....
You created every part of me;
you put me together in my mother's womb.
I praise you because you are to be feared;
all you do is strange and wonderful.
I know it with all my heart....
Examine me, O God, and know my mind;
test me, and discover my thoughts.
Find out if there is any evil in me
and guide me in the everlasting way.   *Psalm 139: 1-3, 13-14, 23-24*

> "...you put me together in my mother's womb."

God's plan

I look at my almost-grown children and am filled with amazement as I watch them get ready to step into the unknown future that beckons to them. They are unique – down to the tiniest detail, more complicated and intricate than anything modern science can imagine.

Yet I remember placing my hand on my wife's swelling belly for each one, feeling the just-forming life growing and moving within, and wondering, "Who are you?"

I find it comforting to think that my knowledge of them is a mere suggestion of the knowledge God has of them. I'm reassured to think that the God who put together these marvellous creations surely has a purpose in mind for them. They are here for a reason.

Lord, help all children learn their purpose on this earth, and give them the strength to meet it.

He always had the nature of God, but he did not think that by force he should try to remain equal with God. Instead of this, of his own free will he gave up all he had, and took the nature of a servant. He became like a human being and appeared in human likeness. He was humble and walked the path of obedience all the way to death – his death on the cross. For this reason God raised him to the highest place above and gave him the name that is greater than any other name.

Philippians 2: 6-11

> "…and walked the path of obedience…"

True obedience

Robert was diagnosed with multiple sclerosis some fifteen years ago. He probably wanted to cling to his identity as a fully able person. He could have stood resolute in anger at how this disease has humbled him. And I'm sure he has had (and maybe still has) such moments.

But, having been "humbled" into early retirement, Robert chose instead a path of "obedience." "Obedience" comes from the Latin word for "to hear." Since finding himself out of work and in a wheelchair, Robert has chosen *to hear* the voices of the less fortunate – from his wheelchair! He has become a full-time volunteer, investing his energy, wit and wisdom in a multitude of local community projects.

Robert is, for me, a tiny window into the mystery of God-with-us.

**God, help me see reflections of your presence
in those around me.**

The child's father and mother were amazed at the things Simeon said about him. Simeon blessed them and said to Mary, his mother, "This child is chosen by God for the destruction and the salvation of many in Israel. He will be a sign from God which many people will speak against and so reveal their secret thoughts. And sorrow, like a sharp sword, will break your own heart."

Luke 2: 33-35

> "Sorrow…will break your own heart."

Living with sorrow

How could Mary continue? To watch her own child move away from her, out into the world. To see him rejected, mocked, tortured and crucified. How could she survive this horror? How could she carry so much hurt and still have room in her broken heart for the pain of other people?

And as we live and suffer, how can we become wise and loving, not hardened and bitter?

My friend lost her husband and raised the family alone. Yet her laughter was infectious, her generosity boundless and her tears real when others were in grief. Her life enriched us all. Perhaps, if I do not turn from my own pain, I can feel the pain of others and touch them in their sorrow.

Dear God, help me to live with my own sorrow, so that I can help ease the sorrow of others.

Isa 50: 5-9; Ps 116; James 2: 14-18; Mk 8: 27-35

We are familiar with the names of the rich and famous, leaders of nations and sports stars. Thanks to the media, we know how these people look, act and live. But beyond the superficial, do we *really* know who they are?

It can be the same with our Christian faith. "I believe in God." "I follow the Ten Commandments." "I keep the doctrines and rules of the Church." But Jesus asks Peter, "Who do you say that I am?" This question follows us on our life journey, a quest to come to terms with the identity of Jesus. Who is Jesus *for me*? Where do I find him?

The New Testament gives us a glimpse into Jesus' identity. The answer to Saul's outrage against Christians is "I am Jesus, whom you are persecuting" (Acts 9). In the final judgment, Jesus says, "Just as you did it to one of the least of these, you did it to me" (Mt 25). Jesus identifies himself with the persecuted and the poor. He identifies with the hungry, the thirsty, the naked and the captive because he is good news to them.

Jesus is known through the gospels and in the sacramental presence of the eucharist. We find him in the Body of Christ, the body of the poor and those who struggle for justice. At eucharist, we can ask ourselves, "With whom do we identify?"

**Jesus, I want to know you.
Open my eyes to who you really are.**

A Roman officer had a servant who was very dear to him; the man was sick and about to die. When the officer heard about Jesus, he sent some Jewish elders to ask him to come and heal his servant....

[Jesus] was not far from the house when the officer sent friends to tell him, "Sir, don't trouble yourself. I do not deserve to have you come into my house.... Just give the order, and my servant will get well. I, too... have soldiers under me. I order this one, 'Go!' and he goes; I order that one, 'Come!' and he comes...."

Jesus was surprised and said, "I tell you, I have never found faith like this, not even in Israel!" The messengers went back to the officer's house and found his servant well.

Luke 7: 1-10

> "I order this one, 'Go!' and he goes..."

True humility

This Roman officer is someone I have met many times – sometimes simply by looking in the mirror.

Our modern world is full of people who say, "Go!" and someone goes, and "Come!" and someone comes. We all seem to have someone above us who tells us what to do, and people below us whom we tell what to do. That's the natural way the world is, we believe. That's reality. Freedom, of course, is having as few people as possible telling us what to do and as many people as possible doing what we tell them.

Now here's the difference. The Roman officer knows his real place in the world and is humble. We are puffed up with the illusion of our importance and are vain.

Lord, the Roman soldier could see clearly who he was. Give me the wisdom to see myself truly, as I am.

J ust as [Jesus] arrived at the gate of the town, a funeral procession was coming out. The dead man was the only son of a woman who was a widow, and a large crowd from the town was with her. When the Lord saw her, his heart was filled with pity for her, and he said to her, "Don't cry." Then he walked over and touched the coffin, and the men carrying it stopped. Jesus said, "Young man! Get up, I tell you!" The dead man sat up and began to talk, and Jesus gave him back to his mother.

They all were filled with fear and praised God. "A great prophet has appeared among us!" they said; "God has come to save his people!" This news about Jesus went out through all the country and the surrounding territory.

Luke 7: 11-17

> "God has come to save his people!"

God's presence

"The man who laughs / Has simply not yet had / The terrible news" wrote one of my favourite playwrights, Bertolt Brecht, in a time of war. Filled with contradictory characters and paradoxical extremes, his work echoes realities in my own world.

I recall times when I've felt like the widow in today's reading: lost and quite alone. When I think that nothing could make things worse, inevitably the other shoe falls: a contract is lost, a diagnosis is confirmed.

But then, in the most surprising ways, I am lifted from my self-concern. Not by dramatic miracles, but by "envelopes of light," as a songwriter describes them – by a surprise phone call, a breathtaking sunrise, a sudden smile, a piece of music that says gently, "Don't cry, I am here."

**When I need you most, Lord, may I recognize
your grace-filled presence in the details of my life.**

Love is patient and kind; it is not jealous or conceited or proud; love is not ill-mannered or selfish or irritable; love does not keep a record of wrongs; love is not happy with evil, but is happy with the truth. Love never gives up; and its faith, hope and patience never fail.

When I was a child, my speech, feelings, and thinking were all those of a child; now that I am an adult, I have no more use for childish ways. What we see now is like a dim image in a mirror; then we shall see face-to-face. What I know now is only partial; then it will be complete – as complete as God's knowledge of me. Meanwhile these three remain: faith, hope and love; and the greatest of these is love.

I Corinthians 12: 31 – 13: 13

"Love never gives up…"

Choosing to love

I had to pass an examination to get a driver's licence. I went through extensive interviews before I got a job. My spouse and I took counselling before we married. But there are no requirements at all to meet for bringing a child into the world. Why?

Perhaps because parenting is too complex for any test. There are no rehearsals to prepare parents for when a daughter falls in with the wrong crowd, or a son has an accident….

Someone told me once, "Love opens your heart to be hurt."

Joan and I didn't know what we were doing when we had children. But we did our best. Even when it hurt. Because we loved them. And we always will. No matter what…

**Love is never easy, God.
But you know this much better than I do.**

I n that town was a woman who lived a sinful life. She heard that Jesus was eating in the Pharisee's house, so she brought an alabaster jar full of perfume and stood behind Jesus, by his feet, crying and wetting his feet with her tears. Then she dried his feet with her hair, kissed them, and poured the perfume on them. When the Pharisee saw this, he said, "If this man really were a prophet, he would know what kind of sinful life this woman lives!"

Jesus said, "I came into your home, and you gave me no water for my feet, but she has washed my feet with her tears and dried them with her hair…. I tell you, then, the great love she has shown proves that her many sins have been forgiven."

Luke 7: 36-50

> "…a woman who lived a sinful life."

Sin and forgiveness

I am envious of this woman. She can admit she is a sinner and can also grieve over it. Like most modern people, the word "sin" is not one I feel comfortable using. Words like "broken" and "wounded" work better. There's something about them that makes me seem, well, less responsible for my "sins." After all, broken or wounded things have usually had things done to them, rather than by them.

Today's reading reminds me of a terrible sin I committed many years ago. A friend needed help and I did not give it. Now that friend has died and I can never give it. Will there be forgiveness for me?

Lord, I am sorry for the good I do not do.
Please forgive me.

I urge you to live a life that measures up to the standard God set when he called you. Be always humble, gentle, and patient. Show your love by being tolerant with one another. Do your best to preserve the unity which the Spirit gives by means of the peace that binds you together....

Each one of us has received a special gift in proportion to what Christ has given.... It was he who "gave gifts to people"; he appointed some to be apostles, others to be prophets, others to be evangelists, others to be pastors and teachers. He did this to prepare all God's people for the work of Christian service, in order to build up the body of Christ. And so we shall all come together to that oneness in our faith and in our knowledge of the Son of God; we shall become mature people, reaching to the very height of Christ's full stature.

Ephesians 4: 1-7, 11-13

> "It was he who 'gave gifts to people...'"

Hidden gifts

What a wonder it is – watching our children grow! My husband and I know this time of early childhood will pass quickly. Sometimes we are tempted to dream away the present by wondering about the future. What will our children be when they grow up? Will they be successful and happy?

One thing we know for sure: the source of their talents is a mystery. When we try to pin down what gifts we have passed on to our children, we are often surprised. They have gifts that are beyond our abilities and interests, that challenge us to grow in new directions.

God willing, they will develop into the people God intended them to be. May I have the wisdom to step out of the way.

**May all children be given the space
to grow into their God-given gifts.**

273

S omeone will ask, "How can the dead be raised to life? What kind of body will they have?" You fool! When you plant a seed in the ground, it does not sprout to life unless it dies. And what you plant is a bare seed, perhaps a grain of wheat or some other grain, not the full-bodied plant that will later grow up....

This is how it will be when the dead are raised to life. When the body is buried, it is mortal; when raised, it will be immortal. When buried, it is ugly and weak; when raised, it will be beautiful and strong. When buried, it is a physical body; when raised, it will be a spiritual body.... Those who belong to the earth are like the one who was made of earth; those who are of heaven are like the one who came from heaven.

I Corinthians 15: 35-37, 42-50

"...it does not sprout to life unless it dies."

Transformation

I slap a lump of ordinary greyish material on my wheel, centre it and pull up the sides to make a bowl. After the new shape is fired in an electric kiln, the clay turns hard and white. I cover it with a dull, chalky substance and place it in an outdoor raku kiln. When the kiln reaches the appropriate temperature, I pull out the vessel, still red hot, and place it in a nest of leaves and papers that immediately catch fire. Changes in temperature cause the glaze to crackle as smoke from the fire turns the pattern black. It is then plunged into cold water and the soot is rubbed away to reveal a beautiful bowl.

Transformation can be painful and unsettling, but sometimes the results can't be achieved any other way.

God, help me to trust the transformations in my life.

Wis 2: 12, 17-20; Ps 54; James 3: 16 – 4: 3; Mk 9: 30-37

Few of Jesus' statements are as puzzling as this one: "Whoever wants to be first must be last of all and servant of all." It ran against the grain in his day as much as it does today. Is it not a recipe for poor self-esteem? For being a perpetual doormat? For being exploited by everyone?

This statement invites us into God's life in a particular way. The early Christian hymn recorded in the letter to the Philippians talks about how Jesus emptied himself and became obedient to death on the cross. In response, God exalted him. The hymn describes the dynamic that is at the heart of life in the Trinity: each person of God is constantly pouring out the divine self in love and service to the other persons. Each person is constantly welcoming the other, ceding their place to the other, making room.

When we were baptized, we were incorporated into this self-emptying life of love that is the Trinity. We're already part of that dynamic. But it requires a radical "un-selfing" on our part that only makes sense in a religious world in which the person who loses their life will find it.

What makes this not just tolerable, but life-giving, is that every one of us is called to this un-selfing. Just as the persons of the Trinity are, we who live in God are called to give our all on this path to glory.

Holy Trinity, you model for us how to love.
Help me to love in this way.

Lord, who may enter your Temple?
Who may worship on Zion, your sacred hill?
Those who obey God in everything
and always do what is right,
whose words are true and sincere,
and who do not slander others.
They do no wrong to their friends
nor spread rumours about their neighbours....
They always do what they promise,
no matter how much it may cost.
They make loans without charging interest
and cannot be bribed to testify against the innocent.
Whoever does these things will always be secure.   *Psalm 15: 1-5*

"Those who obey God in everything..."

Everyday saints

The psalmist's portrait of a person of unswerving integrity reminds me of my mother, who died over 20 years ago. A post-war British immigrant, she was an unassuming person who never sought the limelight. Yet everything she did reflected her strength of character and her sheer, ordinary goodness. Widowed in her 40s, she rose to the challenges of raising two children on her own. Her professional life as a nurse was marked by a compassion that extended far beyond duty. Her family and her many friends knew she could always be counted on for love, support, forgiveness and encouragement. She was, I think (though she would laugh at the notion), a holy person.

My mother's example offers me hope when I am faced with my daily responsibilities – that I, too, may share in God's holiness.

Lord, thank you for the everyday saints and heroes you send into my life.

Jesus' mother and brothers came to him, but were unable to join him because of the crowd. Someone said to Jesus, "Your mother and brothers are standing outside and want to see you."

Jesus said to them all, "My mother and brothers are those who hear the word of God and obey it."

Luke 8: 19-21

"Your mother and brothers are standing outside…"

Redefining family

This story used to make me squirm: "Gentle Jesus, meek and mild" more or less dismissing his family – and not because they've done anything wrong. After all, they simply want to see him. His words seem harsh and unfair.

But I'm a parent now whose children are closer to independent adult life than to the dependent life of a child. The time is coming when they will go.

Today I hear no anger in Jesus' voice. Maybe there is even a little sadness as he speaks. Now I think the story is simply telling us that we all grow up. Children have to leave home and make their own way in the world and families have to redefine themselves. That's the nature of human life.

Lord, I have held my children close.
Help me to let them go.

One of the elders asked me, "Who are these people dressed in white robes, and where do they come from?" "I don't know, sir. You do," I answered.

He said, "These are the people who have come safely through the terrible persecution. They have washed their robes and made them white with the blood of the Lamb. That is why they stand before God's throne and serve him day and night in his temple. He who sits on the throne will protect them with his presence. Never again will they hunger or thirst; neither sun nor any scorching heat will burn them, because the Lamb, who is in the centre of the throne, will be their shepherd, and he will guide them to springs of life-giving water. And God will wipe away every tear from their eyes."

Revelation 7: 9-17

> "And God will wipe away every tear from their eyes."

We all cry

"And God will wipe away every tear from their eyes." People of every race, tribe and nation: what do we have in common? I guess one answer is that we all cry. In a lifetime, we cry so many tears.

Tears of laughter, of pain, of joy, of loneliness. Tears for newborn babies, tears for dead sons. Tears for new brides, tears for spouses left alone. Tears for old friends we'll never see again.

Arabs cry, and Jews. Serbs cry, too, and Croats. Children cry, and mothers. And so do fathers cry, on cold winter nights, alone at kitchen tables. Even Jesus cried, we are told, in Gethsemane.

When others cry, I'll try to remember they're just like me – a child of God, in need of God's healing touch.

Dear God, help me dry the tears from others' eyes.

Teach us how short our life is,
so that we may become wise.
How much longer will your anger last?
Have pity, O Lord, on your servants!
Fill us each morning with your constant love,
so that we may sing and be glad all our life....
Lord our God, may your blessings be with us.
Give us success in all we do!

Psalm 90: 3-6, 12-14, 17

> "Teach us how short our life is..."

The gift of time

Recently, a well-meaning relative gave my four-year-old daughter a clock. "It's time you learned to tell the time!" she claimed. I cringed. This period of life when clocks have no power over us is so short! My daughter wanders through the day oblivious to schedules and deadlines. I delight when she is surprised that the day is coming to an end. (Although I admit this can be frustrating when we are trying to get out the door!)

I know there is a wisdom that comes with understanding that life is short. My daughter will learn this soon enough. For now, I hope to let her enjoy the magic of living in the moment. And I will try to meet her there.

Lord, help me to truly live this moment.

God sets the time for birth and the time for death,
the time for planting and the time for pulling up,
the time for killing and the time for healing,
the time for tearing down and the time for building.
God sets the time for sorrow and the time for joy,
the time for mourning and the time for dancing,
the time for making love and the time for not making love,
the time for kissing and the time for not kissing.
God sets the time for finding and the time for losing,
the time for saving and the time for throwing away,
the time for tearing and the time for mending,
the time for silence and the time for talk.
God sets the time for love and the time for hate,
the time for war and the time for peace....
God has set the right time for everything.   *Ecclesiastes 3: 1-11*

"God has set the right time for everything."

The right time

The measured poetry of today's reading is a contrast to the pattern of my life. Just to read it slows me down, causing me to pause and reconsider. Its simple rhythm calls me into rare and quiet reflection.

I am known as one of those people who like to "make things happen." This, however, has been both a blessing and a curse. Sometimes it's my saving grace; sometimes it gets me into trouble.

In my effort to take charge, at times I've overlooked subtleties, stepped on toes and put my foot in my mouth – which, of course, has led to swallowing a lot of pride. This reading reminds me that the rhythm of God's wisdom is constant – even when I can't hear it.

God, you have given me ears.
May I use them to tune into your rhythm.

I thank you, Lord, with all my heart;
I sing praise to you before the gods.
I face your holy Temple,
bow down, and praise your name
because of your constant love and faithfulness,
because you have shown that your name
and your commands are supreme.
You answered me when I called to you;
with your strength you strengthened me.
All the kings in the world will praise you, Lord,
because they have heard your promises.
They will sing about what you have done
and about your great glory.   *Psalm 138: 1-5*

"With your strength you strengthened me."

In times of need

A winter of illness had drawn me to the point of despair. Unable to attend to the roles and responsibilities that had long defined my life, I felt worthless. There was little left to give me a sense of purpose or meaning. Hopelessness and helplessness became my daily companions.

Into that pocket of despondency drifted a memory of God's promise of constant love. Despite my emptiness, this memory touched my heart and delighted me. With it came the reassurance that I did not have to rely on my own strength, but that I could trust God's strength. God's love and faithfulness are constant.

Initially, I felt overwhelmed. Then, as I opened myself to God's promise, hope surged through me, bringing me to life again.

**Lord, may I always turn to you,
especially when I feel weak and without hope.**

Num 11: 25-29; Ps 19; James 5: 1-6; Mk 9: 38-43, 45, 47-48

We are all called to be prophets: to announce the good news of God's deep love for each one of us. How wonderful it would be if we could be crystal clear in the announcement of this message, particularly in the behaviour we show to others.

The first reading, from Numbers, provides insight into the working of God's spirit through us. The reading highlights our tendency

to try to define clearly who is a prophet and who can speak on behalf of God. Yet the suggestion in the readings from Numbers and Mark is that it is our actions that are meaningful – not whether we are part of some inner circle.

So who can speak on behalf of God? We live in times when the rich and famous are often portrayed as the blessed. Yet the letter from James suggests the opposite. Any who have riches are to use them for the benefit of others.

When we examine Jesus' words, we realize that our actions are more important than a simple claim to follow Jesus. As followers of Jesus, we are called to bring blessing to others. The life and love we receive from God are intimately connected to our call to be prophets and our life of service in the body of Christ.

Lord, it's easy to say that I follow you.
Help me to live that call.

An argument broke out among the disciples as to which one of them was the greatest. Jesus knew what they were thinking, so he took a child, stood him by his side, and said to them, "Whoever welcomes this child in my name, welcomes me; and whoever welcomes me, also welcomes the one who sent me. For the one who is least among you all is the greatest."

John spoke up, "Master, we saw a man driving out demons in your name, and we told him to stop, because he doesn't belong to our group." "Do not try to stop him," Jesus said to him and to the other disciples, "because whoever is not against you is for you."

Luke 9: 46-50

"Whoever welcomes this child in my name…"

Seeing the person

These words sound great from the pulpit: "The least among you all is the greatest!" Then I leave church and drive home. I go past people sleeping on the street and squeegee kids pressing me to give them money. So many people with so many needs. How can I possibly "welcome" them all?

Jesus' words are so easy to agree with, but so hard to live. The demands of life seem to conspire to make us treat each other like objects.

Every Saturday morning I stop for coffee. I'm usually part of a long lineup, but the woman behind the counter treats each of us with genuine good humour and kindness. In her own way she shows me the truth: recognize and treat others as persons, just like me.

**Lord, help me stop and consider my actions.
Have I forgotten that people, indeed, come first?**

At that time the disciples came to Jesus, asking, "Who is the greatest in the kingdom of heaven?" So Jesus called a child to come and stand in front of them, and said, "I assure you that unless you change and become like children, you will never enter the kingdom of heaven. The greatest in the kingdom of heaven is the one who humbles himself and becomes like this child. And whoever welcomes in my name one such child as this, welcomes me.

"See that you don't despise any of these little ones. Their angels in heaven, I tell you, are always in the presence of my Father in heaven."

Matthew 18: 1-5, 10

> "...unless you change and become like children..."

Childlike wonder

Buddy is a four-month-old Jack Russell terrier that nuzzled his way into my heart two months ago. Now I can't imagine life without him.

Someday I may write a book entitled *Everything I Needed to Know, I Learned from My Dog*. Why? Because Buddy is helping me to rediscover my child's heart. Watching him romp and play, I throw adult caution to the wind and join in his fun. Through his explorations and adventures, I realize that every tree, every bush, every blade of grass is magical. Buddy lives in the present moment and revels in each new discovery. He also shows no hesitation when lavishing his love and devotion upon me.

Wonder. Passion. Delight. My child's heart struggles to break free, to live again!

God, today may I rediscover wonder, delight and magic in my life.

As they went on their way, a man said to Jesus, "I will follow you wherever you go." Jesus said to him, "Foxes have holes, and birds have nests, but the Son of Man has no place to lie down and rest." He said to another man, "Follow me." But that man said, "Sir, first let me go back and bury my father." Jesus answered, "Let the dead bury their own dead. You go and proclaim the Kingdom of God." Someone else said, "I will follow you, sir; but first let me go and say good-bye to my family." Jesus said to him, "Anyone who starts to plow and then keeps looking back is of no use for the Kingdom of God."

Luke 9: 57-62

> "I will follow you wherever you go."

Faith and understanding

My youngest son is a "spirited" child. He lives at the extremes of his emotions, and his actions usually follow suit! While I delight in channelling the marvellous creativity of his passions to goodness, I fear the potential of his misdirected energies.

My son is a lot like the disciples in today's reading. James and John have an endearing zeal, with energy and faith in what they can accomplish in Jesus' name. But they don't yet understand exactly what he is asking of them.

Jesus tells his would-be followers what it takes to "get with the program" of his kingdom: immediate, wholehearted, unconditional commitment. Can we place whatever we have – passions, talents and family – at the service of whatever he asks?

Lord, all that I am and have is yours today.
Help me to listen for what you want of me!

Y ou are my friends! Take pity on me!
The hand of God has struck me down.
Why must you persecute me the way God does?
Haven't you tormented me enough?
How I wish that someone
would remember my words
and record them in a book!
Or with a chisel carve my words in stone
and write them so that they would last forever.
But I know there is someone in heaven
who will come at last to my defence.
Even after my skin is eaten by disease,
while still in this body I will see God.
I will see him with my own eyes,
and he will not be a stranger.   *Job 19: 21-27*

> "…and he will not be a stranger."

Secure in God's love

I was deeply hurt the first time she asked, "Who is that man?" She meant me, her son-in-law of 15 years. As her memory disintegrates, names, words, ideas become increasingly difficult to articulate.

At first there were flashes of anger and frustration when she was still aware of the depth of her difficulties. Now her visitors, even her four daughters, must constantly remind her who they are.

Ninety years old and, like Job, weary and broken, she lives in a world she can no longer comprehend. Her stories fragment; today, yesterday and long ago blur. Now we must remember for her. Nevertheless, this painful journey takes her ever closer to the one who will never be a stranger to her.

God, as I become a stranger to those whose memories fade, hold me securely in your love.

Lord, you have examined me
and you know me.
You know everything I do;
from far away you understand
all my thoughts.
You see me,
whether I am working or resting;
you know all my actions...
You created every part of me;
you put me together
in my mother's womb.
I praise you because you are to be feared;
all you do is strange and wonderful.
I know it with all my heart.

Psalm 139: 1-3, 7-10, 13-14

> "...you put me together in my mother's womb."

God's love revealed

Today's psalm makes me think of a friend who was born with a life-threatening birth defect. She tells me how, for many years, the words of this psalm made her sad, and even angry at God.

Why did God – who created every part of her – let her body develop as it did? What sort of loving God would allow this to happen?

Strangely enough, the answers to my friend's questions came from her body itself. The limitations she experienced taught her to face the challenges and setbacks that life brings us, and to turn them into opportunities for growth. Within her "birth defect," my friend discovered God truly loves her – as she is. And this gives her comfort.

**God, give me the courage to face my limitations
and learn from them.**

Jesus was filled with joy by the Holy Spirit and said, "Father, Lord of heaven and earth! I thank you because you have shown to the unlearned what you have hidden from the wise and learned. Yes, Father, this was how you were pleased to have it happen.

"My Father has given me all things. No one knows who the Son is except the Father, and no one knows who the Father is except the Son and those to whom the Son chooses to reveal him."

Then Jesus turned to the disciples and said to them, "How fortunate you are to see the things you see! I tell you that many prophets and kings wanted to see what you see, but they could not, and to hear what you hear, but they did not."

Luke 10: 17-24

> "…this was how you were pleased to have it happen."

Trusting in God's gift

Tensely I watched as my daughter began riding her first two-wheeler. I had come to rely on those little training wheels, and was reluctant to let them go. "Whoa, a little wobbly there, honey… Ooops, don't go too fast now." She, on the other hand, was much more brash about the outcome of this whole·experience. "Don't hold me, Daddy! I'm okay. Let go!"

How I wish I could! Like many self-appointed "wise and learned" types, I'm bound by my fears. My little one, having conquered her fear of the dark, of "boogeymen," and now of falling, was once again utterly determined to ride on freely. Her trust in God's gift of life was as solid as a rock.

"Wise and learned" indeed.

**God, renew me and help me to see the world again –
with a child's wild passion and love of life.**

Gen 2: 7, 8, 18-24; Ps 128; Heb 2: 9-11; Mk 10: 2-16

When the United Nations set its Millennium Development Goals [www.un.org/millenniumgoals] in 2000, many of these addressed the plight of our world's children, a sign that children in our time are among the least in society, without power, status or even value. So it was in biblical times. Yet Jesus welcomes children and invites us to "receive the kingdom of God as a little child." Turning the least in our society away – children, women, displaced persons – will not bring us to the kingdom, for it belongs to them, too. The kingdom is a gift.

Today's readings offer another clue about the kingdom. In Genesis we are reminded that all living creatures have life through God; all creatures (humans, cattle, birds and animals) are created of the same stuff, the dust of the ground. The human gives a name to every creature given by God. Speaking another's name invokes a certain intimacy and establishes a relationship and responsibility toward the one named.

In today's gospel Jesus warns that it is hardness of hearts that ruptures relationships between man and woman who were created to be one flesh, suitable companions for each other. Our attitude of heart has the potential to support or break apart any relationship.

Let us walk this earth with humility, in relationships marked by love, acceptance, justice and responsibility. In this way we might hope to be grateful recipients of the kingdom of God.

God of love, soften my heart to hear and live your word.

The teacher of the Law asked Jesus, "Who is my neighbour?" Jesus answered, "There was once a man who was going down from Jerusalem to Jericho when robbers attacked him, stripped him, and beat him up, leaving him half dead.... A priest was going down that road; but when he saw the man, he walked on by on the other side. A Levite also came there, went over and looked at the man, and then walked on by on the other side. But a Samaritan who was travelling that way came upon the man, and when he saw him, his heart was filled with pity. He went over to him, poured oil and wine on his wounds and bandaged them."

Luke 10: 25-37

> "...his heart was filled with pity."

Not just a nice story

My high school English class got into a discussion about bullying. One of the school's leading athletes told about seeing others publicly humiliated in the locker room. The most vocal social justice advocate told about racial slurs on the bus. When I asked them what they did, they were silent. They squirmed. "It's part of life." "What can we do?" "They won't listen."

I kept those kids after class, got the names of the bullies and spoke to them. I did it for the bullied kids, but more so to challenge those "star" students. In our look-out-for-number-one world, they need to see adults living their faith. They need to see that the Good Samaritan isn't just a nice story!

**Lord, let me model your love for others –
in my actions as well as in my words.**

As Jesus and his disciples went on their way, he came to a village where a woman named Martha welcomed him in her home. She had a sister named Mary, who sat down at the feet of the Lord and listened to his teaching. Martha was upset over all the work she had to do, so she came and said, "Lord, don't you care that my sister has left me to do all the work by myself? Tell her to come and help me!"

The Lord answered her, "Martha, Martha! You are worried and troubled over so many things, but just one is needed. Mary has chosen the right thing, and it will not be taken away from her."

Luke 10: 38-42

> "You are worried and troubled over so many things…"

God and my messy life

My daughter has a book about an owl that, one night, is delighted to see the moon rising. But when the moon seems to follow him home, Owl gets increasingly alarmed. "You must stay up over the sea, where you look so fine," he says. "You really must not come home with me. My house is small. You would not fit through the door."

I'm a lot like Owl. I am happy for God to stay "up over the sea," or safely in church. But what if God wants to come home with me, into my life? It's a bit of a mess; I'm not ready. I don't have much to offer.

Like Martha, when I am "troubled over so many things," I can't hear what God is saying.

Lord, silence the voice that says, "I am not good enough." Help me to listen to your voice instead.

One day Jesus was praying in a certain place. When he had finished, one of his disciples said to him, "Lord, teach us to pray, just as John taught his disciples."

Jesus said to them, "When you pray, say this: 'Father: May your holy name be honoured; may your kingdom come. Give us day by day the food we need. Forgive us our sins, for we forgive everyone who does us wrong. And do not bring us to hard testing.'"

Luke 11: 1-4

> "When you pray, say this…"

Searching for the right words

The poet Tennyson has given me an insight into the risks of reading Scripture. He wrote: "Words, like Nature, half reveal/And half conceal the Soul within." Today's reading both reveals and conceals my understanding of God.

When I think of God, I don't think of my "father." Now don't get me wrong; I loved and respected my father. And, surprisingly, I speak of him more now after his death than I did when he was alive.

But when I pray, I struggle to find the right words with which to address God. God is rarely the "Dad" of my quirky family story. God is certainly present – caring and accessible as my dad was. Yet God also remains a soul-challenging, word-defying mystery.

**Dear God, may I always search for ways
to communicate with you.**

Jesus said to his disciples, "I say to you: Ask, and you will receive; seek, and you will find; knock, and the door will be opened to you. For those who ask will receive, and those who seek will find, and the door will be opened to anyone who knocks. Would any of you who are fathers give your son a snake when he asks for fish? Or would you give him a scorpion when he asks for an egg? As bad as you are, you know how to give good things to your children. How much more, then, will the Father in heaven give the Holy Spirit to those who ask him!"

Luke 11:5-13

> "Ask, and you will receive..."

Keep knocking

"Daddy, look! Daddy, watch this!" No matter how tired or busy I am, and despite my body language that may say, "Don't bother me!" my children keep on seeking my attention. They keep knocking at the door. They seem to have an unquenchable faith in me – a stronger faith than I have in myself!

I grew up thinking a father had to be the strong, distant, silent type. Now that I'm a father, I'm trying to change this image – both for myself and as I seek an ever-attentive and caring God.

When God seems silent in my life, I tend to stop asking. I stop knocking at the door. If only I could have the kind of faith in God that my children have in me.

Dear God, give me the faith to keep on knocking at the door, even when you seem silent.

Others wanted to trap Jesus, so they asked him to perform a miracle to show that God approved of him. But Jesus knew what they were thinking, so he said to them, "Any country that divides itself into groups which fight each other will not last very long; a family divided against itself falls apart. So if Satan's kingdom has groups fighting each other, how can it last? You say that I drive out demons because Beelzebul gives me the power to do so. If this is how I drive them out, how do your followers drive them out? Your own followers prove that you are wrong! No, it is rather by means of God's power that I drive out demons, and this proves that the kingdom of God has already come to you. ...Anyone who is not for me is really against me; anyone who does not help me gather is really scattering...."

Luke 11:15-26

> "A family divided against itself falls apart."

Healing the division

How many of us experience "a divided family": divisions between siblings; between partners; between in-laws; between parents and children. Whatever the cause of the division, if left to fester, it takes on a life of its own. Feelings are hurt. Communications break down. Relationships falter. A family falls apart and all suffer.

But if things are turned around; if our differences are seen in light of our common goal; if "the kingdom of God has already come to you," then we cannot remain divided. We are united in God's love. With this truth in mind – truly central in our minds and hearts – we have the power to overcome the divisions that tear us apart.

Can I allow myself to be absorbed into God rather than being so self-absorbed?

God, give me the courage to go beyond the misunderstandings that I experience.

When Jesus had said this, a woman spoke up from the crowd and said to him, "How happy is the woman who bore you and nursed you!" But Jesus answered, "Rather, how happy are those who hear the word of God and obey it!"

Luke 11: 27-28

> "...happy are those who hear the word of God..."

True nurture

What is this woman in the crowd really saying? And why doesn't Jesus allow Mary, his mother, these few words of praise?

Jesus seems to be saying that it's not just the physical act of bearing and nursing a child that matters. What matters in my parenting is how I hear the word of God: in my children's questions and their searching. In their anger, sadness and hurt. In what they say and what they leave unsaid. In their eyes that plead for understanding. In their tight, angry bodies that need to be hugged and comforted.

Giving birth and caring for the physical needs of my children has come fairly easily to me. Nurturing their spirits – by hearing and responding to their deeper needs – is proving much harder.

God, grant me the strength to recognize your word as it is spoken today. May I respond with love.

Wis 7: 7-11; Ps 90; Heb 4: 12-13; Mk 10: 17-30

What is more important to you than anything else? For the young man in today's gospel it was his possessions. He knew and followed the commandments and wanted to inherit eternal life… but not if it meant giving up what he owned – which was exactly what it did mean in his case.

Jesus' statement that a camel can go through the eye of a needle more easily than a rich person can enter heaven goes against the common beliefs of his time (and often ours). People then believed that wealth was a sign of God's blessing. No wonder the disciples were shocked. To this day, people try to explain away the plain meaning of Jesus' words here. But Jesus knew that rich people often put their trust in what they have rather than in God.

Jesus demands a lot from his followers. In fact, he demands everything! If we wish to follow Jesus fully, then Jesus must be at the core of our lives. If family, career or some otherwise noble ideal is more important to us than Jesus, then that other thing is our god, not Jesus.

Jesus calls each of us to examine our lives and let go of anything that is more important to us than he is. The central focus will vary from person to person, but the call to follow Jesus at all costs remains the same for each of us.

Lord Jesus, help me to follow you with all my heart, without holding back.

"How evil are the people of this day! They ask for a miracle, but none will be given them except the miracle of Jonah. In the same way that the prophet Jonah was a sign for the people of Nineveh, so the Son of Man will be a sign for the people of this day. On the Judgment Day the Queen of Sheba will stand up and accuse the people of today, because she travelled all the way from her country to listen to King Solomon's wise teaching; and there is something here, I tell you, greater than Solomon. On the Judgment Day the people of Nineveh will stand up and accuse you, because they turned from their sins when they heard Jonah preach; and I assure you that there is something here greater than Jonah!"

Luke 11: 29-32

> "They ask for a miracle..."

Everyday miracles

Miracles happen every day – at least, if you believe the advertising industry. Sales pitches regularly offer "miraculous" remedies for every possible ailment – from insomnia to baldness to financial woes. If only life's problems could be so easily solved!

Miracles *do* happen, however. Sometimes it's just that I'm too busy, too bored or too depressed to notice.

In my first year of university there was a student from Malaysia in our residence. The first snowfall that autumn scarcely registered with most of us jaded Canadians. But Pui-Lin had never in her life seen snow! Wide-eyed wonder turned to delighted laughter as she ran outside to touch and taste this mysterious new substance. To Pui-Lin, clearly, that snowfall was a miracle!

God of wonder, open my eyes to the daily miracles, great and small, that reveal your presence in the world.

When Jesus finished speaking, a Pharisee invited him to eat with him; so he went in and sat down to eat. The Pharisee was surprised when he noticed that Jesus had not washed before eating. So the Lord said to him, "Now then, you Pharisees clean the outside of your cup and plate, but inside you are full of violence and evil. Fools! Did not God, who made the outside, also make the inside? But give what is in your cups and plates to the poor, and everything will be ritually clean for you."

Luke 11: 37-41

> "...you clean the outside of your cup and plate..."

Appearances are deceiving

Imagine a person who didn't care about appearances. I'm lucky to have known such a person. He was a junk man who wore green clothes and usually had three days' growth of beard and an ever-present "roll-your-own" stuck to his lower lip. He was thoroughly wonderful, kind and gentle; a great storyteller.

After my mother's funeral, Harry and his family came back to our house. Soon, everyone was listening to Harry's stories – as he knocked his ashes into the cuff of his pants, too polite to ask for the ashtray we had forgotten to offer. He brought life that day – as always, with grace.

Many people saw him, with his old clothes and five o'clock shadow, and didn't know they were looking at a king.

Dear God, let me not worry about what is on the outside – of me, or of those I meet.

I f the Spirit leads you, then you are not subject to the Law....

The Spirit produces love, joy, peace, patience, kindness, goodness, faithfulness, humility and self-control. There is no law against such things as these. And those who belong to Christ Jesus have put to death their human nature with all its passions and desires. The Spirit has given us life; he must also control our lives.

Galatians 5: 18-25

> "If the Spirit leads you..."

Room for the Spirit

One of my colleagues often uses the expression "Leave room for the Holy Spirit." At first this puzzled me, as she has the knack for covering all the bases. Everything she does seems brilliantly planned and executed.

Watching her work, I've come to recognize what makes her a remarkable mentor: she knows that she can't control everything. She listens to others with an intensity and respect that honours their input. I've seen her shift an agenda – with delight and enthusiasm – to incorporate the ideas of co-workers.

There have been times when I have been asked to take the helm and I've had my ego bruised when things didn't go my way. I must remember to leave room for the Holy Spirit to guide my words and actions.

Holy Spirit, lead me. I am willing to follow.

The Lord chose another seventy-two men and sent them out two by two, to go ahead of him to every town and place where he himself was about to go. He said to them… "Go! I am sending you like lambs among wolves. Don't take a purse or a beggar's bag or shoes…. Whenever you go into a house, first say, 'Peace be with this house.' If someone who is peace-loving lives there, let your greeting of peace remain on that person; if not, take back your greeting of peace. Stay in that same house, eating and drinking whatever they offer you, for workers should be given their pay. Don't move around from one house to another. Whenever you go into a town and are made welcome, eat what is set before you, heal the sick in that town, and say to the people there, 'The kingdom of God has come near you.'"

Luke 10: 1-9

> "Whenever you go into a house…"

Open to others

Jesus tells the disciples to go into a person's home and to decide if the person there is peace-loving or not. Spending time getting to know someone implies an openness, a vulnerability – and the possibility of getting hurt. But that's the risk that Jesus asks of his disciples. And of me.

Most of my friends would agree that I am too trusting. I meet people with an open heart, with a willingness to get to know them, and to be known by them.

There have been occasions when I've been hurt in my relationships. Yes, I know I could have been less trusting, and protected myself more. But getting to know others has helped me learn more about myself – and to become capable of loving more fully.

**Loving God, teach me to remain open to others –
in order to learn how to give more deeply of myself.**

Jesus said, "Be on guard against the yeast of the Pharisees – I mean their hypocrisy. Whatever is covered up will be uncovered, and every secret will be made known. So then, whatever you have said in the dark will be heard in broad daylight, and whatever you have whispered in private in a closed room will be shouted from the housetops.

"Do not be afraid of those who kill the body but cannot afterward do anything worse. I will show you whom to fear: fear God, who, after killing, has the authority to throw into hell....

"Aren't five sparrows sold for two pennies? Yet not one sparrow is forgotten by God. Even the hairs of your head have all been counted. So do not be afraid; you are worth much more than many sparrows!"

Luke 12: 1-7

> "...every secret will be made known."

Known and loved

Everything covered will be uncovered – what a terrifying thought! Imagine if all the petty arguments I've had with my partner, or the quiet cruelties I've practised when I was angry, were broadcast on the evening news. What if the contempt for certain people that sits secretly in my heart were made visible to all, especially the people I want most to impress! What if everyone could see how casually I have dismissed people I considered unimportant.

But this very threat makes Jesus' words about the sparrows that much more consoling. In spite of all my failings, I am deeply and intimately cherished by God, not just in my thoughts and my feelings, but in my body, too – down to the last hair on my head.

**Lord, help me to dig out all that is hidden
and give it over to you, trusting in your love.**

O Lord, our Lord,
your greatness is seen in all the world!
Your praise reaches up to the heavens;
it is sung by children and babies....
When I look at the sky, which you have made,
at the moon and the stars,
which you set in their places –
what are human beings, that you think of them;
mere mortals, that you care for them?
Yet you made them inferior only to yourself;
you crowned them with glory and honour.
You appointed them rulers
over everything you made.

Psalm 8: 1-6

> "When I look at the sky, which you have made…"

Words that last

The sky was big, the night was dark, and I was afraid. I stood on the shore of the lake, surrounded by dense forest, myriad stars reflecting on the water. Unfortunately, I was less aware of the beauty around me than of my fear of the walk through the bush to get back to the cabin.

I was with a friend who was everything I wasn't: big, strong and powerful. As we looked out at the lake, he said, "I'm scared of the dark." His words were a gift to me. If he was scared, I could be, too.

Like light still visible from stars long dead, his words remain, though he does not. Often when I'm scared, I remember his words, and they help me believe that I'm stronger than I feel.

**Lord, help me to accept myself as I am –
with my strengths and fears alike.**

Isa 53: 10-11; Ps 33; Heb 4: 14-16; Mk 10: 35-45

Listening to the scriptures can be a risky activity. There we are, sitting in church, just trying to slow down a little bit and collect some good thoughts to help us through the week.

Then we hear something like "whoever wishes to become great among you must be your servant" and we start to think there is another way to live. We imagine a world where we really act on our belief that each one of us is treasured by God. Before we know it, we feel uncomfortable about our search to make it to the top, to be the most important, to be well liked. We even ache about the troubles we have in our own lives. Church has become disturbing. Our ears and our hearts have been opened to hear the challenges and we struggle to respond.

We have a responsibility to help spread the message found in those disturbing, uncomfortable scriptures. But we don't have to be experts in evangelization – we are called to work with our brothers and sisters to build up the kingdom of God here in this place. We can go back to those scriptures to tap into the strength that is waiting for us as we "approach the throne of grace with boldness, so that we may receive mercy and find grace to help in time of need."

**God of wisdom, may your word disturb
and inspire and strengthen me.**

S ing to the Lord, all the world!
  Worship the Lord with joy;
  come before him with happy songs!
Acknowledge that the Lord is God.
He made us, and we belong to him;
we are his people, we are his flock.
Enter the Temple gates with thanksgiving;
go into its courts with praise.
Give thanks to him and praise him.
The Lord is good;
his love is eternal
and his faithfulness lasts forever.

Psalm 100: 1-5

> "He made us, and we belong to him…"

All God's children

When my friend visited Iraq, he took a lot of photographs. After he returned home, he showed us the pictures he'd taken. Most of them were of kids and families he'd come to know in Baghdad. One of the boys in the pictures reminded me of my grandson who lives in Chicago.

"He made us, and we belong to him." It's not hard for me to look at both my grandson and that little Iraqi boy and see that they are children of God. But there was a time when I read, "We are his people," and I thought that it applied only to Jews and, by extension, Christians.

Now I can see that it includes *every* person who lives and has ever lived. God cannot make some and not others.

**Lord, give me wisdom and courage,
that I may defend your creation with joyful, happy songs.**

B e ready for whatever comes, dressed for action and with your lamps lit, like servants who are waiting for their master to come back from a wedding feast. When he comes and knocks, they will open the door for him at once. How happy are those servants whose master finds them awake and ready when he returns! I tell you, he will take off his coat, have them sit down, and will wait on them. How happy they are if he finds them ready, even if he should come at midnight or even later!"

Luke 12: 35-38

> "Be ready for whatever comes..."

Ready for what comes

The table was set, dinner ready in the kitchen. But where were our out-of-town visitors? Their expected arrival time was 6 p.m. The clock ticked away, but no guests arrived. Worried and anxious, we finally ate some of the dinner, but we had little appetite. Then the telephone rang with reassuring news: our friends had been held up by bad weather and would be arriving eventually!

When they finally knocked on the door, at midnight or even later, the weary travellers were comforted to find us awake and eager to greet them.

When we're talking about friends and house guests, it's easy to be ready for whatever comes. What about other, less welcome visitors – sickness, bad luck, unemployment – that also show up sooner or later on our doorsteps?

**O Lord, help me to be ready
for whatever is waiting for me.**

I was made a servant of the gospel by God's special gift…. I am less than the least of all God's people; yet God gave me this privilege of taking to the Gentiles the Good News about the infinite riches of Christ, and of making all people see how God's secret plan is to be put into effect. God, who is the Creator of all things, kept his secret hidden through all the past ages, in order that at the present time, the angelic rulers and powers in the heavenly world might learn of his wisdom in all its different forms. God did this according to his eternal purpose, which he achieved through Christ Jesus our Lord. In union with Christ and through our faith in him we have the boldness to go into God's presence with all confidence.

Ephesians 3: 1-12

"…with all confidence."

God's special gift

Henri Nouwen tells this story: While living and working within a community of adults with developmental disabilities, he was invited to speak at a national conference on the meaning of ministry. Bob, a member of Henri's community, travelled with him to the conference, as he sometimes did.

At the end of Henri's talk, Bob unexpectedly joined Henri at the podium and made a short, impromptu presentation of his own. It was not eloquent or profound by most people's measures, but it said more about the meaning of ministry than all of Henri's well-crafted words.

Bob's boldness was the clearest witness possible to the welcome he felt, both from Henri and from God. Indeed, he brought the Good News of Christ to the conference participants that day!

**God, may I help one person today discover
the confidence that comes from experiencing your love.**

I ask God to give you power through his Spirit to be strong in your inner selves, and I pray that Christ will make his home in your hearts through faith. I pray that you may have your roots and foundation in love, so that you, together with all God's people, may have the power to understand how broad and long, how high and deep, is Christ's love. Yes, may you come to know his love – although it can never be fully known – and so be completely filled with the very nature of God.

To him who by means of his power working in us is able to do so much more than we can ever ask for, or even think of: to God be the glory in the church and in Christ Jesus for all time, forever and ever! Amen.

Ephesians 3: 13-21

> "...have your roots and foundation in love..."

Rooted in love

When asked *how* I became interested in spirituality, I paused, then replied, "Through my parents." And I explained how we'd pick lily-of-the-valley to place before the statue of Mary each May. And during Advent the little stable that my father built stood empty, waiting for each wooden figure to arrive in turn. Epiphany was celebrated with a special pie: the one who found the dried pea would be "king" for the evening! Easter meant hot cross buns and special treats.

But beneath all these "traditions," one memory stands out. Every evening my mother would sit on our beds and read from the Bible. Her love for the scriptures has shaped my own search for meaning, helping me discover the height and the breadth of God's love.

**Thank you, God, for those who have shown,
and who continue to reveal, your love for our world.
May I do the same for others.**

Jesus said, "When you see a cloud coming up in the west, at once you say that it is going to rain – and it does. And when you feel the south wind blowing, you say that it is going to get hot – and it does. Hypocrites! You can look at the earth and the sky and predict the weather; why, then, don't you know the meaning of this present time?

"Why do you not judge for yourselves the right thing to do? If someone brings a lawsuit against you and takes you to court, do your best to settle the dispute before you get to court. If you don't, you will be dragged before the judge, who will hand you over to the police, and you will be put in jail... until you pay the last penny of your fine."

Luke 12:54-59

"You can look at the earth and the sky..."

Signs of the times

When I was growing up on the Pacific coast, we knew how to predict the weather. "If you can see the mountains," we said, "it's going to rain. If you can't see the mountains, it *is* raining."

Jesus cites similar sayings from his own time. But then he challenges his listeners: "Why do you read weather signs, but not the signs of the times?" Perhaps they were in denial – to use a psychological term invented 20 centuries later!

People in denial refuse to recognize signs. When my mother was dying, the signs were clear: increasing shortness of breath, lapses into unconsciousness, loss of lucidity. But my father and I couldn't accept them – until the telephone call came, in the middle of the night.

I wonder what I may be in denial about these days.

**If I don't hear you speaking, Lord, is it because
I don't want to hear your message?**

J esus told them this parable: "There was once a man who had a fig tree growing in his vineyard. He went looking for figs on it but found none. So he said to his gardener, 'Look, for three years I have been coming here looking for figs on this fig tree, and I haven't found any. Cut it down! Why should it go on using up the soil?' But the gardener answered, 'Leave it alone, sir, just one more year; I will dig around it and put in some fertilizer. Then if the tree bears figs next year, so much the better; if not, then you can have it cut down.'"

Luke 13: 1-9

> "Leave it alone, sir, just one more year..."

Left alone to grow

I transplanted a tree once. Soon, however, it looked quite dead. I kept watering it, but then I stopped. The next spring, what did I see? New growth! It needed time, some nutrients – sometimes it takes a while for fertilizer to work.

People can be like that, too. My friend Harry teaches a young woman. She's had a tough life. Not one high school credit. Lots of piercings, though: ears, nose – you name it. Not many smiles, either. But boy, can that kid write. She's just finishing her high school credits now. I saw her this morning and she smiled. She really did. And said she wants to be a journalist.

Many people had "cut her down," given up on her. Harry? He gave her a little time... and some fertilizer.

Dear God, when I see people who appear to be dead, don't let me cut too quickly.

Jer 31: 7-9; Ps 126; Heb 5: 1-6; Mk 10: 46-52

Sometimes, in the psalms, we cry out to God to come and save us. In today's readings, we proclaim the great God who has kept his promise to do so. Jeremiah reminds us of God's promise in the first reading; Jesus' cure of Bartimaeus in the gospel is a sign that God, in Jesus, is indeed doing great things among the people.

In the words of Jeremiah, God promises to gather his people and bring them home, even the blind and the lame. In the gospel, Jesus does just that. Jesus cures Bartimaeus of his blindness and frees him to go his own way. But the gospel tells us that Bartimaeus followed Jesus on Jesus' way instead. Jesus is indeed gathering the people of God.

At today's celebration of the eucharist, this work of Jesus continues. Look around. Who is present? If we look carefully we may see people from the farthest parts of the earth gathered into this one assembly. We see people of all ages and abilities. We have come through the waters of baptism to feast at the Lord's table. Together we cry out for our needs and the needs of the world and we are consoled at the table of God's word. On our lips are songs of joy, because God has done great things for us, each and every one.

**Generous God, you always keep your promises.
I trust in you.**

B e kind and tender-hearted to one another, and forgive one another, as God has forgiven you through Christ.

Since you are God's dear children, you must try to be like him. Your life must be controlled by love, just as Christ loved us and gave his life for us as a sweet-smelling offering and sacrifice that pleases God....

Do not let anyone deceive you with foolish words; it is because of these very things that God's anger will come upon those who do not obey him. So have nothing at all to do with such people. You yourselves used to be in the darkness, but since you have become the Lord's people, you are in the light. So you must live like people who belong to the light.

Ephesians 4: 32 – 5: 8

> "Be kind and tender-hearted to one another..."

Kind and tender-hearted

"Everyone here is so kind!" exclaimed my son. Just days into our summer holidays on Prince Edward Island, he'd noticed how gentle and polite people were with one another. The Island – with its rolling hills, spectacular ocean views and slower pace of life – seemed to work its magic on me, too. Before long I'd noticed that I was treating others with greater kindness and consideration also.

Back from our holidays, I easily slipped into the pressure-cooker of work deadlines and sports schedules, homework and music lessons. Now, as we approach the shorter, darker days of winter, I recall the healing brought by the sea, the sunshine and the Islanders' kindness. And I hope I can bring healing to others by being kinder and more tender-hearted today.

Lord, heal my heart so I can bring your healing love to those who live in darkness.

Happy are those who obey the Lord,
who live by his commands.
Your work will provide for your needs;
you will be happy and prosperous.
Your wife will be like a fruitful vine in your home,
and your children will be like young olive trees around your table.
A man who obeys the Lord
will surely be blessed like this.
May the Lord bless you from Zion!
May you see Jerusalem prosper
all the days of your life!

Psalm 128: 1-5

> "...you will be happy and prosperous."

Remembering blessings

I'm always amazed that, when I'm not feeling well, I stop doing the very things that help me feel better. During these times I'm unable to see any good in my life; it's almost as if I want to be miserable. I avoid talking to my friends, skip my exercise regime, stay away from my creative work, and resist any form of prayer. Instead, I seek out comfort food and watch mindless television shows.

This doesn't happen often or last too long – just enough for me to appreciate the difficulties imposed by depression. Though I *know* what to do to help myself, at times I simply can't do it.

If I can't move forward, I can still look backward, and recall the blessings that I've already received.

**God, help me to see the good in my life
when I'm feeling low.**

Someone asked [Jesus], "Sir, will just a few people be saved?" He answered, "Do your best to go in through the narrow door; because many people will surely try to go in but will not be able. The master of the house will get up and close the door; then when you stand outside and begin to knock on the door, and say, 'Open the door for us, sir!' he will answer you, 'I don't know where you come from!' Then you will answer, 'We ate and drank with you; you taught in our town!' But he will say again, 'I don't know where you come from. Get away from me, all you wicked people...!' Then those who are now last will be first, and those who are now first will be last."

Luke 13: 22-30

> "Do your best to go in through the narrow door..."

The last will be first

The squeegee kid walked up to my car and offered to clean the windshield. I'd just had it done at the last red light so I shook my head. He shrugged and smiled. "Have a good day anyway," he called as he moved on. Just then the light turned green, and the guy in an expensive car behind me leaned on his horn.

Why was the affluent man so angry about a second's delay? Why was the kid, who had so little of the world's goods, content to take my shake of the head and offer back a smile?

The first shall be last. The self-important often miss out on ordinary human contact. The last shall be first. Those who don't take themselves too seriously can share their humanity with others.

**Lord, help me to avoid self-importance,
to see everyone with your perspective.**

S ee how much the Father has loved us! His love is so great that we are called God's children – and so, in fact, we are. This is why the world does not know us: it has not known God. My dear friends, we are now God's children, but it is not yet clear what we shall become. But we know that when Christ appears, we shall be like him, because we shall see him as he really is. Everyone who has this hope in Christ keeps himself pure, just as Christ is pure.

1 John 3: 1-3

> "...it is not yet clear what we shall become."

God's children

My four-year-old daughter changes her mind about her future career on a daily (if not hourly) basis. This week she has made plans to become a veterinarian, figure skater, astronaut, archaeologist and/or entomologist.

Today she asks me what I would like to be "when I grow up." I laugh. I figure that since I've moved into my fourth decade, the answer to that question is pretty well a done deal. She reminds me to think again.

It seems the writer of today's reading agrees. I am reminded that defining myself in terms of what I *do* or what I might *be* is really of little consequence. What really matters is who I am: a member of God's family.

Jesus, teach me to live with the openness of knowing that I am part of your family.

I am telling you the truth: a grain of wheat remains no more than a single grain unless it is dropped into the ground and dies. If it does die, then it produces many grains. Those who love their own life will lose it; those who hate their own life in this world will keep it for life eternal. Whoever wants to serve me must follow me, so that my servant will be with me where I am. And my Father will honour anyone who serves me."

John 12: 23-26

> "If it does die, then it produces many grains."

Dying to self

Jesus challenges us to risk. To risk is to enter the realm of uncertainty, and that may mean the death of my long-held beliefs. I find myself caught up in expected, comfortable patterns of behaviour. I do not like to disturb myself, or those around me, by choosing the unexpected, the uncomfortable.

However, just as the seed, in the dark of the soil, is broken open, so too must I enter the unknown areas of my life, in order to grow. It is precisely in breaking through the bonds that hold me captive that the seeds of God's kingdom can germinate.

Spiritual author and activist Marianne Williamson once wrote, "Our deepest fear is not that we are inadequate. Our deepest fear is that we are powerful beyond measure."

Lord, give me the courage to look for your presence in situations where I am uncomfortable.

Jesus went to eat a meal at the home of one of the leading Pharisees…. He noticed how some of the guests were choosing the best places, so he told this parable: "When someone invites you to a wedding feast, do not sit down in the best place. It could happen that someone more important than you has been invited, and your host would have to come and say to you, 'Let him have this place.' Then you would have to sit in the lowest place. Instead, when you are invited, go and sit in the lowest place, so that your host will come to you and say, 'Come on up, my friend, to a better place….' For those who make themselves great will be humbled, and those who humble themselves will be made great."

Luke 14: 1, 7-11

> "Come on up, my friend, to a better place…"

The way of humility

When my kids were young, I often sounded like a broken record: "Don't boast. Let what you do speak for you." I'm sure my kids were sick of hearing it. It's a tough one, though. Everything in society says, "Me first!" "Look out for Number 1." "It's a dog-eat-dog world."

It's hard to resist joining those voices. After all, what parents don't want their child to be successful, to have a secure place in the world? And what if your child listens to you, takes the lower place, and then is not seen?

That's the risk, I guess – living life believing that even if your worth is unnoticed at the wedding feast, God recognizes and values you way down at the table by the kitchen door.

**Lord, teach me the way of humility
and give me the courage to live it.**

Deut 6: 2-6; Ps 18; Heb 7: 23-28; Mk 12: 28-34

When I hear the word "commandment" I usually think of orders, about being told what to do or not do. The most famous biblical example is the Ten Commandments, but there are many others in both Testaments. Yet when Jesus is asked which of the many versions in the Jewish tradition is the greatest of all, he does not respond with any of these commandments. Instead, he directs us to an attitude: the attitude of love.

By not specifying individual actions, Jesus leaves the matter open-ended. If God simply desires that we perform certain deeds, then it is possible to fulfill our obligations. I go to church, I give to the poor, I pray every day. But I can never finish having an attitude. In particular, I can  never get to the point where I can honestly say, "I've loved enough."

At the same time, Jesus puts forward two commandments as the greatest, not just one. The two are inseparable: you cannot love God if you do not love others. Paul combines the two into a single command to love your neighbour and explains that "Love does no wrong to a neighbour; therefore, love is the fulfilling of the law" (Romans 13: 10).

We come together as a Christian community not just to fulfill a duty, but to express our love for God. We leave here with a firm commitment to love others. These two loves combined will bring us closer to God's reign in our world.

Infinite God, may your love overflow in me.

Lord, I have given up my pride
and turned away from my arrogance.
I am not concerned with great matters
or with subjects too difficult for me.
Instead, I am content and at peace.
As a child lies quietly in its mother's arms,
so my heart is quiet within me.
Israel, trust in the Lord
now and forever!

Psalm 131: 1-3

"As a child lies quietly in its mother's arms…"

Giving over

What a lovely feeling it is to have a child fall asleep in my arms. My girls are too big for that now, so it's a pleasure to spend time with my neighbour's one-year-old son for the afternoon. We play together far past naptime. Then, without warning, his tiny arms circle my neck and he doesn't let go. His head nuzzles its way onto my shoulder. Within moments, he is asleep.

It is wonderful to share this sudden stillness. I feel blessed by this moment of unexpected tranquility. I wonder if God yearns to hold me this way.

Today I will try to quiet my soul, to let go of the worries of the moment, and to give myself over to the possibility of peace.

**Loving God, help me let go of my worries
to find a place of rest with you.**

... The poor will eat as much as they want;
those who come to the Lord will praise him....
All nations will remember the Lord.
From every part of the world they will turn to him;
all races will worship him.
The Lord is king, and he rules the nations.
All proud people will bow down to him;
all mortals will bow down before him.
Future generations will serve him;
they will speak of the Lord.

Psalm 22: 25-31

"All the nations will remember the Lord."

Too comfortable?

I remember sitting on my comfortable sofa in my warm living room, listening to a radio commentary on the Olympic Games. The reporter spoke of how the host city had poured new cement armrests on the park benches – making it hard for the homeless to sleep comfortably in the parks. He described how the street people were being moved out of the city parks to temporary shelters in the suburbs – out of sight of the reporters and camera crews.

The city defended its actions by pointing to the potential revenue through increased tourism in the years following the Games. After all, the entire world would be watching the Olympics. What would they see? What would they remember?

Today's reading says the Lord does not neglect the poor. I wonder, do we?

**Lord, when I want to remain on my comfortable perch,
unsettle me.**

"Those who come to me cannot be my disciples unless they love me more than they love father and mother, wife and children, brothers and sisters, and themselves as well. Those who do not carry their own cross and come after me cannot be my disciples. If one of you is planning to build a tower, you sit down first and figure out what it will cost, to see if you have enough money to finish the job. If you don't, you will not be able to finish the tower after laying the foundation; and all who see what happened will make fun of you. 'You began to build but can't finish the job!'

"In the same way," concluded Jesus, "none of you can be my disciple unless you give up everything you have."

Luke 14: 25-33

> "…unless you give up everything you have."

Letting go

I remember when my little brother took his first step. He let go of my hand and tottered toward another pair of outstretched hands. It was a day of celebration!

Learning to swim, I was afraid to take my feet off the bottom, but one day I suddenly did. What a joy to discover my body was buoyant!

This letting go of what gives me security – to discover new freedom – is a lifelong invitation. Jesus challenges me to let go of everything that prevents me from growing in relationship with God – a particular friendship, my need to be in control, my comfortable routine.

Change will be painful. It will "cost," but ultimately it will lead me to new freedom and joy.

Lord, still my heart. May I recognize where you are calling me to greater freedom today.

When many tax collectors and other outcasts came to listen to Jesus, the Pharisees and the teachers of the Law started grumbling, "This man welcomes outcasts and even eats with them!" So Jesus told them this parable: "Suppose one of you has a hundred sheep and loses one of them – what do you do? You leave the other ninety-nine sheep in the pasture and go looking for the one that got lost until you find it. When you find it, you are so happy that you put it on your shoulders and carry it back home. Then you call your friends and neighbours together and say to them, 'I am so happy I found my lost sheep. Let us celebrate!' In the same way, I tell you, there will be more joy in heaven over one sinner who repents than over ninety-nine respectable people who do not need to repent."

Luke 15: 1-10

> "I am so happy I found my lost sheep."

Lost and found

Did anyone ever come looking for me, their "lost sheep"? Perhaps they did, and I just never knew it. Lost sheep, by definition, aren't very aware of what's going on around them.

While I don't remember any dramatic rescues, I know there have been people who went out of their way for me when they didn't have to. There were people whose time and attention made such a difference at crucial moments in my life. Was I their "lost sheep"?

I like to think of myself as the "heroic rescuer." Maybe I learned to be a rescuer by first being the one rescued. I've never thought of myself as a lost-sheep-found. But maybe that's what we all are – found-sheep who go on to be lost-sheep-finders.

Thank you, God, for the people who have looked out for me, whether I was aware of it or not.

The man led me back to the entrance of the Temple. Water was coming out from under the entrance and flowing east, the direction the Temple faced…. He said to me, "This water flows through the land to the east and down into the Jordan Valley and to the Dead Sea. When it flows into the Dead Sea, it replaces the salt water of that sea with fresh water. Wherever the stream flows, there will be all kinds of animals and fish. The stream will make the water of the Dead Sea fresh, and wherever it flows, it will bring life…. On each bank of the stream all kinds of trees will grow to provide food. Their leaves will never wither, and they will never stop bearing fruit… because they are watered by the stream that flows from the Temple."
Ezekiel 47: 1-2, 8-9, 12

> "…it will bring life…"

Faced with loss

A few summers ago, I stood on a hill high above the village of Quidi Vidi in my native Newfoundland. Everything was still under the blue sky: the small boats, the piles of nets, the water itself.

My chest heaved as I remembered busier, noisier, happier times when cod nourished our bodies and nurtured our souls. I thought of my cousins Jim, Steve and Jerry, men with calloused hands who knew every rock and underwater ledge, but who will never fish again. Then I felt the loss was unbearable.

I've mourned in this way every summer for a decade now. Looking at the Atlantic Ocean, I want to cling to hope, but it's very hard in the face of such stillness.

God, help me to remember that you are with your earth, your water and your people at all times.

"**A**nd so I tell you: make friends for yourselves with worldly wealth, so that when it gives out, you will be welcomed in the eternal home. Whoever is faithful in small matters will be faithful in large ones; whoever is dishonest in small matters will be dishonest in large ones. If, then, you have not been faithful in handling worldly wealth, how can you be trusted with true wealth? And if you have not been faithful with what belongs to someone else, who will give you what belongs to you?

"No servant can be the slave of two masters; such a slave will hate one and love the other or will be loyal to one and despise the other. You cannot serve both God and money."

Luke 16: 9-15

"You cannot serve both God and money."

Which master?

Here we are in our consumption-driven culture: get the big house, get the satellite, get the SUV. Don't forget the condo in Florida. Meanwhile, the spouse has become a stranger, and the kids are left adrift. No one can serve two masters.

My friend's daughter started to fall off the rails: marks falling, unhappy, directionless. My friend was losing her.

So the mother quit her job. Sold the house, and took her daughter to Asia. Showed her poverty, people's struggle to live. Their desperate struggle to live.

The daughter is now studying medicine in order to go back. The laughter returned; the meaning returned.

No one can serve two masters. This woman served the right one. There's a lesson in that for me.

Dear God, help me search for what's important, and to know to ignore what's not.

1 Kgs 17: 10-16; Ps 146; Heb 9: 24-28; Mk 12: 38-44

I n today's readings we encounter two widows who, though among the poorest of the poor, gave "all [they] had to live on." We don't know what became of them, but they had great trust to be able to share despite such an uncertain future.

Compassion and care for others surely prompt our own giving, although seldom is such radical generosity asked. Perhaps, like the scribes, our giving may sometimes be tinged with a need for recogni-

tion or affirmation. Contributing to charitable works is important, but we can also be generous in sharing ourselves in simple ways. Smiling and seeking eye contact when saying thank you, giving a compliment or offering "the peace of Christ."

Sometimes, like the widow of Zarephath, we may feel we have little personal strength or resources to share, especially when we experience stress or hardship. But, as Elijah reassured her, "Do not be afraid." God will reward our giving with unstinting bounty.

After being diagnosed with a serious illness, I took the unlikely step of beginning a gratitude journal. It helped me to see and receive the simple gifts of each day – birds singing, a pot of soup from a friend. Gradually, fear faded and trust grew, as did an ability to reach out to others.

With the psalmist, we can affirm, "The Lord lifts up those who are bowed down."

**O God, you are my strength.
Help me to share that strength with others.**

Jesus said, "Things that make people fall into sin are bound to happen, but how terrible for the one who makes them happen! It would be better for him if a large millstone were tied around his neck and he were thrown into the sea than for him to cause one of these little ones to sin.…

"If your brother sins, rebuke him, and if he repents, forgive him. If he sins against you seven times in one day, and each time he comes to you saying, 'I repent,' you must forgive him."

The apostles said, "Make our faith greater." The Lord answered, "If you had faith as big as a mustard seed, you could say to this mulberry tree, 'Pull yourself up by the roots and plant yourself in the sea!' and it would obey you."

Luke 17: 1-6

> "…and if he repents, forgive him."

Forgive me

Last week, I was having one of those days. The last straw came when one of my boys knocked over a lamp while jumping in the living room.

I lost my temper and sent him outside so I could cool off and assess the damage. A few minutes later he appeared at the door and said, "I'm sorry, Mom. But remember that Jesus says we must forgive seven times in one day? So will you forgive me, Mommy?"

His words made me stop dead in my tracks. Not only was he able to integrate Jesus' teaching into his life, but he forced me to take it seriously, too. We hugged and I said those magic words, "I forgive you." The rest of the day went much better!

**Lord, when I am slow to forgive,
help me to remember your words and deeds.**

" Suppose one of you has a servant who is plowing or looking after the sheep. When he comes in from the field, do you tell him to hurry along and eat his meal? Of course not! Instead, you say to him, 'Get my supper ready, then put on your apron and wait on me while I eat and drink; after that you may have your meal.' The servant does not deserve thanks for obeying orders, does he? It is the same with you; when you have done all you have been told to do, say, 'We are ordinary servants; we have only done our duty.'"

Luke 17:7-10

> "…we have only done our duty."

Doing my duty

After my little ones finally drift off to sleep, I often head toward the thankless tasks of managing the household… with a scowl on my face. Clean up the supper dishes, sort the mountain of dirty (or are they clean?) clothes, wade through the flotsam and jetsam of toys, chase the cat hair that roams the house like a nomad, feed the cat (if we still have one)… Sometimes I think Sisyphus had an easier job, eternally rolling that stone up the hill.

Perhaps it would be better if I stopped hoping someone would thank me for every little task I do. I know I make a difference in our home. I know my family is thankful. And I know their thanks will come in time.

Dear God, may I learn to serve others with loving hands rather than a grumbling heart.

Jesus was going into a village when he was met by ten men suffering from a dreaded skin disease. They stood at a distance and shouted, "Jesus! Master! Have pity on us!" Jesus saw them and said to them, "Go and let the priests examine you."

On the way they were made clean. When one of them saw that he was healed, he came back, praising God in a loud voice. He threw himself to the ground at Jesus' feet and thanked him. The man was a Samaritan. Jesus spoke up, "There were ten who were healed; where are the other nine? Why is this foreigner the only one who came back to give thanks to God?" And Jesus said to him, "Get up and go; your faith has made you well."

Luke 17: 11-19

> "When one of them saw that he was healed…"

Gratitude for healing

My husband died of cancer at the age of 36 and I was left alone to care for our three young children. I was overwhelmed with the experience of our loss and with the effort of trying to bring some order to the chaos we experienced. Grief, anger and loneliness seemed to consume me.

Now several years have passed. Recently, in a phone call with my mum, I was filled with a deep sense of gratitude. "Thank you," I said, "for accepting me when I wasn't the easiest person to be around. Your love brought healing in ways I never thought possible."

God's healing often happens through friends and family. Do I recognize it, and remember to give thanks?

**God, heal me so that I can believe again in love.
Help me bring your healing love to others.**

make a request to you on behalf of Onesimus, who is my own son in Christ.... I am sending him back to you now, and with him goes my heart. I would like to keep him here with me, while I am in prison for the gospel's sake, so that he could help me in your place. However, I do not want to force you to help me; rather, I would like for you to do it of your own free will. So I will not do anything unless you agree.... So, if you think of me as your partner, welcome him back just as you would welcome me. If he has done you any wrong or owes you anything, charge it to my account. Here, I will write this with my own hand: I, Paul, will pay you back.

Philemon 7-20

> "...welcome him back just as you would welcome me."

An open door

For about 20 years, strangers kept arriving on my aunt's doorstep in Northern Ireland. They were friends of my mother's, travelling to Britain for holidays, graduate studies or various personal crises. They had only one thing in common: they all came with my mother's recommendation. She had learned that they were going to a strange place. They needed a place to stay while they got themselves organized. So my mother sent word about them to her sister. My aunt welcomed them into her home as if they were family. Like my mother, Paul was a letter writer. And he made a similar request of Philemon: to welcome an escaped slave, not as a criminal deserving punishment, but as a friend, a brother, a member of the family.

Forgive me, God, when I judge people by society's standards. Encourage me to value people just because you do.

A s it was in the time of Noah so shall it be in the days of the Son of Man. Everybody kept on eating and drinking, and men and women married, up to the very day Noah went into the boat and the flood came and killed them all. It will be as it was in the time of Lot. Everybody kept on eating and drinking, buying and selling, planting and building. On the day Lot left Sodom, fire and sulfur rained down from heaven and killed them all. That is how it will be on the day the Son of Man is revealed....

Those who try to save their own life will lose it; those who lose their life will save it."

Luke 17: 26-37

> "...fire and sulfur rained down..."

Motivation to change

The last time we had a smog alert in our city, my son and I were driving down a crowded highway. On the radio they were discussing how cars and fossil fuels are the main reason for the pollution.

"Do you think we're ever going to change our ways?" I asked. "We know what we're doing is wrong, and yet we keep on doing it." My son replied, "I think people need to feel pain before they'll change. As long as they're still comfortable, there's no reason to change."

From the mouths of babes! How comfortable I am: not only regarding social issues, but in my faith life, also. I pay attention when I'm hurting; when I'm comfortable, I go on automatic pilot.

**Lord, draw me out of my complacency.
Inspire me to action and growth.**

Jesus told his disciples a parable to teach them that they should always pray and never become discouraged. "In a certain town there was a judge who neither feared God nor respected people. And there was a widow in that same town who kept coming to him and pleading for her rights. For a long time the judge refused to act, but at last he said to himself, 'Because of all the trouble this widow is giving me, I will see to it that she gets her rights. If I don't, she will keep on coming and finally wear me out!'"

And the Lord continued, "Now, will God not judge in favour of his own people who cry to him day and night for help?"

Luke 18: 1-8

> "I will see to it that she gets her rights."

Gutsy determination

In biblical times, "widows and orphans" were understood to be the vulnerable ones, those needing care and protection by others (usually males) in society. But here, in today's reading, a widow stands up for her rights and her request is met by a corrupt (male) judge! What an example of gutsy determination!

I think of the women who have spoken up for their rights and for the rights of others. Not for what they might want or need – but for their *rights*. The right to vote. The right to walk on city streets in safety. The right for them and their children to live without fear of abuse in their homes. The right to be full, contributing members of their church communities.

I hope to learn from their example.

**Dear God, give me the courage to ask –
not for my needs or wants, but for my rights to be met.**

Dan 12: 1-3; Ps 16; Heb 10: 11-14, 18; Mk 13: 24-32

Today's gospel anticipates the dramatic events of the end times, when, after a time of suffering, the world as we know it will pass away. When I consider some of our global relationships and the state of our planet, I see much suffering. Some of us are wealthy, while many more are very poor. Some have power and others have no voice. The earth is damaged by pollution and over-consumption. I sometimes wonder if we will ever fully live out God's call to love our neighbours and to be good stewards of creation.

Instead of a message of doom, however, this gospel reading offers hope. It offers a future hope in the second coming of Christ and also a present hope in the promise that while heaven and earth will pass away, Christ's words will not. This latter promise is fulfilled even after two thousand years, as the Church continues to proclaim the good news of the kingdom of God, a kingdom of love, compassion, kindness and mercy.

Even in the midst of suffering humanity and the harm done to creation, the Word of God continues to be alive and active in us. As we wait in hope for the fulfillment of the kingdom of God in Christ's return in glory, let us give thanks for the living Word of God empowering us to respect creation and to build a more just, loving and peaceful world.

**God, creator of all, I do not treasure your creation
as I should. Help me become a better steward.**

A s Jesus was coming near Jericho, there was a blind man sitting by the road. When he heard the crowd passing by, he asked, "What is this?"

"Jesus of Nazareth," they told him. He cried out, "Jesus! Son of David! Have mercy on me!" The people told him to be quiet. But he shouted even more loudly, "Son of David! Have mercy on me!" So Jesus ordered the blind man to be brought to him. When he came near, Jesus asked him, "What do you want me to do for you?"

"Sir," he answered, "I want to see again." Jesus said to him, "Then see! Your faith has made you well." At once he was able to see, and he followed Jesus, giving thanks to God. When the crowd saw it, they all praised God.

Luke 18: 35-43

> "Your faith has made you well."

A healing faith

If it's possible, Jessa's prayers were even more startling than this blind man's persistent cries. Last spring, during her junior year in college, Jessa died of cystic fibrosis. She knew death was coming – and sooner rather than later. Like the blind man, Jessa, too, called out to Jesus.

At the campus memorial service, several friends offered remembrances of her. Two of them read prayers written in Jessa's journal just months before she died. I was amazed. Jessa did not pray to be miraculously healed. She sought a deeper miracle: to see life through eyes of hope and gratitude.

As I listened to all who shared memories of her, I knew that Jessa, too, had heard Jesus say to her, "Your faith has made you well."

**Jesus, shape my prayers so that I, too,
long for what will truly make me well.**

There was a chief tax collector there named Zacchaeus, who was rich…. He was a little man and could not see Jesus because of the crowd. So he ran ahead and climbed a sycamore tree to see Jesus…. [Jesus] looked up and said, "Hurry down, Zacchaeus, because I must stay in your house today." Zacchaeus hurried down and welcomed him with great joy. All the people who saw it started grumbling, "This man has gone as a guest to the home of a sinner!" Zacchaeus stood up and said to the Lord, "Listen, sir! I will give half my belongings to the poor, and if I have cheated anyone, I will pay back four times as much." Jesus said, "Salvation has come to this house today…. The Son of Man came to seek and to save the lost."

Luke 19: 1-10

> "The Son of Man came to seek and to save the lost."

Down from my perch

As a short person, I've always been fond of Zacchaeus and his approach to problems. Can't see? Climb a tree!

But when Zacchaeus climbs a tree to see Jesus more clearly, he ends up giving half of his goods to the poor and instituting a four-for-one repayment scheme for some shady transactions in his past. Wait a minute! Solving one problem created a more demanding challenge!

I prefer the safety of a detached spirituality, straddling a tree limb high above the crowds. But Jesus wants more. He invites me down from my "tree," to place my feet on solid ground. Like Zacchaeus, I'm called to do something concrete about the poor, to make restitution for the wrongs I've done. Sometimes staying in the tree is easier!

**Jesus, I can't turn my life around overnight.
Help me to take one concrete step toward you each day.**

Praise the Lord!
Praise God in his Temple!
   Praise his strength in heaven!
Praise him for the mighty things he has done.
Praise his supreme greatness.
Praise him with trumpets.
Praise him with harps and lyres.
Praise him with drums and dancing.
Praise him with harps and flutes.
Praise him with cymbals.
Praise him with loud cymbals.
Praise the Lord, all living creatures!
Praise the Lord!

Psalm 150: 1-6

> "Praise the Lord, all living creatures!"

Praise the Lord!

Today's psalm describes a celebration of praise that is so good, even the animals join in with the musicians. It sounds like a party in Narnia!

But when we take the time to notice it, we see that animals are always praising God. They can't help it. An animal's praise is extinguished only when a species is extinguished.

Today, conservative estimates of the effects of global warming on animals suggest a loss of between 15 and 37 percent of all species.

That's losing a lot of praise if we don't take steps to care for our world. What would it take, for example, to live up to the minimum requirements of the Kyoto accord? To surpass them?

**Lord, give me the wisdom and the courage
to accept responsibility for creation.**

He came closer to the city, and when he saw it, he wept over it, saying, "If you only knew today what is needed for peace! But now you cannot see it! The time will come when your enemies will surround you with barricades, blockade you, and close in on you from every side. They will completely destroy you and the people within your walls; not a single stone will they leave in its place, because you did not recognize the time when God came to save you!"

Luke 19:41-44

> "...he wept over it..."

Caring enough to cry

Tears of compassion? Tears of frustration?

Time and again, Jesus' followers just don't get it. How frustrated he must have been. But his tears did not dry up; he did not become cynical. His tears are the sign that he still cares.

I'm a teacher and a parent. Both roles bring tears of frustration and of compassion. Sometimes, as a teacher, it's difficult not to become cynical – about governments, difficult students, parents. And yes, as a parent, to be cynical about teachers.

It's so hard to keep caring. But I must. I must preserve my compassion – for those students who don't understand, and for those parents who are, above all, concerned for their children and don't know whom to trust.

I must preserve my tears.

Dear Lord, help me care enough to be frustrated, and to love enough to show compassion.

Jesus went into the Temple and began to drive out the merchants, saying to them, "It is written in the Scriptures that God said, 'My Temple will be a house of prayer.' But you have turned it into a hideout for thieves!"

Every day Jesus taught in the Temple. The chief priests, the teachers of the Law, and the leaders of the people wanted to kill him, but they could not find a way to do it, because all the people kept listening to him, not wanting to miss a single word.

Luke 19: 45-48

> "Every day Jesus taught in the Temple."

Religion and politics

We had a guest preacher at our church one morning. His sermon blasted the provincial government's process of negotiating a treaty with the province's native bands. After the service a number of people were visibly angry.

"He shouldn't mix religion and politics," they said. I wonder if they read the same Bible as I do. Jesus overturned the traders' tables in the Temple. And it wasn't just a hit-and-run protest. "Every day," Luke says, "Jesus taught in the Temple."

For sheer political audacity, a comparison today would be someone going to Afghanistan, while the Taliban still had supreme power, to stand in a public square and openly accuse them of wrongdoing. Such a prophet probably wouldn't last long. Neither did Jesus.

God, give me the courage to say what you call me to say, regardless of personal risk.

Teacher, Moses wrote this law: 'If a man dies and leaves a wife but no children, that man's brother must marry the widow....' Now, on the day when the dead rise to life, whose wife will she be...?"·

Jesus answered them, "The men and women of this age marry, but the men and women who are worthy to rise from death and live in the age to come will not then marry.... They are the children of God, because they have risen from death. And Moses clearly proves that the dead are raised to life. In the passage about the burning bush he speaks of the Lord as 'the God of Abraham, the God of Isaac, and the God of Jacob.' He is the God of the living, not of the dead, for to him all are alive."

Luke 20: 27-40

> "...the God of the living, not of the dead..."

The life within

As November days darken, my garden becomes tangled with reminders that this is a season of decay. Like the Sadducees, I am concerned about the details of death: What plants will survive the snow? Which ones will be killed by a harsh winter? What can I do to ensure that most will survive?

It is hard to trust that there is a rhythm and wisdom to this season, hard to believe there is a spark of life hidden in this decaying garden. It is difficult to wait for the signs of life that will appear again next spring.

As the chill and dark increase, I'll try to remember Jesus' promise: that our God is the God of the living. The promise of life is always present.

God of life, as November days grow short,
help me see the spark of life in all things.

Dan 7: 13-14; Ps 93; Rev 1: 5-8; Jn 18: 33-37

A long, dusty avenue climbs a little knoll. On either side of it, thick, roofless adobe walls suggest the ancient grandeur of Pachacamac. At this site on the arid coastal plain of Peru some 40 km south of Lima, adobe bricks by the millions had been formed by hand, one at a time. Enormous structures rose slowly from the desert.

The largest buildings, scholars note, were devoted to religious purposes. The temples and pyramids of Pachacamac mark the spiritual strivings of its inhabitants. They all gave witness to their builders' belief in the divine, with and in the creation around them.

Civilizations rise and fall. God's project of salvation "is a plan that," in the words of Pope Benedict XVI, "is revealed little by little throughout history." Across time and cultures, this mystery is disclosed to us. We hear in the gospel today the voice of one who came "to testify to the truth."

Do others hear that voice? Pope Pius XI saw a rising tide of secularization sweeping the world. In the hope of countering this trend, he instituted the Solemnity of Christ the King in 1925.

Can we be counted among those belonging to the truth, truly listening to his voice? Let us strive to serve God's plan by building his kingdom brick by brick through our daily actions.

God, help me to remember that I, too, have a job to do in building your kingdom.

J esus looked around and saw rich people dropping their gifts in the Temple treasury, and he also saw a very poor widow dropping in two little copper coins. He said, "I tell you that this poor widow put in more than all the others. For the others offered their gifts from what they had to spare of their riches; but she, poor as she is, gave all she had to live on."

Luke 21: 1-4

"...two little copper coins."

A challenge

Christmas is just over a month away. I've tried to trim down my gift list to a reasonable length, but still it is long. And, as I do every year, I wonder: Is all this really necessary? I never manage to avoid the last-minute rush of obligatory gift-giving. Why do I fall into keeping watch on who gave what to whom and at what price?

At the heart of today's reading is the image of the widow's gift: "two little copper coins." I see her cradling them: humbly, secretly, in the palm of her hand. I hear them dropping: clink, clink. Small notes of graced giving amid the cacophony of commercialism. Those two coins challenge me to look at my attitude toward gift-giving this Christmas.

Lord, help me to give simply and sincerely, straight from my heart.

S ome of the disciples were talking about the Temple, how beautiful it looked with its fine stones and the gifts offered to God. Jesus said, "All this you see – the time will come when not a single stone here will be left in its place; every one will be thrown down."

"Teacher," they asked, "when will this be? And what will happen in order to show that the time has come for it to take place?"

Jesus said, "Watch out; don't be fooled. Many men, claiming to speak for me, will come and say, 'I am he!' and, 'The time has come!' But don't follow them. Don't be afraid when you hear of wars and revolutions; such things must happen first, but they do not mean that the end is near."

Luke 21:5-11

> "...not a single stone here will be left..."

Home or temple?

My friend was as I remembered her: light-hearted, full of laughter and energy. It had been years since we'd seen each other. By chance, we met one another in a restaurant.

"Oh yes," she added – as we ended our list of births, deaths and marriages – "then there was the house fire. We lost everything. But thank God no one was hurt."

Later, as I entered my own home, I remembered her words and was humbled. While I like being surrounded by beautiful things, today's reading and my friend's words give me pause. Have I built a home, or a temple of things that I cannot imagine losing?

**God, let my faith in you be the foundation
for all that I build.**

S ing a new song to the Lord;
he has done wonderful things!
By his own power and holy strength
he has won the victory.
The Lord announced his victory;
he made his saving power known to the nations.
He kept his promise to the people of Israel
with loyalty and constant love for them.
All people everywhere have seen the victory of our God....
Roar, sea, and every creature in you;
sing, earth, and all who live on you!
Clap your hands, you rivers;
you hills, sing together with joy before the Lord,
because he comes to rule the earth.

Psalm 98: 1-3, 7-9

"Clap your hands, you rivers..."

Stewards of the earth

Every day the news is filled with terrible stories about our planet. The air and water are bad and getting worse. Animals and plants are dying off at unprecedented rates. The depleted land groans with exhaustion and the wind and rain show us their anger in devastating ways. Even the sun, source of light and warmth, has become dangerous to us.

We have done a terrible job at being God's stewards, and the world is suffering.

I can imagine all creation longing for God to take charge, to fire the selfish incompetents who have run things into the ground. As the psalmist says, even the rivers and hills would sing and clap with joy!

**Lord, give me the strength to serve your world
as a good steward.**

"When you see Jerusalem surrounded by armies, then you will know that it will soon be destroyed.... Terrible distress will come upon this land, and God's punishment will fall on this people....

"There will be strange things happening to the sun, the moon, and the stars. On earth whole countries will be in despair, afraid of the roar of the sea and the raging tides. People will faint from fear as they wait for what is coming over the whole earth, for the powers in space will be driven from their courses. Then the Son of Man will appear, coming in a cloud with great power and glory. When these things begin to happen, stand up and raise your heads, because your salvation is near."

Luke 21: 20-28

> "...stand up and raise your heads..."

Facing death

When I saw the blockbuster movie *Titanic*, I marvelled at the cinematography and special effects. But what stirred my emotions most deeply was sharing the final moments of people's lives.

Faced with imminent death, I wonder how I would react. Would I curl up in despair, or be moved by compassion for others? Would I faint with fear, race into frenzied panic, or calmly stand and await my fate?

Perhaps it depends on my behaviour throughout my whole life. Have I waited for others to rescue me? Have I used my energy and intelligence to advance only my own interests? Have I cared deeply for others and placed my faith in God's saving power? The answers may predict how I would act in a crisis.

**Lord of Life, teach me to live today
as if it were my last day on earth.**

As Jesus walked along the shore of Lake Galilee, he saw two brothers who were fishermen, Simon (called Peter) and his brother Andrew, catching fish in the lake with a net. Jesus said to them, "Come with me, and I will teach you to catch people." At once they left their nets and went with him. He went on and saw two other brothers, James and John, the sons of Zebedee. They were in their boat with their father Zebedee, getting their nets ready. Jesus called them, and at once they left the boat and their father, and went with him.

Matthew 4: 18-22

> "...they left their nets and went with him."

Open to the call

How did the father of James and John feel? Did he take comfort in knowing his boys were following the call they heard in their hearts? Was he worried about what it might cost them? The rejection, the lack of security, the possibility of death?

Zebedee must have raised his sons to be open to God's call, to be faithful to whatever God asked. In the end, he let them go.

I, too, watch as my children struggle to find their way. I encourage them to ask the deeper questions, to be compassionate, to speak up for those who can't defend themselves. I know that they'll be hurt along the way. And I try to prepare myself for the day they leave to follow their dreams.

**Lord, guide me as I help my children
to live with a heart open to your call.**

The angel showed me the river of the water of life, sparkling like crystal, and coming from the throne of God and of the Lamb and flowing down the middle of the city's street. On each side of the river was the tree of life, which bears fruit twelve times a year... and its leaves are for the healing of the nations. Nothing that is under God's curse will be found in the city.

The throne of God and of the Lamb will be in the city, and his servants will worship him. They will see his face, and his name will be written on their foreheads. There shall be no more night, and they will not need lamps or sunlight, because the Lord God will be their light, and they will rule as kings forever and ever.

Revelation 22: 1-7

> "...the Lord God will be their light..."

God's light

Do you know what real darkness is like? When I was very small, we had no electricity on our farm. On long winter nights we depended on coal oil lamps and a gas lantern for light. There was barely enough light for cleaning eggs, or darning socks, or doing homework at the kitchen table.

And if I needed something from my bedroom, I ascended the stairs into true darkness – the kind where unknown forces lurked under beds and monsters waited in the closets.

As a grown-up, I've had to face new monsters: loneliness, financial problems, poor health. What if I accepted God's bright light and let it shine upstairs and downstairs, under the bed and into the closets of my life, to help dispel my fears?

Lord, let your light shine in my life. Let me see clearly.

Jer 33: 14-16; Ps 25; I Thess 3: 12 – 4.2; Lk 21: 25-28, 34-36

This is a time of much anticipation. Advertisements bombard us with things to buy for Christmas. Children compile lists of toys they hope to receive on that day. And many look forward to New Year's Day as an opportunity for a fresh start.

But the Church starts its new year today. The start of the liturgical year also calls us to anticipate what is coming, but with a different emphasis. In our worship together we do not anticipate presents or resolutions for the New Year. Instead, we anticipate the coming of Jesus.

There are three aspects to Jesus' coming in the Advent season. One looks to the past, as we anticipate the celebration of his birth among us 2,000 years ago. The second looks to the present, as we prepare ourselves to receive him anew in our lives today. The third looks to the future, for his coming again.

Today's readings emphasize the third aspect. Jeremiah predicts the coming of the Branch, a reference to the Messiah who would save Israel. In the gospel, Jesus speaks of his own return with signs and wonders. But it is not the signs that are important: it is the redemption that Jesus brings.

As we begin the Advent season, let us prepare our hearts not just to celebrate Christmas, but to receive Jesus when he comes again in glory.

Lord Jesus, I could use a fresh start.
Open my eyes and my heart to new possibilities!

When Jesus entered Capernaum, a Roman officer met him and begged for help: "Sir, my servant is sick in bed at home, unable to move and suffering terribly."

"I will go and make him well," Jesus said.

"Oh no, sir," answered the officer. "I do not deserve to have you come into my house. Just give the order, and my servant will get well. I, too, am a man under the authority of superior officers, and I have soldiers under me. I order this one, 'Go!' and he goes...."

When Jesus heard this, he was surprised and said to the people following him, "I tell you, I have never found anyone in Israel with faith like this...." Jesus said to the officer, "Go home, and what you believe will be done for you."

Matthew 8: 5-11, 13

> "I do not deserve to have you come into my house."

Beyond divisions

This story, a couple of millennia later, strikes me as rather charming. But think of it: the officer belongs to the occupying force; he's the enemy. Now he's asking the local prophet for a favour. And, voilà! It's done for him. What does this say about "us" and "them"?

Years ago, I got into a fight with a kid who was the outsider. After that fight, we seemed to get along, but I found myself criticized by my friends for talking to him. After all, he was "the enemy."

We like it that way: us and them. Good guys and bad. It's a hard thing Jesus asks of me — to go beyond these divisions, to love my enemies. A very hard thing.

**Lord, help me be open to all people,
even when they've hurt me.**

Jesus was filled with joy by the Holy Spirit and said, "Father, I thank you because you have shown to the unlearned what you have hidden from the wise and learned....

"My Father has given me all things. No one knows who the Son is except the Father, and no one knows who the Father is except the Son and those to whom the Son chooses to reveal him."

Then Jesus turned to the disciples and said, "How fortunate you are to see the things you see! I tell you that many prophets and kings wanted to see what you see, but they could not, and to hear what you hear, but they did not."

Luke 10: 21-24

"How fortunate you are to see…"

Seeing and hearing

Yes, I guess the disciples were fortunate – they were actually there with Jesus.

I think back to times when we played the game "Who would you like to meet from history?" Usually it came down to Jesus. I, too, would like to see what his followers saw, and hear what they heard.

But I have a suspicion Jesus might ask me about what I see and hear today. The geese calling to me on fall mornings. My children's banter around the table. The voice coming from the scarred, whiskered face asking for spare change.

Yes, I would dearly love to sit and talk with Jesus. For now, I guess I need to pay close attention to what I do see, what I do hear all around me.

**Dear God, help me to see and hear you
in all of your creatures.**

Jesus said, "I feel sorry for these people, because they have been with me for three days and now have nothing to eat. I don't want to send them away without feeding them, for they might faint on their way home." The disciples asked, "Where will we find enough food in this desert to feed this crowd?"

"How much bread do you have?" Jesus asked. "Seven loaves," they answered, "and a few small fish." Jesus took the seven loaves and the fish, gave thanks to God, broke them, and gave them to the disciples; and the disciples gave them to the people. They all ate and had enough. Then the disciples took up seven baskets full of pieces left over.

Matthew 15: 29-37

> "How much bread do you have?"

God will provide

I really don't know what to think about miracles, but today's reading reminds me of my buddy Riaz. I teach with him; I think he invented math and physics. He's a great guy, very generous.

Riaz is from Pakistan. I told him it's an irony that the best Christian in the place is a Muslim. Whenever anyone needs something, Riaz looks skyward and says, "He will provide."

One day, I had no lunch and Riaz insisted that I take half his sandwich. "Riaz, I don't want to take your lunch!" I protested. "He will provide!" replied Riaz.

The next thing I know, someone doesn't want their salad and someone else gives us fries. We had more food than anyone!

Riaz fed us both on one little sandwich.

**Lord, let me be as faithful and as generous
as my dear friend Riaz.**

A day is coming when the people will sing this song
in the land of Judah:
Our city is strong!
God himself defends its walls....
You, Lord, give perfect peace
to those who keep their purpose firm
and put their trust in you.
Trust in the Lord forever;
he will always protect us.
He has humbled those who were proud;
he destroyed the strong city they lived in,
and sent its walls crashing into the dust.

Isaiah 26: 1-6

> "A day is coming when the people will sing this song..."

Past, present and future

Learning a new language is always a challenge. Invariably, I have to figure out what tense I'm in, and the tense I am trying to use, before I can apply myself to the mundane demands of grammar. It's why I love language.

Isaiah presents a song in the present tense, but stresses that it is something to be sung at some unspecified time in the future. For the residents of Judah, security and peace were only future promises, not their present experience.

I'm challenged to find comfort in the God of all my tenses: past, present and future, even though my most compelling need is decidedly in the here and now.

**God of the present, the past, and my future,
may I discover you now and for always.**

As Jesus walked along, two blind men started following him. "Have mercy on us, Son of David!" they shouted.... Jesus asked them, "Do you believe that I can heal you?"

"Yes, sir!" they answered. Then Jesus touched their eyes and said, "Let it happen, then, just as you believe!" – and their sight was restored.

Jesus spoke sternly to them, "Don't tell this to anyone!" But they left and spread the news about Jesus all over that part of the country.

Matthew 9: 27-31

> "Jesus spoke sternly to them..."

Seeing the truth

I know that, in today's reading, Matthew is writing about the extraordinary power of faith. But that's not the part of the story that touches me. I delight in the small detail at the end where Jesus, after performing this amazing miracle, sternly admonishes the two men to keep his gift a secret.

Brimming with gratitude, the men, just like kids who have found a puppy under the Christmas tree, run off and tell absolutely everyone they meet about Jesus – in spite of his admonition.

This could only have happened if the newly sighted men could see the deep compassion behind the stern words. Who among us could keep such a secret?

Lord, give me eyes to see your love.

God sent the angel Gabriel to a town in Galilee named Nazareth. He had a message for a young woman [whose] name was Mary.... The angel said, "Peace be with you! The Lord is with you!"

Mary was deeply troubled by the angel's message, and she wondered what his words meant. The angel said, "Don't be afraid, Mary; God has been gracious to you. You will become pregnant and give birth to a son, and you will name him Jesus. He will be great and will be called the Son of the Most High God...."

Mary said, "I am a virgin. How, then, can this be?" The angel answered, "The Holy Spirit will come on you, and God's power will rest upon you. For this reason the holy child will be called the Son of God."

Luke 1: 26-38

> "Mary was deeply troubled by the angel's message..."

The voice of an angel

Angels! Mary is visited by an angel with a message that is so very clear. And when Mary asks questions, she gets clear answers. But what of me? Where are my clear answers? It is often difficult to hear the voice of God or to see God's hand at work in my life.

This is the great challenge of our secular age. In the cold of winter, amid global economic turmoil and bombarded by images of violence, can I hear the voice of an angel – in the laughter shared with a friend, in the offer of help from a colleague, in the hand of a child reaching out to hold mine?

And more, can I be the clear voice of the angel in my dealings with others?

**Lord, help me see your hand at work in my life.
Help me choose to be a part of that work.**

Baruch 5: 1-9; Ps 126; Phil 1: 3-6, 8-11; Lk 3: 1-6

With the approach of the Christmas party season, we can get lost in trivialities: things like what to buy or how we look. The readings today recommend an interior transformation that will make us attractive to everyone, regardless of what we wear.

Baruch calls for Jerusalem to be joyful because the reason for her sadness is over – her children are returning home from exile.

The psalmist, like Baruch, also encourages the people to change their attitude from hopelessness to hope and to trust in God because God will make them happy again.

Paul's letter also calls the people to adjust their behaviour to ensure they are doing what truly matters in life and are ready to meet Christ. Preparation for the coming of Christ is essential, as John the Baptist proclaims in the gospel today. To prepare, we must change, as the Advent season reminds us.

The readings show us we can change when our desire is sincere, for we can count on the help of God. Let us thank God for the opportunities of change that God gives us, so we may become, this Advent season and always, signs of joy and peace for those we meet.

Lord God, change my heart that I may change my ways.

S ome men came carrying a paralyzed man on a bed, and they tried to carry him into the house and put him in front of Jesus. Because of the crowd, however, they could find no way to take him in. So they carried him up on the roof, made an opening in the tiles, and let him down on his bed into the middle of the group in front of Jesus. When Jesus saw how much faith they had, he said to the man, "Your sins are forgiven, my friend.... I tell you, get up, pick up your bed, and go home!"

At once the man got up in front of them all, took the bed he had been lying on, and went home, praising God. They were all completely amazed! "What marvellous things we have seen today!"
Luke 5: 17-26

"Some men came carrying a paralyzed man..."

A helping hand

Who carried the paralyzed man to Jesus for healing? Relatives? Neighbours? People from his old workplace? Did the man or woman who came up with the idea have to rope in the others? Whoever they were, it would have been easy to give up when they ran into the crowd blocking their way into the house. If they had, the sick person would never have reached Jesus.

When someone I know is paralyzed with grief, misfortune or fear, I realize that, with persistence and inventiveness, I can help in their healing process. It's sobering to realize that both the Lord, and the person in need, may depend on me to find a way around the practical and emotional obstacles that stand in the way of healing.

Lord, give me the courage and imagination to carry those who lack the power to help themselves.

What do you think a man does who has one hundred sheep and one of them gets lost? He will leave the other ninety-nine grazing on the hillside and go and look for the lost sheep. When he finds it, I tell you, he feels far happier over this one sheep than over the ninety-nine that did not get lost. In just the same way your Father in heaven does not want any of these little ones to be lost."

Matthew 18: 12-14

> "...go and look for the lost sheep."

A God who cares

We're so used to the somewhat sentimental image of the Good Shepherd that it's easy to overlook the passionate nature of God's love for us. We may trust God's love, but this parable tells us of God's commitment to us – a commitment that is ever active and ever faithful.

There is a sense of relief and joy when the shepherd finds the sheep that has wandered away. Also, we know that the lost sheep will be cared for tenderly, not blamed and scolded. God's love accepts us, cherishes us, cares for all our needs. It rejoices when we return to his friendship.

Knowing this God of love, we in turn are to seek out those who hunger and thirst, and care for them in like manner.

Lord, help me to stay near to you,
but if I stray from you, look for me quickly.

Soon afterward Mary got ready and hurried off to a town in the hill country of Judea. She went into Zechariah's house and greeted Elizabeth. When Elizabeth heard Mary's greeting, the baby moved within her. Elizabeth was filled with the Holy Spirit and said in a loud voice, "You are the most blessed of all women, and blessed is the child you will bear! For as soon as I heard your greeting, the baby within me jumped with gladness. How happy you are to believe that the Lord's message to you will come true!"

Mary said, "My heart praises the Lord; my soul is glad because of God my Saviour...."

Luke 1: 39-47

> "You are the most blessed of all women..."

A powerful greeting

When Elizabeth greets Mary, she calls her "most blessed of all women." The words seem tame, but only two other women in Scripture are greeted this way. Jael (Judges 5: 24) and Judith (Judith 13: 18) each killed an enemy general, thereby liberating their people.

Recently, a bumper sticker made me think of Solveig: "Well-behaved women rarely make history." Solveig never killed anyone, but for 20 years she was the most persistent, articulate and unwilling-to-be-well-behaved woman in North America, working to end apartheid. During her lifetime, she saw the Magnificat happen: the kings brought down and the lowly lifted up.

Mary and Solveig deserve today's greeting – not for their readiness to use violence, but for their determination to sing the justice of God with their whole lives.

God, let me know when being well-behaved keeps me from being faithful to you.

" I assure you that John the Baptist is greater than anyone who has ever lived. But the one who is least in the Kingdom of heaven is greater than John. From the time John preached his message until this very day the Kingdom of heaven has suffered violent attacks, and violent men try to seize it. Until the time of John all the prophets and the Law of Moses spoke about the kingdom; and if you are willing to believe their message, John is Elijah, whose coming was predicted. Listen, then, if you have ears!"

Matthew 11: 11-15

"From the time John preached his message…"

Waiting

In one of his books for children, Dr. Seuss describes a waiting place where people are "waiting perhaps for their Uncle Jake or a pot to boil, or a Better Break…." I always seem to be waiting… for rest from the relentless demands of being a single parent, for a phone call from a friend to cheer me up, for reconciliation with members of my family.

John upset people by telling them to stop waiting for the kingdom – it had already arrived! But they didn't want to listen; they might be called to look at their lives and perhaps change the way they were living.

Each year I await the birth of Jesus. How easy it is to forget that he is already here. How hard it is to stop waiting and to start living… now.

Lord, give me the courage to believe that you are with me here, and to live the truth of your kingdom now.

The holy God of Israel,
the Lord who saves you, says:
"I am the Lord your God,
the one who wants to teach you for your own good
and direct you in the way you should go.
If only you had listened to my commands!
Then blessings would have flowed for you
like a stream that never goes dry.
Victory would have come to you
like the waves that roll on the shore.
Your descendants would be as numerous as grains of sand,
and I would have made sure they were never destroyed."

Isaiah 48: 17-19

"If only you had listened..."

A wake-up call

"If you're too tired to drive home after the party, sleep over there, okay?" Jeremy rolled his eyes. "Sure, Dad," he said. But after the party, Jeremy decided he was fine to drive. Five minutes from home, he must have dozed off. He hit a pole and totalled the car, but he walked away with just a few scratches.

Upon arriving at the scene, his dad hugged him fiercely. He was thinking, "If only he had listened to me!" Aloud he said, "I'm so glad you're okay."

More things were shattered that early morning than the family car. Jeremy and his dad were jolted into a new, deeper relationship – one where "I'm sorry" and "I love you" became the cornerstones of mutual respect and caring.

**Lord, my mistakes can bring me closer to you.
Help me learn from them as I keep trying to listen
to your commands.**

There arose the fiery prophet Elijah, whose words blazed like a torch. He brought a famine on the people, and many of them died because of his persistence. Speaking in the name of the Lord, he kept the rain from coming, and on three occasions he called down fire. Elijah, your miracles were marvellous! No one else can boast of such deeds.... You were taken up to heaven in a fiery whirlwind, a chariot drawn by fiery horses. The scripture says that you are ready to appear at the designated time, to cool God's anger before it breaks out in fury; that you "will bring parents and children together again," and restore the tribes of Israel. Fortunate are those who live to see you come, as well as those who have already died in love, for we too shall live.

Sirach 48: 1-4, 9-11

> "...will bring parents and children together again..."

A world in disarray

Famine. Drought. Storms of fire. Terrible things all, and convincing evidence that God is angry and the world is in disarray. But these are not the worst signs of the world's imbalance. No, a world where "parents and children are not together" is a truly disordered and hopeless one.

We live in such a world. We don't value children and we view parenting as a private hobby, like stamp collecting. I have seen young children treated as the ultimate accessory, and I have seen them shamefully neglected. I have seen children treated as miniature adults as they cry out silently for the protection and love they need, but don't get.

If it takes an Elijah to make a change, to "bring parents and children together again," let him come!

Lord, our world needs good mothers and fathers.
Help me do my part as I strive to be the best parent I can be.

Zeph 3: 14-18; Ps: Is 12; Phil 4: 4-7; Lk 3: 10-18

"**M**iss…" I look up from my desk to see an earnest, anxious student. She is clutching a lopsided array of dog-eared papers and weighty textbooks. "Miss…" she begins again. Her tired eyes implore me to listen closely. I wait. "My parents are going to kill me. I am failing your course. What do I need to do to pass?"

John the Baptist finds himself in a similar situation in today's gospel. He is surrounded by an equally anxious flock of students. They, too, are weary. They carry with them an impressive array of Old Testament wisdom, yet fail to grasp the key. They do not know how to rejoice. They crave rules and regulations and will not rest until they are given something to "do."

Both John and I are good teachers. We recognize that fear-filled hearts do not hear. Swift intervention is in order. "Whoever has two coats must share… Collect no more than the amount prescribed… Be satisfied with your wages… Hand in an extra assignment."

Soon Jesus will come. He will have compassion for the fear-filled student. He will tell parables to calm troubled hearts and use verbs in all of his sentences. Love your God… love your neighbour… love yourself. His listeners will be like grain tossed by a winnowing fork. Soon their hearts will be open, pliable – ready to heal and to hear. Soon they will be ready to rejoice.

Lord Jesus, show me the way.
I am not the best student, so please be patient!

This is the list of the ancestors of Jesus Christ, a descendant of David, who was a descendant of Abraham.

From Abraham to King David: Abraham, Isaac, Jacob, Judah and his brothers; then Perez and Zerah... Hezron, Ram, Amminadab, Nahshon, Salmon, Boaz... Obed... Jesse, and King David.

From David to the time when the people of Israel were taken into exile in Babylon: David, Solomon... Rehoboam, Abijah, Asa, Jehoshaphat, Jehoram, Uzziah, Jotham, Ahaz, Hezekiah, Manasseh, Amon, Josiah, and Jehoiachin and his brothers.

From the time after the exile in Babylon to the birth of Jesus: Jehoiachin, Shealtiel, Zerubbabel, Abiud, Eliakim, Azor, Zadok, Achim, Eliud, Eleazar, Matthan, Jacob, and Joseph, who married Mary, the mother of Jesus, who was called the Messiah.

Matthew 1: 1-17

> "This is the list of the ancestors of Jesus Christ..."

Connections

Family trees give me pause. Last summer I went to a family reunion and met many cousins I'd never known while growing up. The reason we never knew each other was because of a perceived slight that happened at my grandmother's wake – 63 years ago! Many families will recognize this severing of family ties.

What happens in families happens in neighbourhoods, races and countries, too. And we're the worse for it. Disconnected.

The story of Jesus' lineage is a poetic attempt at providing connections. The names themselves read like poetry. I think we, too, need that same poetry of connections in our own lives. Not necessarily back to kings, but to our own kin – both living and dead.

Lord, give me patience, love and respect for others so we can stay connected.

This was how the birth of Jesus Christ took place. His mother Mary was engaged to Joseph, but before they were married, she found out that she was going to have a baby by the Holy Spirit.... An angel of the Lord appeared to [Joseph] in a dream and said, "Joseph, descendant of David, do not be afraid to take Mary to be your wife. For it is by the Holy Spirit that she has conceived. She will have a son, and you will name him Jesus – because he will save his people from their sins."

Now all this happened in order to make come true what the Lord had said through the prophet, "A virgin will become pregnant and have a son, and he will be called Immanuel" (which means, "God is with us").

Matthew 1: 18-24

> "...and he will be called Immanuel."

God-with-us

The gospel writers pack so much into such a short phrase, capturing the meaning of the entire Christmas season in the word "Immanuel." If, at Jesus' birth, "God is with us," then we have reason to rejoice and sing and celebrate. God is not far away, perched on some celestial throne with hosts of angels around. Rather, "God is with us."

So when I clean the house, shovel the snow, put up the tree, and bake for friends and family, God is with me in everything I do. Sometimes I forget, but God doesn't forget. God is always present. In preparing for Christmas, let me recall that "God is with us" and let me live my life in God's presence.

Dear God, help us be aware each day of the ways you are "with us." Help us remember "Immanuel."

One day Zechariah was doing his work as a priest in the Temple, taking his turn in the daily service…. An angel of the Lord appeared to him, and said to him, "Don't be afraid, Zechariah! God has heard your prayer, and your wife Elizabeth will bear you a son. You are to name him John…."

Zechariah said to the angel, "How shall I know if this is so? I am an old man, and my wife is old also." "I am Gabriel," the angel answered…. "Because you have not believed, you will be unable to speak; you will remain silent until the day my promise to you comes true."

The people were waiting for Zechariah. When he came out, he could not speak to them, and so they knew that he had seen a vision in the Temple. Unable to say a word, he made signs to them with his hands.

Luke 1: 5-25

"Unable to say a word, he made signs to them…"

Silence and wonder

Today's reading calls me to silence. In the pre-Christmas rush, so many different messages vie for my attention. But hearing Zechariah's story, I find my heart drawn to stillness. With him, I feel moved to a silent awe that seeks to be attentive to the mysterious working of God.

Zechariah had no choice. He had to wait – in silence – for a birth that was beyond his rational understanding. Within all the clamour of the season, can I allow myself a few moments of silence to wait for the simple birth of Jesus?

God's decision that Jesus enter our world as a helpless infant goes beyond my understanding. Instead, given quiet space, it calls me to an attitude of profound wonder.

**God, prepare my heart in silence
for the coming mystery of your birth.**

The Lord sent another message to Ahaz: "Ask the Lord your God to give you a sign. It can be from deep in the world of the dead or from high up in heaven."

Ahaz answered, "I will not ask for a sign. I refuse to put the Lord to the test."

To that Isaiah replied, "Listen, now, descendants of King David. It's bad enough for you to wear out the patience of people – do you have to wear out God's patience too? Well then, the Lord himself will give you a sign: a young woman who is pregnant will have a son and will name him 'Immanuel.'"

Isaiah 7: 10-14; 8:10

"...to give you a sign."

Trust in God

Enemies were preparing to attack and King Ahaz was terrified. "Trust me," God said. "If you find trust hard, just ask me for a sign of my power and I'll give it to you." But Ahaz was like me: afraid that trusting in God would call for heroism, and heaven knows he was no hero, and neither am I.

But that's the point. God can carry me to heroic heights of courage and depths of compassion. It seems to me that this is the sign of Immanuel: that God's power and love are with me whenever I ask for them.

Over these last hectic days before Christmas, I will trust that God will help me to be courageous or compassionate when I am needed to be.

Lord, teach me to trust in your power.
Today I ask for a sign of your power and love.

hear my lover's voice.
He comes running over the mountains,
racing across the hills to me....
My lover speaks to me.
Come then, my love;
my darling, come with me.
The winter is over; the rains have stopped;
in the countryside the flowers are in bloom.
This is the time for singing....
Let me see your lovely face
and hear your enchanting voice.

Song of Songs 2: 8-14

> "This is the time for singing…"

With eyes of love

The whole world looks different when you're in love!

I remember a warm autumn day: I was sitting on a rock by the river with my new girl. With her at my side, the colours seemed brighter and I felt that wonderful feeling of being truly alive. Being in love made me realize how beautiful the world really was!

Now, when the world seems grey, it's usually me that has changed. If only I could see with the eyes of one newly in love… every day. If only I could recognize the beauty of all that I'm given… every day.

And that "new girl" of mine? Well, that was 27 years ago, and we still sit on that rock, and it's still a beautiful river.

**Dear God, open my heart to new love every day,
and open my eyes to the beauty that surrounds me.**

Mary said, "My heart praises the Lord; my soul is glad because of God my Saviour, for he has remembered me, his lowly servant! From now on all people will call me happy, because of the great things the Mighty God has done for me. His name is holy; from one generation to another he shows mercy to those who honour him. He has stretched out his mighty arm and scattered the proud with all their plans. He has brought down mighty kings from their thrones, and lifted up the lowly. He has filled the hungry with good things, and sent the rich away with empty hands. He has kept the promise he made to our ancestors, and has come to the help of his servant Israel. He has remembered to show mercy to Abraham and to all his descendants forever!"   *Luke 1: 46-56*

"...he has remembered me, his lowly servant!"

Youthful servants

Children figure prominently in these ritual-filled days before Christmas. Given Mary's young age when she first spoke these amazing words, this strikes me as appropriate. Today's reading forces me to reconsider the connection between wisdom and age.

I usually find it hard to accept such wisdom from "kids," although there are some notable exceptions. I am amazed to recall that Mozart was eight years old when he wrote his first symphony, and 14 when be began writing string quartets. That's the same age as Joan of Arc when "voices" changed her life, and French history. Here in Canada, Craig Kielburger was only 12 years old when he established Free the Children, an organization whose aim is to improve the condition of child workers in the Third World. He was nominated for a Nobel Peace Prize in 2007.

Youthful, lowly servants, indeed!

Dear God, help me to understand that people of all ages are in tune with you. I'd like to be one of them!

Micah 5: 2-5; Ps 80; Heb 10: 5-10; Lk 1: 39-45

Today's gospel tells the wondrous story of Mary's visit to her cousin Elizabeth and Elizabeth's recognition that the baby Mary is carrying will be the long-awaited Saviour. The passage closes with Elizabeth's declaration of Mary's blessedness – "And blessed is she who believed…."

What does it mean to be "blessed"? Some of those who knew Mary might have thought she was not blessed at all. After all, she was pregnant under what seemed suspicious circumstances and she was most likely gossiped about and shunned. But Mary's blessedness had to do with something much deeper – with having a heart that was open to God and to God's mysterious ways. In the Bible, the word "blessed" is sometimes translated as "happy." We tend to associate happiness with superficial things. The biblical association of blessedness with happiness offers us a more meaningful understanding of both words.

We also are blessed when we believe, like Mary, that God's promises to us will be fulfilled. As we approach Christmas, let us treasure up and draw strength from the most comforting of promises, that God is Emmanuel – "God with us." In all the ups and downs, the trials and joys of our lives and relationships, God is always with us. Our awareness of this can be the source of the most profound happiness. Blessed are we who believe and live our days with this assurance!

**Loving God, I take comfort in your promises
and rejoice in your blessings.**

John's father Zechariah was filled with the Holy Spirit, and he spoke God's message: "Let us praise the Lord, the God of Israel! He has come to the help of his people and has set them free. He has provided for us a mighty Saviour....

"You, my child, will be called a prophet of the Most High God. You will go ahead of the Lord to prepare his road for him, to tell his people that they will be saved by having their sins forgiven. Our God is merciful and tender. He will cause the bright dawn of salvation to rise on us and to shine from heaven on all those who live in the dark shadow of death, to guide our steps into the path of peace."

Luke 1:67-79

> "He will cause the bright dawn of salvation to rise…"

A new world vision

My thoughts of Christmas are deeply linked with candles and the flickering light of a fire… sitting quietly in a room decorated with a Christmas tree, being with family and friends. Outside it may be snowing and cold, but inside there is warmth and light.

Zechariah had a vision of a world where God would give light to all who lived in darkness. We, too, dream of a different kind of world. But our present world is such a wilderness – there are so many who have no family, who have no food on the table. How can I reach out to share the love and light I enjoy? Zechariah's words give us the courage to see things in a new way, to hope, to see that change is possible.

Lord, let my hands, my thoughts and my prayers help others to enjoy your light and peace.

Is 52: 7-10; Ps 98; Heb: 1-6; Jn 1:1-18

I s there anything more defenceless than a tiny newborn? Totally dependent on others for every need, a baby is the perfect image of vulnerability. How amazing it is, then, that God should choose to come to us as a helpless infant, born into the humblest of circumstances.

But *why*? Why would God do such a thing? Because... God loves us. Beyond reason, beyond imagining, God loves us and wants to

share in the smallest and most ordinary happenings of our lives. God doesn't want merely to exist alongside us but to be part of everything that we are. And so God became one of us, to love each of us intimately, passionately and without limits.

And while it is good and right to bask in that love, today's feast also calls us to something greater. God became one of us not only to make evident God's great love for us, but also to show us how to *live out of* that love. Christmas is not just for one day: it's for the whole year. Learning to live each day with patience, kindness, gentleness, faithfulness and self-giving – this is the true gift of Christmas.

And so, on this holy day when we celebrate the Love that became flesh and dwelt among us, may we commit ourselves anew to the daily challenge of passing on the gift of Christmas to our families, our communities and the whole world.

Thank you, God. Thank you, Jesus. Thank you, Spirit of holiness. Live in me, and may my life reveal you.

Watch out, for there will be those who will arrest you and take you to court…. For my sake you will be brought to trial before rulers and kings, to tell the Good News to them and to the Gentiles. When they bring you to trial, do not worry about what you are going to say or how you will say it; when the time comes, you will be given what you will say. For the words you will speak will not be yours; they will come from the Spirit of your Father speaking through you."

Matthew 10: 17-22

"…do not worry about what you are going to say…"

Spirit words

When I was younger, speaking in public was one of my biggest nightmares. Fortunately, mid-life has allowed me to become considerably less inhibited in that regard.

But often, in more personal situations, I still find it hard to know what to say. What words of comfort can I offer to the friend whose child has just died? Do I have the courage to speak words of protest when I recognize an injustice in my workplace or my community? Am I able to extend a much-needed word of reconciliation in the face of misunderstanding or a strained relationship?

I need to recognize those circumstances where silence is not an option, and to trust that God will help me find the necessary words.

**O Lord, be in my heart and on my lips, so that
I may speak words of healing where they are needed.**

We write to you about the Word of life, which has existed from the very beginning. We have heard it, and we have seen it with our eyes; yes, we have seen it, and our hands have touched it. When this life became visible, we saw it; so we speak of it and tell you about the eternal life which was with the Father and was made known to us. What we have seen and heard we announce to you also, so that you will join with us in the fellowship that we have with the Father and with his Son Jesus Christ. We write this in order that our joy may be complete.

1 John 1: 1-4

> "When this life became visible, we saw it…"

Word of life

I was thrilled when my brother and his wife asked me to help during the delivery of their first child. Yet it's hard to pinpoint what was so remarkable about being present "when this life became visible."

Was it the tenderness of my brother as he supported his wife in her labour, or was it the calm confidence of the midwives as they coaxed life forward? Was it my sister-in-law's intense concentration, or her exhilaration as she finally held her baby? Indeed, there is a powerful mystery that surrounds the beginning of life.

Jesus' birth is an opportunity to be attentive to the birth of joy in our midst. When I drift into post-Christmas letdown, I will try to remember what it was like to welcome this new child.

Jesus, as I celebrate your birth, I am filled with joy.

An angel of the Lord appeared in a dream to Joseph and said, "Herod will be looking for the child in order to kill him. So get up, take the child and his mother and escape to Egypt...."

When Herod realized that the visitors from the East had tricked him, he was furious. He gave orders to kill all the boys in Bethlehem and its neighbourhood who were two years old and younger....

In this way what the prophet Jeremiah had said came true: "A sound is heard in Ramah, the sound of bitter weeping. Rachel is crying for her children; she refuses to be comforted, for they are dead."

Matthew 2: 13-18

"...she refuses to be comforted, for they are dead."

The shadow of death

Every Christmastime, when images of "sweet baby Jesus" prevail, I struggle to suppress the images of horror provoked by today's reading: every boy under two executed, no exceptions.

These children were lost without a trace: no family albums, no videos, just the quickly fading memories of first words spoken, an unused cot in the corner.

Years later, their older brothers and sisters would struggle to remember something of the baby they knew for two years, before the soldiers arrived.

Across the joy of Jesus' birth falls the shadow of the violence that such light continues to provoke through time and space.

Dear Lord, your presence is often met with fear and violence. May I be a messenger of your peace.

There was a man named Simeon.... He was a good, God-fearing man and was waiting for Israel to be saved. The Holy Spirit was with him and had assured him that he would not die before he had seen the Lord's promised Messiah. Led by the Spirit, Simeon went into the Temple. When the parents brought the child Jesus into the Temple to do for him what the Law required, Simeon took the child in his arms and gave thanks to God: "Now, Lord, you have kept your promise, and you may let your servant go in peace. With my own eyes I have seen your salvation, which you have prepared in the presence of all peoples: A light to reveal your will to the Gentiles and bring glory to your people Israel."

Luke 2: 22-35

> "...you may let your servant go in peace."

Go in peace

I've heard it said that we die once we have accomplished that for which we are given life. Simeon accomplished his task: he saw and recognized the promised Messiah. And his response revealed the Messiah to others.

Throughout scripture, as in our lives, God is revealed in everyday life. The light – God's Word – reveals what is true and good in my world. However, certain forces often obscure my path and throw me off track. The choices I make – the small decisions made each day – are choices for the light or for the dark. How will my life reveal the God of hope, of new possibilities in the decisions I make today?

God, help me to recognize the true light in my life and let it show me the way to truth and love.

1 Sam 1: 11, 20-22, 24-28; Ps 84; 1 Jn 3: 1-2, 21-24; Lk 2: 41-52

Returning thanks is not just something we do at our eucharistic liturgy, but something embedded in the daily life of our families.

Hannah reminds us that every child is a gift from God. As parents, we not only give thanks to God for the gift of our children, but also we must give them back to God. Our return gift is not usually a one-time event, as it is for Hannah, but a daily handing over of our children to God so they can grow in body and spirit toward maturity.

Mary and Joseph experience the awakening in their child Jesus to his life's direction. On the brink of adulthood – at the age of 12, a Jewish boy celebrates his bar mitzvah (becoming "one to whom the commandments apply") – Jesus takes responsibility for his vocation as a teacher of God's ways. Though Mary and Joseph do not quite understand what Jesus is up to, their love makes room for him to follow the path that will eventually take him from home and family to his death not far from this same Jerusalem temple.

John's letter recalls that though we might now be parents, we remain children of God. We are all gifts from God, begotten in love and called to give back that love not only to God, but to one another. Following this path, we will become like our Father in heaven.

O God, your love is everlasting. Make room in my heart so I can share that love with those around me.

n the beginning the Word already existed; the Word was with God, and the Word was God. From the very beginning the Word was with God. Through him God made all things; not one thing in all creation was made without him. The Word was the source of life, and this life brought light to people. The light shines in the darkness, and the darkness has never put it out....

The Word became a human being and, full of grace and truth, lived among us. We saw his glory, the glory which he received as the Father's only Son....

No one has ever seen God. The only Son, who is the same as God and is at the Father's side, he has made him known.

John 1: 1-18

> "The Word became a human being..."

Word made flesh

Words are easy. It's flesh and blood – being a human person – that are the hard things. What risks must I take, what price must I pay, to make my words become flesh and blood?

I have a friend who walks with the shuffling gait of an old man. He's a war hero, but those who remember his bravery and his dashing good looks are now dead. He is old before his time: leg blown apart by shrapnel, spirit seared by the horrors he has seen. Like Jesus, he paid the price of making his words become flesh.

And me? How much am I willing to risk? How far will I go to make my words become flesh, to become a true human being?

**Dear God, help me find the courage
to make my words become flesh.**

Contributors

Kelly Adams
Tony Adams
Ian Adnams
Ella Allen
Ralph Amato
Dale C. Balkovec
Mary Bastedo
Rosalee Bender
Rick Benson
Margaret Bick
Louisa Blair
Barbara Bozak
Ina Mae Brooks
Kevin Burns
Alex Campbell
Mary Ellen Chown
Wanda Conway
Mike Cooke
Regina Coupar
Jim Creskey
Rebecca Cunningham
Barbara K. d'Artois
Claudette Derdaele
Carmen Diston
Helga Doermer
Michael Dougherty
Patrick Doyle
Robert Dueweke
Raymond Earle
Susan Eaton
Corbin Eddy
Karen Fee
Tanya Ferdinandusz
Patrick Gallagher
Bernadette Gasslein
George Gilliland

Barbara Green
Caryl Green
Mary Ellen Green
Joe Gunn
Calvin Halley
Maryanne Hannan
Maura Hanrahan
Charles Harrel
Krystyna Higgins
Brenda Merk Hildebrand
Karen Johnson
Roger Keeler
Phil Kelly
Nancy Keyes
Marilyn Kreyer
Christine Mader
Bertha Madott
Anne Louise Mahoney
Marguerite McDonald
Beth McIsaac Bruce
Jim McLaughlin
Jim McSheffrey
Marilyn Moore
Judy Morris
RoseMarie Morris
Steve Mueller
Caroline Nolan
Rosemary O'Hearn
Connie Paré
Beth Porter
Jean-Pierre Prévost
Michael Reist
Sherie Rusler Croft
Kathy Shaidle
John Spicer
April Strauch

Marilyn Sweet
Jim Taylor
Marie-Louise Temier-Gommers
Michael Traher
Joseph Vorstermans
Donald Walker
Pamela Walker
David Weiss
Teresa Whalen Lux
Susie Whelehan
Geoffrey Whitney-Brown

Photographs

Cléo: 205
Crestock: 65, 93, 177, 233
Gilles Larche: 156
Ingram: 37, 79, 142, 310, 331
iStock: 128, 254, 268, 317, 345
Jocelyn Boutin: 170, 226
Jupiter Images: 16, 23, 30, 51, 100, 121, 135, 212, 282, 296, 338, 359
Monique Nadeau: 289
Plaisted: 44, 72, 86, 107, 163, 366, 368
Skjold: 198, 247, 303, 373
W.P. Wittman: 9, 58, 114, 149, 184, 191, 219, 240, 261, 275, 324, 352

 This book has been printed on 100% post consumer waste paper, certified Eco-logo and processed chlorine free.